ŚRĪMAD-BHAGAVAD-GĪTĀ

ŚRĪMAD-
BHAGAVAD-GĪTĀ

With Text, Word-for-Word Translation,
English Rendering, Comments and Index

by
SWAMI SWARUPANANDA

Advaita Ashrama
(Publication Department)
5 Dehi Entally Road • Kolkata 700 014

Published by
Swami Tattwavidananda
Adhyaksha, Advaita Ashrama
Mayavati, Champawat, Uttarakhand, Himalayas
from its Publication Department, Kolkata
Email: mail@advaitaashrama.org
Website: www.advaitaashrama.org

Second Edition, March 2016
10M3C

ISBN 978-81-7505-096-9 (Limp)
ISBN 978-81-7505-262-7 (Deluxe)

Printed in India at
Trio Process
Kolkata 700 014

FOREWORD

The Śrīmad-Bhagavad-Gītā occurs in the Bhīṣma Parva of the Mahābhārata and comprises 18 chapters from the 25th to the 42nd. The discourse between Arjuna and Kṛṣṇa on the battlefield, on the eve of the war which forms the subject-matter of the work, was strung together in seven hundred verses and put in its place in the body of this great history by Vyāsa.

The Gītā opens with Dhṛtarāṣṭra's query to Sañjaya about the progress of events. In the second chapter of the Bhīṣma Parva, we find Vyāsa offering the power of sight to the blind king, that he might see the war. Dhṛtarāṣṭra declined to have it, saying he did not care to have eyes with which only to see the death of his own people; but he would like to hear what was happening. On this the great Ṛṣi Vyāsa said, that all the occurrences in connection with the war would be reflected in the mind of Sañjaya, and he would faithfully report them to Dhṛtarāṣṭra.

The Gītā is called an Upaniṣad, because it contains the essence of Self-knowledge, and because its teachings, like those of the Vedas, are divided into three sections, *Karma* (work), *Upāsanā* (devotion), and *Jñāna* (knowledge).

The first chapter is introductory. The second is a summary of the whole work, e.g., in II. 48 and the connected Ślokas, selfless work devoid of desire for fruits, is taught for the purification of the heart; in II. 61 and the connected Ślokas devotion is taught to the pure-hearted, to qualify them further for the highest *Sannyāsa,* which last is taught in II. 71 and the connected Ślokas.

It is also usual to divide the work into three sections illustrative of the three terms of the *Mahāvākya* of the Sāma-Veda, "Thou art That" (Chānd. Upa., VI. viii. 7). In this view the first six chapters explain the path of work without desire for fruits, and the nature of "Thou". The next six chapters deal with devotion and the nature of "That". The last six describe the state of the highest knowledge and the nature of the middle term of the *Mahāvākya,* in other words, the means of re-establishing the identity of "Thou" and "That".

The central teaching of the Gītā is the attainment of Freedom, by the performance of one's *Svadharma* or duty in life. "Do the duty without an eye to the results thereof. Thus shouldst thou gain the purification of heart which is essential for *Mokṣa*"—seems to be the keynote of Kṛṣṇa's teachings to Arjuna.

It is well known why the Gītā came into existence. It was owing to Arjuna's unwillingness to do his duty as a Kṣatriya—to fight for a just cause—because it involved the destruction of his own people. Not that Arjuna did not recognise the justice and right of the cause, but he would rather renounce the world and try for *Mokṣa* than kill his relatives and friends. Kṛṣṇa's characterisation of this weakly sentimental attitude of Arjuna is well known. He called it "Un-*Ārya*-like delusion, contrary to the attainment alike of heaven and honour" and exhorted Pārtha to "yield not to unmanliness" but to "cast off this mean faint-heartedness" (II. 2–3). "Could a coward who fails to do his duty, be worthy to attain *Mokṣa*?"—seems to be Kṛṣṇa's rejoinder. Could a man not purified by the fire-ordeal of *Svadharma,* could a renegade, a slave, attain *Mokṣa*? No! says the Lord. And this is the lesson we Indians have forgotten all these years, though we have been reading and discussing the Gītā all the time.

S.

KEY TO TRANSLITERATION AND PRONUNCIATION

	sounds like		sounds like
अ	a o in s*o*n	ड	ḍ d
आ	ā in m*a*ster	ढ	ḍh dh in go*dh*ood
इ	i i in *i*f	ण	ṇ n in u*n*der
ई	ī ee in f*ee*l	त	t French t
उ	u u in f*u*ll	थ	th th in *th*umb
ऊ	ū oo in b*oo*t	द	d th in *th*en
ऋ	ṛ somewhat between r and ri	ध	dh theh in brea*the h*ere
ए	e a in ev*a*de	न	n n
ऐ	ai y in m*y*	प	p p
ओ	o oh	फ	ph ph in loo*p-h*ole
औ	au ow in n*ow*	ब	b b
क	k k	भ	bh bh in a*bh*or
ख	kh ckh in blo*ckh*ead	म	m m
ग	g g (hard)	य	y
घ	gh gh in lo*g-h*ut	र	r r
ङ	ṅ ng	ल	l l
च	c ch (not k)	व	v in a*v*ert
छ	ch chh in cat*ch h*im	श	ś sh
ज	j j	ष	ṣ sh in *sh*ow
झ	jh dgeh in he*dgeh*og	स	s s
ञ	ñ n (somewhat)	ह	h h
ट	ṭ t	.	ṁ ng
ठ	ṭh th in an*t-h*ill	:	ḥ half h

CONTENTS

PREFACE TO THE SECOND EDITION

We are pleased to present this digitized second edition of the book with some corrections. Hope this will be warmly received by the readers as the previous edition.

March 2016 Publisher

PREFACE TO THE FIRST EDITION

Swami Swarupananda, a disciple of Swami Vivekananda and the first president of the Advaita Ashrama, Mayavati, and former editor of the *Prabuddha Bharata,* compiled the present edition of the Bhagavad-Gītā with the collaboration of his brother Sannyāsins at Mayavati, and some of the Western disciples of Swami Vivekananda. The manuscripts were begun in 1901, and were ready for the press by the end of 1903, but through unavoidable circumstances the publication was delayed. It was only after the passing away of Swami Swarupananda that the work was brought out in monthly instalments in the *Prabuddha Bharata,* and this work is now presented to the public in convenient book form, after being carefully edited and enlarged with additional comments.

The object of the compiler was to make accessible to the Indian public who are educated in English but have a limited knowledge in Sanskrit, and also to the Western world, an edition of the Celestial Gītā, in which they will feel sufficient interest to follow the original text, and thus create a taste for the study and interpretation of holy Sanskrit literature. How far the compiler has been successful in his object can be gleaned from the following pages. His thoughtful comments following the commentaries of the great Ācāryas, and illuminating sidelights thrown on intricate places, will, we trust, be of much help to the study of the Gītā, especially to a beginner. An elaborate Index has been subsequently added.

A word of explanation as to the paraphrase is necessary here: Though the literal meaning of each word is given, yet to avoid the awkwardness of language and confusion of sense to a beginner, the equivalents of case terminals of such words as are used to qualify some other words in the sentence, are omitted in most cases.

We hope this edition will meet a much-felt want, not only in India but in all English-speaking countries.

THE EDITORS AND PUBLISHERS

ADVAITA ASHRAMA
MAYAVATI, HIMALAYAS
18th October, 1909

MEDITATION

ॐ पार्थाय प्रतिबोधितां भगवता नारायणेन स्वयं
व्यासेन ग्रथितां पुराण-मुनिना मध्ये-महाभारतम्।
अद्वैतामृत-वर्षिणीं भगवतीमष्टादशाध्यायिनी-
मम्ब त्वामनुसन्दधामि भगवद्गीते भव-द्वेषिणीम्॥ १

ॐ Om अम्ब O Mother, भगवद्गीते O Bhagavad-Gītā, अनुसन्दधामि I meditate upon त्वाम् thee भगवतीम् the Supreme Goddess अद्वैतामृत-वर्षिणीं showering the nectar of non-duality भव-द्वेषिणीम् destroyer of rebirth अष्टादशाध्यायिनीं having eighteen chapters ग्रथितां incorporated मध्ये-महाभारतं in the Mahābhārata पुराण-मुनिना by the ancient sage व्यासेन Vyāsa पार्थाय प्रतिबोधितां with which Pārtha was enlightened भगवता by the Lord नारायणेन Nārāyaṇa स्वयम् Himself.

1. Om! O Mother, O Bhagavad-Gītā, I meditate upon thee the Supreme Goddess showering the nectar of non-duality, the destroyer of rebirth, having eighteen chapters incorporated in the Mahābhārata by the ancient sage Vyāsa, with which Pārtha was enlightened by the Lord Nārāyaṇa Himself.

नमोऽस्तु ते व्यास विशाल-बुद्धे
फुल्लारविन्दायत-पत्र-नेत्र।
येन त्वया भारत-तैल-पूर्णः
प्रज्वालितो ज्ञानमयः प्रदीपः ।। २

व्यास O Vyāsa विशाल-बुद्धे of mighty intellect फुल्लारविन्दायत-पत्र-नेत्र with eyes as large as the petals of a full-blown lotus नमः salutation ते to thee अस्तु be येन by whom त्वया (i.e) by thee प्रदीपः the lamp भारत-तैल-पूर्णः full of the oil of the Mahābhārata (and) ज्ञानमयः consisting of wisdom प्रज्वालितः was lighted.

2. O Vyāsa of mighty intellect and with eyes as large as the petals of a full-blown lotus, salutation be to thee, by whom (i.e) by thee the lamp full of the oil of the Mahābhārata (and) consisting of wisdom, was lighted.

प्रपन्न-पारिजाताय तोत्र-वेत्रैक-पाणये।
ज्ञान-मुद्राय कृष्णाय गीतामृत-दुहे नमः ।। ३

नमः Salutation कृष्णाय to Kṛṣṇa प्रपन्न-पारिजाताय the wish-yielding tree of those who take refuge in Thee तोत्र-वेत्रैक-पाणये who holdest in one hand a whip and a cane (for driving cows) ज्ञान-मुद्राय (Jñānamudrā: a position of the hands in which the tips of the fore-finger and the thumb of each hand touch each other; an attitude associated with the highest Yogis and Gurus) the holder of Jñānamudrā (and) गीतामृत-दुहे the milker of the Gītā-nectar.

3. Salutation to Kṛṣṇa the wish-yielding tree of those who take refuge in Thee, who holdest in one hand a whip and a cane (for driving cows), the holder of Jñānamudrā (and) the milker of the Gītā-nectar.

सर्वोपनिषदो गावो दोग्धा गोपाल-नन्दनः।
पार्थो वत्सः सुधीर्भोक्ता दुग्धं गीतामृतं महत्॥ ४

सर्वोपनिषद: All the Upaniṣads गाव: the cows, गोपालनन्दन: the son of the cowherd (Kṛṣṇa) दोग्धा the milker, पार्थ: Pārtha (Arjuna) वत्स: the calf, सुधी: man of purified intellect भोक्ता the drinker, महत् the supreme गीतामृतं nectar of the Gītā दुग्धम् milk.

4. All the Upaniṣads are the cows, the son of the cowherd is the milker, Pārtha is the calf, the man of purified intellect is the drinker, and the supreme nectar of the Gītā is the milk.

वसुदेव-सुतं देवं कंस-चाणूर-मर्दनम्।
देवकी-परमानन्दं कृष्णं वन्दे जगद्गुरुम्॥ ५

वन्दे I salute देवं God कृष्णं Kṛṣṇa वसुदेव-सुतं the son of Vasudeva कंस-चाणूर-मर्दनं the destroyer of Kaṁsa and Cāṇura देवकी-परमानन्दं the supreme bliss of Devakī (mother of Kṛṣṇa) जगद्गुरुम् the Guru (Teacher) of the Universe.

5. I salute Kṛṣṇa the son of Vasudeva, God, the destroyer of Kaṁsa and Cāṇura, the supreme bliss of Devakī (and) the Guru of the Universe.

भीष्म-द्रोण-तटा जयद्रथ-जला गान्धार-नीलोत्पला
शल्य-ग्राहवती कृपेण वहनी कर्णेन वेलाकुला।
अश्वत्थाम-विकर्ण-घोर-मकरा दुर्योधनावर्तिनी
सोत्तीर्णा खलु पाण्डवै रण-नदी कैवर्तकः केशवः ॥ ६

सा that रण-नदी battle-river भीष्म-द्रोण-तटा with Bhīṣma and Droṇa as the banks जयद्रथ-जला with Jayadratha as the water गान्धार-नीलोत्पला with the king of Gāndhāra as the blue water-lily शल्य-ग्राहवती with Śalya as the shark कृपेण वहनी with Kṛpa as the current कर्णेन वेलाकुला with Karṇa as the high waves अश्वत्थाम-विकर्ण-घोर-मकरा with Aśvatthāmā and Vikarṇa as terrible Makaras (a kind of marine animal) दुर्योधनावर्तिनी with Duryodhana as the whirlpool खलु indeed उत्तीर्णा crossed over पाण्डवैः by Pāṇḍavas, केशवः Keśava (Kṛṣṇa) कैवर्तकः the ferryman.

6. That battle-river---with Bhīṣma and Droṇa as the banks, with Jayadratha as the water, with the king of Gāndhāra as the blue water-lily, with Śalya as the shark, with Kṛpa as the current, with Karṇa as the high waves, with Aśvatthāmā and Vikarṇa as terrible Makaras (a kind of marine animal), and with Duryodhana as the whirlpool,---was indeed crossed over by Pāṇḍavas; Keśava was the ferryman.

पाराशर्य-वचः-सरोजममलं गीतार्थ-गन्धोत्कटं
नानाख्यानक-केसरं हरि-कथा-सम्बोधनाबोधितम्।
लोके सज्जन-षट्पदैरहरहः पेपीयमानं मुदा
भूयाद्भारत-पङ्कजं कलि-मल-प्रध्वंसि नः श्रेयसे ॥ ७

भारत-पङ्कजं The Mahābhārata-lotus पाराशर्य-वचः-सरोजम् growing on the waters of the words of the son of Parāśara (Vyāsa) अमलं spotless गीतार्थ-गन्धोत्कटं having the Gītā as its strong sweet fragrance नानाख्यानक-केसरं with many a narrative as its stamens हरि-कथा-सम्बोधनाबोधितं fully bloomed because of presenting the message of Hari (the remover of misery) कलि-मल-प्रध्वंसि destroyer of the taint of kali (the age of imperfection) मुदा joyously पेपीयमानं drunk again and again अहरहः day after day सज्जन-षट्पदैः by the honey-bee of the good and the pure लोके in the world नः our श्रेयसे for the supreme good भूयात् may be.

7. The Mahābhārata-lotus growing on the waters of the words of the son of Parāśara (Vyāsa), spotless having the Gītā as its strong sweet fragrance, with many a narrative as its stamens, fully bloomed because of presenting the message of Hari, the destroyer of the taint of kali, joyously drunk again and again day after day, by the honey-bee of the good and the pure in the world--be productive of our supreme good.

मूकं करोति वाचालं पङ्गुं लङ्घयते गिरिम्।
यत्कृपा तमहं वन्दे परमानन्द-माधवम्॥ ८

अहं I वन्दे salute तं that परमानन्द-माधवम् the All-bliss Mādhava (sweetest of the sweet) यत्कृपा whose compassion करोति makes मूकं the mute वाचालं eloquent लङ्घयते causes to cross पङ्गुं the cripple गिरिं mountain.

8. I salute that All-bliss Mādhava whose compassion makes the mute eloquent, causes the cripple to cross mountain.

यं ब्रह्मा वरुणेन्द्र-रुद्र-मरुतः स्तुन्वन्ति दिव्यैः स्तवै-
र्वेदैः साङ्ग-पद-क्रमोपनिषदैर्गायन्ति यं सामगाः।
ध्यानावस्थित-तद्गतेन मनसा पश्यन्ति यं योगिनो
यस्यान्तं न विदुः सुरासुर-गणा देवाय तस्मै नमः॥ ९

नमः Salutation तस्मै to that देवाय God यं whom ब्रह्मा Brahmā (the creator) वरुणेन्द्र-रुद्र-मरुतः Varuṇa, Indra, Rudra and the Maruts स्तुन्वन्ति praise दिव्यैः with divine स्तवैः hymns, यं whom सामगाः the singers of Sāma गायन्ति sing वेदैः by the Vedas साङ्ग-पद-क्रमोपनिषदैः having (six) auxiliaries (Śikṣā etc.), sequence of padas (words and quarters of the stanzas) and the Upaniṣads (crowning knowledge-portions) यं whom योगिनः Yogis पश्यन्ति see मनसा with the mind ध्यानावस्थित-तद्गतेन steadied through meditation and absorbed in Him यस्य whose अन्तं limit सुरासुर-गणाः the hosts of Devas and Asuras विदुः know न not.

9. Salutation to that God whom Brahmā, Varuṇa, Indra, Rudra and the Maruts praise with divine hymns, whom the singers of Sāma sing by the Vedas having (six) auxiliaries (Śikṣā etc.), sequence of padas (words and quarters of the stanzas) and the Upaniṣads, whom Yogis see with the mind steadied through meditation and absorbed in Him, whose limit the hosts of Devas and Asuras know not.

INVOCATION*

O blessed Mother
Who showerest (upon us) the nectar of Advaita
In the form of (these) eighteen chapters!
Thou Destroyer of rebirth!
Thou loving Mother!
Thou Bhagavad-Gītā!
    Upon Thee I meditate.

Thee, O Vyāsa, of lotus-eyes,
And mighty intellect,
Who hast lighted the lamp of wisdom
Filled with the oil of the Mahābhārata,
    Thee we salute.

O Thou who art the Refuge
Of the (ocean-born) Lakṣmī,
Thou in whose right hand is the shepherd's crook,
Who art the milker of the divine nectar of the Gītā,
    To Thee, O Kṛṣṇa, to Thee our salutation!

The Upaniṣads are even as the herd of cows,
The Son of the cowherd as the milker,
Pārtha as the sucking-calf,
And men of purified intellect the drinkers,
    Of this, the supreme nectar, the milk of the Gītā.

* Another rendering of the "Meditation"

Thou son of Vasudeva,
Destroyer of Kaṁsa and Cāṇūra,
The supreme bliss of Devakī,
Guru of the Worlds,
    Thee, O Kṛṣṇa, as God, we salute!

Of that great river of battle which the Pāṇḍavas crossed over,
Bhīṣma and Droṇa were as the high banks;
And Jayadratha as the water of the river;
The King of Gāndhāra the water-lily;
Śalya as the shark, Kṛpa as the current;
Karṇa the mighty waves;
Aśvatthāmā and Vikarṇa dread water-monsters,
And Duryodhana was the very whirlpool;
    But Thou, O Kṛṣṇa, wast the Ferryman!

This spotless product of the words of Vyāsa,
This lotus of the Mahābhārata,—
With the Bhagavad-Gītā as its strong sweet fragrance,
And tales of heroes as its full-blown petals,
Held ever open by the talk of Hari, of Him
Who is destroyer of the taint of *Kali-Yuga*;
This lotus to which come joyously
Day after day the honey-seeking souls—
    May this produce in us the highest good!

Him whose compassion maketh the dumb man eloquent,
And the cripple to cross mountains,

Him the All-blissful Mādhava,
Do I salute!

To that Supreme One Who is bodied forth in Brahmā,
In Varuṇa, in Indra, in Rudra, and Maruts;
That One Whom all divine beings praise with hymns;
Him Whom the singers of Sāma-Veda tell;
Him of Whose glory, sing in full choir, the Upaniṣads and Vedas;
Him Whom the Yogis see, with mind absorbed in perfect meditation;
Him of Whom all the hosts of *Devas* and *Asuras*
Know not the limitations,

To Him, the Supreme God, be salutation,—Him we salute. Him we salute. Him we salute.

ŚRĪMAD-BHAGAVAD-GĪTĀ

प्रथमोऽध्यायः
(अर्जुनविषादयोगः)

FIRST CHAPTER
(The Grief of Arjuna)

धृतराष्ट्र उवाच

धर्मक्षेत्रे कुरुक्षेत्रे समवेता युयुत्सवः ।
मामकाः पाण्डवाश्चैव किमकुर्वत सञ्जय ॥ १

धृतराष्ट्रः Dhṛtarāṣṭra उवाच said:

(भोः) सञ्जय O Sañjaya धर्मक्षेत्रे on the centre of religious activity कुरुक्षेत्रे in Kurukṣetra युयुत्सवः desirous to fight समवेताः assembled मामकाः my people च and पाण्डवाः the Pāṇḍavas किम् what एव indeed अकुर्वत did do.

Dhṛtarāṣṭra said:

1. Tell me, O Sañjaya! Assembled on Kurukṣetra, the centre of religious activity, desirous to fight, what indeed did my people and the Pāṇḍavas do?

True it is that the two parties were gathered together for battle, but was the influence of Kurukṣetra, the sacred centre of religious and spiritual activity from of old, barren of any result? Did not the spiritual influence of the spot affect any of the leaders in a way unfavourable to the occurrence of the battle?—is the purport of Dhṛtarāṣṭra's question.

सञ्जय उवाच

दृष्ट्वा तु पाण्डवानीकं व्यूढं दुर्योधनस्तदा।
आचार्यमुपसङ्गम्य राजा वचनमब्रवीत्॥ २

सञ्जय: Sañjaya उवाच said:

तदा तु But then पाण्डवानीकं the Pāṇḍava forces व्यूढं in battle-array दृष्ट्वा having seen राजा दुर्योधन: King Duryodhana आचार्यम् (द्रोणम्) the teacher (Droṇa) उपसंगम्य approaching वचनम् word अब्रवीत् said.

Sañjaya said:

2. But then King Duryodhana, having seen the Pāṇḍava forces in battle-array, approached his teacher Droṇa, and spoke these words:

Sañjaya's reply beginning with "But then" and describing Duryodhana's action is a plain hint to the old king that his son was afraid. For he went to his teacher (regarded as father) instead of to the commander-in-chief, as a child in fright would run to its parents in preference to others.

पश्यैतां पाण्डुपुत्राणामाचार्य महतीं चमूम्।
व्यूढां द्रुपदपुत्रेण तव शिष्येण धीमता॥ ३

आचार्य O teacher तव शिष्येण by your disciple धीमता talented द्रुपदपुत्रेण son of Drupada व्यूढां arrayed पाण्डुपुत्राणाम् of the sons of Pāṇḍu एतां this महतीं mighty चमूम् army पश्य behold.

3. "Behold, O Teacher! this mighty army of the sons of Pāṇḍu, arrayed by the son of Drupada, thy gifted pupil.

As a scorpion would sting even him whose protection is sought to be free from fear, so did the wicked Duryodhana insult his teacher. His meaning in plain words comes to this: thus think of your stupidity in teaching the science of fight to the son of Drupada and to those of Pāṇḍu. They are now arrayed to kill you!

अत्र शूरा महेष्वासा भीमार्जुनसमा युधि।
युयुधानो विराटश्च द्रुपदश्च महारथः ॥ ४
धृष्टकेतुश्चेकितानः काशिराजश्च वीर्यवान्।
पुरुजित् कुन्तिभोजश्च शैब्यश्च नरपुङ्गवः ॥ ५
युधामन्युश्च विक्रान्त उत्तमौजाश्च वीर्यवान्।
सौभद्रो द्रौपदेयाश्च सर्व एव महारथाः ॥ ६

अत्र Here महेष्वासा: mighty archers युधि in battle भीमार्जुनसमा: equals of Bhīma and Arjuna शूरा: heroes (सन्ति) (are) महारथ: the great warrior युयुधान: (सात्यकि:) Yuyudhāna (Sātyaki) च and विराट: Virāṭa च and द्रुपद: Drupada वीर्यवान् the strong धृष्टकेतु: Dhṛṣṭaketu चेकितान: Cekitāna च and काशिराज: the king of Kāśī नरपुङ्गव: the best of men पुरुजित् Purujit च and कुन्तिभोज: Kuntibhoja च and शैब्य: Śaibya च and विक्रान्त: the powerful युधामन्यु: Yudhāmanyu च and वीर्यवान् the brave उत्तमौजा: Uttamaujas सौभद्र: the son of Subhadrā च and द्रौपदेया: the sons of Draupadī सर्वे all (these) एव verily महारथा: great warriors.

4-6. "Here (are) heroes, mighty archers, the equals in battle of Bhīma and Arjuna—the great warriors Yuyudhāna, Virāṭa, Drupada; the valiant Dhṛṣṭaketu,Cekitāna, and king of Kāśī; the best of men, Purujit, Kuntibhoja, and Śaibya; the powerful Yudhāmanyu, and the brave Uttamaujas, the son of Subhadrā and the sons of Draupadī—all of whom are lords of great chariots.

महारथः great-charioteer: one who is well-versed in the science of war and commands eleven thousand bowmen.

अस्माकं तु विशिष्टा ये तान्निबोध द्विजोत्तम।
नायका मम सैन्यस्य संज्ञार्थं तान् ब्रवीमि ते ।। ७

(हे) द्विजोत्तम (O you) Best of the twice-born अस्माकं of us तु also ये (those) who विशिष्टाः distinguished मम my सैन्यस्य of the army? नायकाः leaders तान् them निबोध know ते संज्ञार्थं for your information तान् them ब्रवीमि I relate.

7. "Hear, also, O Best of the twice-born! the names of those who (are) distinguished amongst ourselves, the leaders of my army. These I relate (to you) for your information.

However well-versed in the science of war you might be, you are after all the best Brāhmaṇa (the twice-born), a lover of peace, that is to say, a coward. It is therefore natural for you to be afraid of the Pāṇḍava force. But take heart, we too have great warriors in our ranks—is the veiled meaning of Duryodhana's words.

भवान् भीष्मश्च कर्णश्च कृपश्च समितिञ्जयः ।
अश्वत्थामा विकर्णश्च सौमदत्तिर्जयद्रथः ।। ८

भवान् Yourself च and भीष्मः Bhīṣma च and कर्णः Karṇa समितिञ्जयः the victorious in war कृपः Kṛpa च and अश्वत्थामा Aśvatthāmā च and विकर्णः Vikarna सौमदत्तिः the son of Somadatta जयद्रथः Jayadratha.

8. "Yourself and Bhīṣma and Karṇa and Kṛpa, the victorious in war. Aṣvatthāmā and Vikarṇa and Jayadratha, the son of Somadatta.

Afraid lest he had said too much, Duryodhana is flattering Drona, by mentioning the latter before even Bhīṣma and qualifying Droṇa's brother-in-law with the phrase "victorious in war", a move likely to touch the heart of mortals.

अन्ये च बहवः शूरा मदर्थे त्यक्तजीविताः ।
नानाशस्त्रप्रहरणाः सर्वे युद्धविशारदाः ।। ९

मदर्थे For my sake त्यक्तजीविताः determined to lay down their lives नानाशस्त्रप्रहरणाः having diverse weapons and missiles सर्वे all युद्धविशारदाः well-skilled in fight अन्ये च and other बहवः many शूराः heroes (सन्ति) (are).

9. "And many other heroes also, well-skilled in fight, and armed with many kinds of weapons, are here, determined to lay down their lives for my sake.

अपर्याप्तं तदस्माकं बलं भीष्माभिरक्षितम् ।
पर्याप्तं त्विदमेतेषां बलं भीमाभिरक्षितम् ॥ १०

अस्माकं Our तत् this भीष्माभिरक्षितम् defended by Bhīṣma बलं army अपर्याप्तं unlimited तु while एतेषां their भीमाभिरक्षितम् defended by Bhīma इदम् this बलं army पर्याप्तं limited.

10. "This our army defended by Bhīṣma (is) impossible to be counted, but that army of theirs, defended by Bhīma (is) easy to number.

In ancient Indian warfare, one commanding a force had for his mainstay a defender about him, whose position was no less important. Here are given the names of the chief defenders, and not of the chief commanders.

The verse is often interpreted to mean that Duryodhana considers his army inefficient and that of the enemy efficient. But this view seems inapposite to the context.

अयनेषु च सर्वेषु यथाभागमवस्थिताः ।
भीष्ममेवाभिरक्षन्तु भवन्तः सर्व एव हि ॥ ११

च (expletive) सर्वेषु In all अयनेषु the divisions (of the army) यथाभागम् in (your) respective positions अवस्थिताः being stationed भवन्तः ye सर्वे all एव हि (used for emphasis) भीष्मम् Bhīṣma एव alone अभिरक्षन्तु protect.

11. "(Now) do, being stationed in your proper places in the divisions of the army, support Bhīṣma alone."

Since I cannot expect from you any initiative, do what you are told to do—seems to be Duryodhana's intention.

तस्य सञ्जनयन्हर्षं कुरुवृद्धः पितामहः ।
सिंहनादं विनद्योच्चैः शङ्खं दध्मौ प्रतापवान् ।। १२

प्रतापवान् The powerful कुरुवृद्धः oldest of the Kurus पितामहः grandsire तस्य his (Duryodhana's) हर्षं cheer सञ्जनयन् causing उच्चैः aloud सिंहनादं lion's roar विनद्य having sounded शङ्खं conch दध्मौ blew.

12. That powerful, oldest of the Kurus, Bhīṣma the grandsire, in order to cheer Duryodhana, now sounded aloud a lion-roar and blew his conch.

All eyes were turned upon Duryodhana and the penetrating intelligence of Bhīṣma detected his fear; and since Droṇa took no notice of Duryodhana's words, knowing his grandson as he did, he had no difficulty in understanding that the latter had spoken to his teacher in a way which called forth Droṇa's coldness instead of his enthusiasm. The grandsire's heart was moved with pity and hence the action on his part described in the above verse. It should here be noted that this action, amounting to a challenge, really began the fight. It was the *Kaurava* side again which took the aggressor's part.

ततः शङ्खाश्च भेर्यश्च पणवानकगोमुखाः ।
सहसैवाभ्यहन्यन्त स शब्दस्तुमुलोऽभवत् ।। १३

ततः Then शङ्खाः conchs च and भेर्यः kettle-drums पणवानकगोमुखाः tabors, trumpets, and cowhorns सहसा

एव quite suddenly अभ्यहन्यन्त blared forth सः that शब्दः noise तुमुलः tremendous अभवत् was.

13. Then following Bhīṣma, conchs, and kettle-drums, tabors, trumpets, and cowhorns blared forth suddenly (from the Kaurava side), and the noise was tremendous.

ततः श्वेतैर्हयैर्युक्ते महति स्यन्दने स्थितौ ।
माधवः पाण्डवश्चैव दिव्यौ शङ्खौ प्रदध्मतुः ॥ १४

ततः then श्वेतैः हयैः with white horses युक्ते yoked महति in the magnificent स्यन्दने chariot स्थितौ stationed माधवः (the Lord of Fortune: Kṛṣṇa) Mādhava च and पाण्डवः (the best of the Pāṇḍu princes: Arjuna) Pāṇḍava दिव्यौ divine शङ्खौ conchs प्रदध्मतुः blew in a splendid manner.

14. Then, also, Mādhava and Pāṇḍava, stationed in their magnificent chariot yoked with white horses, blew their divine conchs with a furious noise.

पाञ्चजन्यं हृषीकेशो देवदत्तं धनञ्जयः ।
पौण्ड्रं दध्मौ महाशङ्खं भीमकर्मा वृकोदरः ॥ १५

हृषीकेशः (The Lord of the senses: Kṛṣṇa) Hṛṣīkeśa पाञ्चजन्यं (the conch named) Pāñcajanya धनञ्जयः (the victor of wealth: Arjuna) Dhanañjaya देवदत्तं (the conch named) Devadatta भीमकर्मा doer of terrific deeds वृकोदरः

(having the belly of a wolf: Bhīma) Vṛkodara महाशङ्खं the large conch पौण्ड्रं (named) Pauṇḍra दध्मौ blew.

15. Hṛṣīkeśa blew the Pāñcajanya, Dhanañjaya, the Devadatta, and Vṛkodara, the doer of terrific deeds, his large conch Pauṇḍra.

अनन्तविजयं राजा कुन्तीपुत्रो युधिष्ठिरः ।
नकुलः सहदेवश्च सुघोषमणिपुष्पकौ ॥ १६

कुन्तीपुत्रः Son of Kunti राजा king युधिष्ठिरः Yudhiṣṭhira अनन्तविजयं (the conch named) Anantavijaya नकुलः Nakula सहदेवः च and Sahadeva सुघोषमणिपुष्पकौ (conchs named) Sughoṣa and Maṇipuṣpaka.

16. King Yudhiṣṭhira, son of Kuntī, blew the conch named Anantavijaya, and Nakula and Sahadeva, their Sughoṣa and Maṇipuṣpaka.

काश्यश्च परमेष्वासः शिखण्डी च महारथः ।
धृष्टद्युम्नो विराटश्च सात्यकिश्चापराजितः ॥ १७

काश्यः च परमेष्वासः And the expert bowman, the king of Kāsi महारथः शिखण्डी च and the great warrior Śikhaṇḍī धृष्टद्युम्नः Dhṛṣṭadyumna विराटः च and Virāṭa अपराजितः सात्यकिः च and the unconquered Sātyaki.

17. The expert bowman, king of Kāsi, and the great warrior Śikhaṇḍī, Dhṛṣṭadyumna, and Virāṭa, and the unconquered Sātyaki;

द्रुपदो द्रौपदेयाश्च सर्वशः पृथिवीपते।
सौभद्रश्च महाबाहुः शङ्खान्दध्मुः पृथक् पृथक्॥ १८

पृथिवीपते O Lord of Earth (Dhṛtarāṣṭra) द्रुपदः (king) Drupada द्रौपदेयाः च and the sons of Draupadī च and महाबाहुः the mighty-armed सौभद्रः son of Subhadrā (Abhimanyu) सर्वशः all पृथक् पृथक् respective शङ्खान् conchs दध्मुः blew.

18. O Lord of Earth! Drupada and the sons of Draupadī, and the mighty-armed son of Subhadrā, all, also blew each his own conch.

स घोषो धार्तराष्ट्राणां हृदयानि व्यदारयत्।
नभश्च पृथिवीञ्चैव तुमुलोऽभ्यनुनादयन्॥ १९

च And सः that तुमुलः tremendous घोषः noise नभः sky पृथिवीं च and earth अभ्यनुनादयन् causing to resound धार्तराष्ट्राणां of Dhṛtarāṣṭra's party हृदयानि hearts व्यदारयत् rent.

19. And the terrific noise resounding throughout heaven and earth rent the hearts of Dhṛtarāṣṭra's party.

Verses 14-19 are full of hints about the superiority of the Pāṇḍava party and the consequent sure defeat of Dhṛtarāṣṭra. The figure to which Sañjaya draws the old king's attention at first taking up Bhīṣma's challenge, is described by him as the Lord of Fortune and the Pāṇḍava—the best of the Pāṇḍu princes. Note also the details in which the chariot, horses, and conchs of the Pāṇḍava party are described; and finally, though the army of the Kauravas was more than a third as much again as that of the Pāṇḍavas, the noise made by the former was only tremendous, whereas that of the latter was not only tremendous but filled the earth and sky with reverberations and rent the hearts of the former.

अथ व्यवस्थितान् दृष्ट्वा धार्तराष्ट्रान् कपिध्वजः ।
प्रवृत्ते शस्त्रसम्पाते धनुरुद्यम्य पाण्डवः ।
हृषीकेशं तदा वाक्यमिदमाह महीपते ।। २०

(हे) महीपते O Lord of Earth (Dhṛtarāṣṭra) अथ then कपिध्वजः monkey-ensigned पाण्डवः Pāṇḍava (Arjuna) धार्तराष्ट्रान् Dhṛtarāṣṭra's party व्यवस्थितान् standing marshalled दृष्ट्वा seeing शस्त्रसम्पाते discharge of missiles प्रवृत्ते about to begin धनुः bow उद्यम्य raising तदा then हृषीकेशं to Hṛṣīkeśa इदम् following वाक्यम् words आह said.

20. Then, O Lord of Earth, seeing Dhṛtarāṣṭra's party standing marshalled and the shooting about to begin, the Pāṇḍava, whose ensign was the monkey, raising his bow, said the following words to Kṛṣṇa:

In view of the sudden change of feeling that is to come over Arjuna it should be noted how full of the war-spirit we find him in this verse.

अर्जुन उवाच

सेनयोरुभयोर्मध्ये रथं स्थापय मेऽच्युत ।। २१
यावदेतान्निरीक्षेऽहं योद्धुकामानवस्थितान् ।
कैर्मया सह योद्धव्यमस्मिन्रणसमुद्यमे ।। २२

अर्जुनः Arjuna उवाच said:

अच्युत (The changeless: Kṛṣṇa) Acyuta उभयोः of both सेनयोः armies मध्ये in the midst मे my रथं chariot स्थापय place अहं I एतान् these योद्धुकामान् desirous to fight अवस्थितान् standing यावत् while निरीक्षे scrutinise अस्मिन् on this रणसमुद्यमे eve of battle कैः सह with whom मया by me योद्धव्यम् the battle should be fought.

Arjuna said:

21-22. Place my chariot, O Acyuta! between the two armies that I may see those who stand here prepared for war. On this eve of battle (let me know) with whom I have to fight.

योत्स्यमानानवेक्षेऽहं य एतेऽत्र समागताः ।
धार्तराष्ट्रस्य दुर्बुद्धेर्युद्धे प्रियचिकीर्षवः ।। २३

अत्र Here (in this Kurukṣetra) युद्धे in battle दुर्बुद्धेः of the evil-minded धार्तराष्ट्रस्य Dhṛtarāṣṭra's son (Duryodhana) प्रियचिकीर्षवः wishing to please ये who एते these समागताः assembled योत्स्यमानान् with the object of fighting अहं I अवेक्षे observe.

23. For I desire to observe those who are assembled here for fight, wishing to please the evil-minded Duryodhana by taking his side on this battle-field.

Arjuna is impatient to see who dared face him in fight!

सञ्जय उवाच

एवमुक्तो हृषीकेशो गुडाकेशेन भारत।
सेनयोरुभयोर्मध्ये स्थापयित्वा रथोत्तमम्॥ २४

भीष्मद्रोणप्रमुखतः सर्वेषां च महीक्षिताम्।
उवाच पार्थ पश्यैतान्समवेतान् कुरूनिति॥ २५

सञ्जयः Sañjaya उवाच said:

भारत (O Descendant of king Bharata: Dhṛtarāṣṭra) Bhārata गुडाकेशेन by (the conqueror of sleep: Arjuna) Guḍākeśa एवं thus उक्तः told हृषीकेशः Hṛṣīkeśa उभयोः of the two सेनयोः armies मध्ये between भीष्मद्रोणप्रमुखतः in front of Bhīṣma and Droṇa च and सर्वेषां (in front) of all महीक्षिताम् rulers of the earth रथोत्तमम् best of chariots स्थापयित्वा having stationed पार्थ (o son of Pṛthā or Kuntī: the name of Arjuna's mother, the first wife of Pāṇḍu) Pārtha समवेतान् gathered together एतान् these कुरून् Kurus पश्य behold इति thus उवाच spoke.

Sañjaya said:

24-25. O Bhārata, commanded thus by Guḍākeśa, Hṛṣīkeśa drove that grandest of chariots to a place between the two hosts, facing Bhīṣma, Droṇa, and all the rulers of the earth, and then spoke thus, "Behold, O Pārtha, all the Kurus gathered together!"

तत्रापश्यत् स्थितान् पार्थः पितॄनथ पितामहान्।
आचार्यान् मातुलान् भ्रातॄन्
पुत्रान् पौत्रान् सखींस्तथा।
श्वशुरान् सुहृदश्चैव सेनयोरुभयोरपि ॥ २६

अथ then पार्थः Pārtha तत्र there उभयोः अपि both the सेनयोः of armies (मध्ये in the midst) स्थितान् stationed पितॄन् uncles पितामहान् grandfathers आचार्यान् teachers मातुलान् maternal uncles भ्रातॄन् brothers (and cousins) पुत्रान् (his own and their) sons पौत्रान् and grandsons तथा and सखीन् comrades श्वशुरान् fathers-in-law सुहृदः च एव and friends as well अपश्यत् saw.

26. Then saw Pārtha stationed there in both the armies, uncles, grandfathers, teachers, maternal uncles, brothers (and cousins), (his own and their) sons, grandsons and comrades, fathers-in-law and friends as well.

तान् समीक्ष्य स कौन्तेयः सर्वान्बन्धूनवस्थितान्।
कृपया परयाविष्टो विषीदन्निदमब्रवीत् ॥ २७

सः He कौन्तेयः the son of Kuntī (Arjuna) अवस्थितान् stationed तान् those सर्वान् all बन्धून् kinsmen समीक्ष्य having seen परया deep कृपया with compassion आविष्टः filled विषीदन् sorrowfully इदम् thus अब्रवीत् spoke.

27. Then he, the son of Kuntī, seeing all those kinsmen stationed in their ranks, spoke thus sorrowfully, filled with deep compassion.

अर्जुन उवाच

दृष्ट्वेमं स्वजनं कृष्ण युयुत्सुं समुपस्थितम् ।
सीदन्ति मम गात्राणि मुखं च परिशुष्यति ।। २८
वेपथुश्च शरीरे मे रोमहर्षश्च जायते ।
गाण्डीवं स्रंसते हस्तात्त्वक् चैव परिदह्यते ।। २९

अर्जुन: Arjuna उवाच said:

कृष्ण (the dark One: He who draws away all misery from His devotees) O Kṛṣṇa समुपस्थितम् present इमं this स्वजनं kinsman युयुत्सुं desirous to fight दृष्ट्वा seeing मम my गात्राणि limbs सीदन्ति are failing मुखं च and mouth परिशुष्यति is parching च and मे my शरीरे in body वेपथु: shivering च and रोमहर्ष: horripilation जायते are taking place हस्तात् from (my) hand गाण्डीवं (my bow) Gāṇḍīva स्रंसते is slipping त्वक् च and (my) skin परिदह्यते is burning all over.

Arjuna said:

28-29. Seeing, O Kṛṣṇa, these my kinsmen gathered here eager for fight, my limbs fail me, and my mouth is parched up. I shiver all over, and my hair stands on end. The bow Gāṇḍīva slips from my hand, and my skin burns.

Compassion overpowered him. Not that it was due to discrimination, but rather to the lack of this. He lost self-control— the first step into the abyss of ignorance.

न च शक्नोम्यवस्थातुं भ्रमतीव च मे मनः ।
निमित्तानि च पश्यामि विपरीतानि केशव ।। ३०

केशव (the slayer of Keśi: Kṛṣṇa) Keśava अवस्थातुं to stand च also न not शक्नोमि I am able मे my मनः mind च and भ्रमति इव seems whirling विपरीतानि adverse निमित्तानि omens च and पश्यामि I see.

30. Neither, O Keśava, can I stand upright. My mind is in a whirl. And I see adverse omens.

न च श्रेयोऽनुपश्यामि हत्वा स्वजनमाहवे।
न काङ्क्षे विजयं कृष्ण न च राज्यं सुखानि च॥ ३१

कृष्ण O Kṛṣṇa आहवे in battle स्वजनम् own people हत्वा killing श्रेयः good च and न nor अनुपश्यामि (I) do see न neither विजयं victory न राज्यं च nor empire सुखानि च and pleasures काङ्क्षे (I) desire.

31. Neither, O Kṛṣṇa, do I see any good in killing these my own people in battle. I desire neither victory nor empire, nor yet pleasure.

किं नो राज्येन गोविन्द किं भोगैर्जीवितेन वा।
येषामर्थे काङ्क्षितं नो राज्यं भोगाः सुखानि च॥ ३२
त इमेऽवस्थिता युद्धे प्राणांस्त्यक्त्वा धनानि च।
आचार्याः पितरः पुत्रास्तथैव च पितामहाः॥ ३३
मातुलाः श्वशुराः पौत्राः श्यालाः संबन्धिनस्तथा॥ ३४

गोविन्द (The presider over and knower of the senses: Kṛṣṇa) Govinda येषाम् अर्थे for whose sake नः by us राज्यं empire भोगाः enjoyments सुखानि च and pleasure काङ्क्षितं desired आचार्याः teachers पितरः uncles पुत्राः sons तथा एव च

and also पितामहाः grandfathers मातुलाः maternal uncles श्वशुराः fathers-in-law पौत्राः grandsons श्यालाः brothers-in-law तथा as well as संबन्धिनः (other) relatives ते they इमे these प्राणान् life धनानि च and wealth त्यक्त्वा having renounced युद्धे in battle अवस्थिताः stand (अतः hence) नः our राज्येन kingdom किं for what purpose भोगैः pleasures वा and even जीवितेन life किं of what avail.

32-34. Of what avail is dominion to us, of what avail are pleasures and even life, if these, O Govinda! for whose sake it is desired that empire, enjoyment, and pleasure should be ours, themselves stand here in battle, having renounced life and wealth—teachers, uncles, sons, and also grandfathers, maternal uncles, fathers-in-law, grandsons, brothers-in-law, besides other kinsmen.

एतान्न हन्तुमिच्छामि घ्नतोऽपि मधुसूदन।
अपि त्रैलोक्यराज्यस्य हेतोः किं नु महीकृते ॥ ३५

मधुसूदन O slayer of Madhu (a demon) घ्नतः अपि even if killed (by them) त्रैलोक्यराज्यस्य dominion over the three worlds (the earth, the intermediate, and the celestial) हेतोः for the sake of अपि even एतान् them हन्तुम् to kill न not इच्छामि (I do) wish महीकृते for earth किं नु far less indeed.

35. Even though these were to kill me, O slayer of Madhu, I could not wish to kill them—not even for the sake of dominion over the three worlds, how much less for the sake of the earth!

निहत्य धार्तराष्ट्रान्नः का प्रीतिः स्याज्जनार्दन ।
पापमेवाश्रयेदस्मान्हत्वैतानाततायिनः ।। ३६

जनार्दन (The destroyer of the *Asura,* Jana; or according to Śaṅkara, He that is prayed to by all for prosperity and salvation: Kṛṣṇa) Janārdana धार्तराष्ट्रान् sons of Dhṛtarāṣṭra निहत्य killing नः ours का what प्रीतिः pleasure स्यात् would be एतान् these आततायिनः felons हत्वा by killing अस्मान् us पापम् sin एव surely आश्रयेत् would take hold.

36. What pleasure indeed could be ours, O Janārdana, from killing these sons of Dhṛtarāṣṭra? Sin only could take hold of us by the slaying of these felons.

Felons: *ātatāyin,* one who sets fire to the house of, administers poison to, falls upon with a sword on, steals the wealth, land, and wife of, another person. Duryodhana did all these to the Pāṇḍava brothers. According to the *Artha-Śāstra,* no sin is incurred by killing an *ātatāyin* even if he be thoroughly versed in Vedānta. But Arjuna seems to argue, "True, there may not be incurred the particular sin of slaying one's own kith and kin by killing the sons of Dhṛtarāṣṭra inasmuch as they are *ātatāyins,* but then the general sin of killing is sure to take hold of us, for the *Dharma-Śāstra* which is more authoritative than the *Artha-Śāstra* enjoins non-killing."

तस्मान्नार्हा वयं हन्तुं धार्तराष्ट्रान् स्वबान्धवान् ।
स्वजनं हि कथं हत्वा सुखिनः स्याम माधव ।। ३७

तस्मात् Therefore स्वबान्धवान् our relatives धार्तराष्ट्रान् sons of Dhṛtarāṣṭra वयं we हन्तुं to kill न not अर्हाः justified माधव O Mādhava हि for स्वजनं kinsmen हत्वा by killing कथं how सुखिनः happy स्याम could (we be).

37. Therefore we ought not to kill our kindred, the sons of Dhṛtarāṣṭra. For how could we, O Mādhava, gain happiness by the slaying of our own kinsmen?

यद्यप्येते न पश्यन्ति लोभोपहतचेतसः ।
कुलक्षयकृतं दोषं मित्रद्रोहे च पातकम् ॥ ३८
कथं न ज्ञेयमस्माभिः पापादस्मान्निवर्तितुम् ।
कुलक्षयकृतं दोषं प्रपश्यद्भिर्जनार्दन ॥ ३९

यद्यपि Though लोभोपहतचेतसः with understanding overpowered by greed एते these कुलक्षयकृतं due to decay of a family दोषं evil च and मित्रद्रोहे in hostility to friends पातकम् sin न no पश्यन्ति see जनार्दन O Janārdana कुलक्षयकृतं due to decay of a family दोषं evil प्रपश्यद्भिः clearly seeing अस्माभिः by us अस्मात् पापात् from this sin निवर्तितुम् to turn away कथं why न ज्ञेयम् should not be learnt.

38-39. Though these, with understanding overpowered by greed, see no evil due to decay of families, and no sin in hostility to friends, why should we, O Janārdana, who see clearly the evil due to the decay of families, not turn away from this sin?

कुलक्षये प्रणश्यन्ति कुलधर्माः सनातनाः ।
धर्मे नष्टे कुलं कृत्स्नमधर्मोऽभिभवत्युत ॥ ४०

कुलक्षये On the decay of a family सनातनाः immemorial कुलधर्माः family religious practices प्रणश्यन्ति disappear धर्मे नष्टे spirituality being destroyed कृत्स्नम् the whole उत also कुलं family अधर्मः impiety अभिभवति overcomes.

40. On the decay of a family the immemorial religious rites of that family die out. On the destruction of spirituality, impiety further overwhelms the whole of the family.

अधर्माभिभवात् कृष्ण प्रदुष्यन्ति कुलस्त्रियः ।
स्त्रीषु दुष्टासु वार्ष्णेय जायते वर्णसङ्करः ॥ ४१

कृष्ण O Kṛṣṇa अधर्माभिभवात् from the prevalence of impiety कुलस्त्रियः the women of the family प्रदुष्यन्ति become corrupt वार्ष्णेय (descendant of the Vṛṣṇi clan: Kṛṣṇa) Vārṣṇeya स्त्रीषु women दुष्टासु being corrupted वर्णसङ्करः caste admixture जायते arises.

41. On the prevalence of impiety, O Kṛṣṇa, the women of the family become corrupt; and women being corrupted, there arises, O Vārṣṇeya, intermingling of castes.

सङ्करो नरकायैव कुलघ्नानां कुलस्य च ।
पतन्ति पितरो ह्येषां लुप्तपिण्डोदकक्रियाः ॥ ४२

सङ्करः Admixture (of castes) कुलघ्नानां of the family-destroyers कुलस्य of the family नरकाय for the hell च also एव indeed हि sure एषां their पितरः ancestors लुप्त-पिण्डोदकक्रियाः deprived of the offerings of rice-ball and water पतन्ति fall.

42. Admixture of castes, indeed, is for the hell of the family and the destroyers of the family; their ancestors fall deprived of the offerings of rice-ball and water.

Verily, confusion of family is the hell of destroyers of family. (For then do)Their own ancestors fall, deprived etc. This refers to the well-known Śrāddha ceremony of the Hindus, the main principle of which consists in sending helpful thoughts to the dead relations as well as to all the occupants of Pitṛ-loka (a temporary abode, immediately after death) accompanied with (to make the thoughts more forcible) concrete offerings. The poor are also fed to secure their good wishes.

दोषैरेतैः कुलघ्नानां वर्णसङ्करकारकैः ।
उत्साद्यन्ते जातिधर्माः कुलधर्माश्च शाश्वताः ॥ ४३

कुलघ्नानां of the family-destroyers वर्णसङ्करकारकैः causing admixture of castes एतैः दोषैः by these misdeeds शाश्वताः immemorial जातिधर्माः caste religious practices कुलधर्माः च and family religious practices उत्साद्यन्ते are destroyed.

43. By these misdeeds of the destroyers of the family, bringing about confusion of castes, are the immemorial religious rites of the caste and the family destroyed.

उत्सन्नकुलधर्माणां मनुष्याणां जनार्दन ।
नरके नियतं वासो भवतीत्यनुशुश्रुम ॥ ४४

जनार्दन O Janārdana उत्सन्नकुलधर्माणां मनुष्याणां of the men whose family religious practices are destroyed नियतं inevitably नरके in hell वासः dwelling भवति is इति thus अनुशुश्रुम have we heard.

44. We have heard, O Janārdana, that dwelling in hell is inevitable for those men in whose families religious practices have been destroyed.

अहो बत महत्पापं कर्तुं व्यवसिता वयम् ।
यद्राज्यसुखलोभेन हन्तुं स्वजनमुद्यताः ॥ ४५

यत् That राज्यसुखलोभेन by the greed of pleasures of kingdom स्वजनम् kinsmen हन्तुं to kill उद्यताः prepared वयम् we (एतत् this) महत् great पापं sin कर्तुं to do व्यवसिताः resolved अहो बत alas.

45. Alas, we are involved in a great sin, in that we are prepared to slay our kinsmen, out of greed for the pleasures for a kingdom!

यदि मामप्रतीकारमशस्त्रं शस्त्रपाणयः ।
धार्तराष्ट्रा रणे हन्युस्तन्मे क्षेमतरं भवेत् ॥ ४६

यदि If अप्रतीकारम् unresisting अशस्त्रं unarmed माम् me शस्त्रपाणयः weapons in hand धार्तराष्ट्राः sons of Dhṛtarāṣṭra रणे in the battle हन्युः should slay तत् that मे my क्षेमतरं better भवेत् would be.

46. Verily, if the sons of Dhṛtarāṣṭra, weapons in hand, were to slay me, unresisting and unarmed, in the battle, that would be better for me.

सञ्जय उवाच

एवमुक्त्वाऽर्जुनः संख्ये रथोपस्थ उपाविशत्।
विसृज्य सशरं चापं शोकसंविग्नमानसः ॥ ४७

सञ्जयः Sañjaya उवाच said:

अर्जुनः Arjuna एवम् thus उक्त्वा saying संख्ये in the battle सशरं with arrows चापं bow (named Gāṇḍīva) विसृज्य casting away शोकसंविग्नमानसः with a mind distressed with sorrow रथोपस्थे on the seat of the chariot उपाविशत् sat down.

Sañjaya said:

47. Speaking thus in the midst of the battle-field, Arjuna, casting away his bow and arrows, sank down on the seat of his chariot, with his mind distressed with sorrow.

इति अर्जुनविषादयोगो नाम प्रथमोऽध्यायः ॥

The end of first chapter, designated,
The Grief of Arjuna.

द्वितीयोऽध्यायः
(सांख्ययोगः)

SECOND CHAPTER
(The Way of Knowledge)

सञ्जय उवाच

तं तथा कृपयाविष्टमश्रुपूर्णाकुलेक्षणम्।
विषीदन्तमिदं वाक्यमुवाच मधुसूदनः ॥ १

सञ्जयः Sañjaya उवाच said:

मधुसूदनः (Destroyer of Madhu) Madhusūdana तथा thus कृपया with pity आविष्टम् overwhelmed अश्रुपूर्णाकुलेक्षणम् eyes dimmed with tears विषीदन्तम् sorrowing तं him (Arjuna) इदं this वाक्यम् word उवाच spoke.

Sañjaya said:

1. To him who was thus overwhelmed with pity and sorrowing, and whose eyes were dimmed with tears, Madhusūdana spoke these words.

Overwhelmed with pity: Not Arjuna, but Arjuna's feeling was master of the situation.

श्रीभगवानुवाच

कुतस्त्वा कश्मलमिदं विषमे समुपस्थितम्।
अनार्यजुष्टमस्वर्ग्यमकीर्तिकरमर्जुन ॥ २

श्रीभगवान् The Blessed Lord उवाच said:
अर्जुन O Arjuna विषमे in (such a) crisis कुत: whence इदं this अनार्यजुष्टम् un-*Ārya*-like (unworthy of a religious man) अस्वर्ग्यम् contrary to the attainment of heaven अकीर्तिकरम् disgraceful कश्मलम् delusion त्वा upon thee समुपस्थितम् comes.

The Blessed Lord said:
2. In such a crisis, whence comes upon thee, O Arjuna, this delusion, un-*Ārya*-like, disgraceful, and contrary to the attainment of heaven ?

Mark with what contempt Kṛṣṇa regards Arjuna's attitude of weakness masked by religious expression!

क्लैब्यं मास्म गमः पार्थ नैतत्त्वय्युपपद्यते।
क्षुद्रं हृदयदौर्बल्यं त्यक्त्वोत्तिष्ठ परन्तप।। ३

पार्थ Son of Pṛthā क्लैब्यं unmanliness मास्म गम: do not get एतत् it त्वयि in thee न उपपद्यते ill becomes परन्तप O scorcher of foes क्षुद्रं mean हृदयदौर्बल्यं faint-heartedness त्यक्त्वा casting off उत्तिष्ठ arise.

3. Yield not to unmanliness, O son of Pṛthā! Ill doth it become thee. Cast off this mean faint-heartedness and arise, O scorcher of thine enemies!

अर्जुन उवाच

कथं भीष्ममहं संख्ये द्रोणं च मधुसूदन।
इषुभिः प्रतियोत्स्यामि पूजार्हावरिसूदन।। ४

अर्जुन: Arjuna उवाच said:

अरिसूदन O destroyer of foes मधुसूदन O slayer of Madhu अहं I संख्ये in battle पूजार्हौ worthy to be worshipped भीष्मम् Bhiṣma द्रोणं च and Droṇa इषुभि: with arrows कथं how प्रतियोत्स्यामि shall fight against.

Arjuna said:

4. But how can I, in battle, O slayer of Madhu, fight with arrows against Bhiṣma and Droṇa, who are rather worthy to be worshipped, O destroyer of foes!

गुरूनहत्वा हि महानुभावान्
श्रेयो भोक्तुं भैक्ष्यमपीह लोके।
हत्वार्थकामांस्तु गुरूनिहैव
भुञ्जीय भोगान् रुधिरप्रदिग्धान्॥ ५

महानुभावान् Great-souled गुरून् masters अहत्वा instead of slaying हि surely इह लोके in this life भैक्ष्यम् bread of beggary अपि even भोक्तुं to eat श्रेय: better तु but गुरून् masters हत्वा killing इह in this world एव even अर्थकामान् wealth and desires भोगान् enjoyments रुधिर-प्रदिग्धान् stained with blood भुञ्जीय enjoy.

5. Surely it would be better even to eat the bread of beggary in this life than to slay these great-souled masters. But if I kill them, even in this world, all my enjoyment of wealth and desires will be stained with blood.

i.e. even in this world I shall be in hell.

न चैतद्विद्मः कतरन्नो गरीयो
यद्वा जयेम यदि वा नो जयेयुः ।
यानेव हत्वा न जिजीविषाम-
स्तेऽवस्थिताः प्रमुखे धार्तराष्ट्राः ।। ६

नः for us कतरत् which of the two गरीयः better एतत् this न च विद्मः and I know not यद्वा whether जयेम we should conquer यदि वा or that नः us जयेयुः they should conquer यान् whom एव very हत्वा after slaying न जिजीविषामः we should not care to live ते those धार्तराष्ट्राः sons of Dhṛtarāṣṭra प्रमुखे in front अवस्थिताः stand.

6. And indeed I can scarcely tell which will be better, that we should conquer them, or that they should conquer us. The very sons of Dhṛtarāṣṭra—after slaying whom we should not care to live—stand facing us.

कार्पण्यदोषोपहतस्वभावः
पृच्छामि त्वां धर्मसंमूढचेताः ।
यच्छ्रेयः स्यान्निश्चितं ब्रूहि तन्मे
शिष्यस्तेऽहं शाधि मां त्वां प्रपन्नम् ।। ७

कार्पण्यदोषोपहतस्वभावः with (my Kṣatriya) nature overpowered by the taint of weak commiseration धर्मसंमूढचेताः with a mind in confusion about Dharma (duty) त्वां Thee पृच्छामि I ask मे for me यत् which श्रेयः good स्यात् is तत् that निश्चितं decidedly ब्रूहि say अहं I ते Thy शिष्यः disciple त्वां Thee प्रपन्नम् taken refuge मां me शाधि instruct.

7. With my nature overpowered by weak commiseration, with a mind in confusion about duty, I supplicate Thee. Say decidedly what is good for me. I am Thy disciple. Instruct me who have taken refuge in Thee.

Dharma is the *ness,* the law of the inmost constitution of a thing. The primary meaning of Dharma is not virtue or religion, but that is only its secondary significance. Fighting in a just cause is the religious duty or Dharma of a Kṣatriya, while the same is a sin to a Brāhmaṇa, because it is contrary to the law of his being. Working out one's *Karma* according to the law of one's own being is therefore the Dharma or religion or way to salvation of an individual. The cloud of *Karma* hides the Self-Sun from view. The means which exhausts this cloud without adding to it and thus helps in one's Self-restoration is one's Dharma.

Thy disciple: Until this declaration has been made, the Master may not give the highest knowledge.

न हि प्रपश्यामि ममापनुद्याद्
यच्छोकमुच्छोषणमिन्द्रियाणाम्।
अवाप्य भूमावसपत्नमृद्धं
राज्यं सुराणामपि चाधिपत्यम्॥ ८

भूमौ In the earth असपत्नम् unrivalled ऋद्धं flourishing राज्यं dominion सुराणाम् over the gods अपि even आधिपत्यम् mastery च and अवाप्य obtaining यत् that मम my इन्द्रियाणाम् of the senses उच्छोषणम् blasting शोकम् sorrow अपनुद्यात् should remove न हि प्रपश्यामि I do not see.

8. I do not see anything to remove this sorrow which blasts my senses, even were I to obtain unrivalled and flourishing dominion over the earth, and mastery over the gods.

सञ्जय उवाच

एवमुक्त्वा हृषीकेशं गुडाकेशः परन्तपः ।
न योत्स्य इति गोविन्दमुक्त्वा तूष्णीं बभूव ह ॥ ९

सञ्जय: Sañjaya उवाच said:

परन्तप: The scorcher of foes गुडाकेश: Guḍākeśa, the conqueror of sleep (Arjuna) हृषीकेशं to Hṛṣikeśa एवम् thus उक्त्वा having spoken न योत्स्ये I shall not fight इति thus गोविन्दम् to Govinda उक्त्वा saying तूष्णीं silent बभूव ह became.

Sañjaya said:

9. Having spoken thus to the Lord of the senses, Guḍākeśa, the scorcher of foes, said to Govinda, "I shall not fight", and became silent.

The object of Sañjaya in using these names is to remind Dhṛtarāṣṭra—who may naturally be a little elated at the prospect of Arjuna's not fighting—that this is only a temporary weakness, since by the presence of the Lord of the senses all ignorance must eventually be dispelled. Arjuna's own nature also is devoid of darkness. Is he not the conqueror of sleep, and the terror of foes?

तमुवाच हृषीकेशः प्रहसन्निव भारत ।
सेनयोरुभयोर्मध्ये विषीदन्तमिदं वचः ॥ १०

भारत Descendant of King Bharata (after whom India is called Bhārata-Varṣa) O Bhārata (Dhṛtarāṣṭra) हृषीकेशः Hṛṣīkeśa -प्रहसन् smiling इव as if उभयोः of the two सेनयोः armies मध्ये in the midst विषीदन्तम् sorrowing तम् to him इदं this वचः word उवाच spoke.

10. To him who was sorrowing in the midst of the two armies, Hṛṣīkeśa, as if smiling, O descendant of Bharata, spoke these words.

Smiling—to drown Arjuna in the ocean of shame. Kṛṣṇa's smile at Arjuna's sorrow is like the lightning that plays over the black monsoon cloud. The rain bursts forth, and the thirsty earth is saturated. It is the smile of the coming illumination.

श्रीभगवानुवाच

अशोच्यानन्वशोचस्त्वं प्रज्ञावादांश्च भाषसे।
गतासूनगतासूंश्च नानुशोचन्ति पण्डिताः ॥ ११

श्रीभगवान् The Blessed Lord उवाच said:

त्वं Thou अशोच्यान् those who should not be mourned for अन्वशोचः hast been mourning प्रज्ञावादान् words of wisdom भाषसे thou speakest च but पण्डिताः the wise गतासून् the dead अगतासून् the living च and न अनुशोचन्ति grieve not.

The Blessed Lord said:

11. Thou hast been mourning for them who should not be mourned for. Yet thou speakest words of wisdom. The (truly) wise grieve neither for the living nor for the dead.

Words of wisdom: Vide I. 35-44.

न त्वेवाहं जातु नासं न त्वं नेमे जनाधिपाः ।
न चैव न भविष्यामः सर्वे वयमतः परम् ।। १२

अहं I जातु ever न तु आसं did not exist (इति) न एव not indeed त्वं thou (न आसीः did not exist) न not इमे these जनाधिपाः kings (न आसन् did not exist) न not अतःपरम् hereafter सर्वे all वयम् we न not भविष्यामः shall exist च also न एव not at all.

12. It is not that I have never existed, nor thou nor these kings. Nor is it that we shall cease to exist in the future.

Of course Kṛṣṇa here does not mean that the body is immortal, but refers to the true Self, behind all bodies.

देहिनोऽस्मिन् यथा देहे कौमारं यौवनं जरा ।
तथा देहान्तरप्राप्तिर्धीरस्तत्र न मुह्यति ।। १३

यथा As देहिनः of the embodied (soul) अस्मिन् देहे in this body कौमारं childhood यौवनं youth जरा old age तथा so also देहान्तरप्राप्तिः the attaining of another body तत्र thereat धीरः the calm soul न मुह्यति is not deluded.

13. As are childhood, youth, and old age, in this body, to the embodied soul, so also is the attaining of another body. Calm souls are not deluded thereat.

According to this, the continuity of the ego is no more interrupted by death than by the passing of childhood into youth and youth into old age in this body.

Calm souls: Those who have become calm by Self-realisation.

मात्रास्पर्शास्तु कौन्तेय शीतोष्णसुखदुःखदाः ।
आगमापायिनोऽनित्यास्तांस्तितिक्षस्व भारत ।। १४

कौन्तेय O son of Kuntī मात्रास्पर्शाः contacts of senses with their objects तु indeed शीतोष्णसुखदुःखदाः producers of (the notions of) cold and heat, pleasure and pain आगमापायिनः with beginning and end अनित्याः impermanent भारत O Bhārata तान् them तितिक्षस्व bear with.

14. Notions of heat and cold, of pain and pleasure, are born, O son of Kuntī, only of the contact of the senses with their objects. They have a beginning and an end. They are impermanent in their nature. Bear them patiently, O descendant of Bharata.

They have a beginning and an end: as distinguished from the permanent Self. The more one is able to identify oneself with the permanent Self, the less one is affected by the agreeable and disagreeable conditions of life.

Impermanent in their nature: That is, the same object which gives pleasure at one moment, gives pain at another, and so on.

यं हि न व्यथयन्त्येते पुरुषं पुरुषर्षभ ।
समदुःखसुखं धीरं सोऽमृतत्वाय कल्पते ।। १५

पुरुषर्षभ O Bull (i.e. chief) among men एते these समदुःखसुखं same in pain and pleasure धीरं calm यं that पुरुषं (lit. dweller in the body) man न व्यथयन्ति afflict not सः he हि surely अमृतत्वाय for immortality कल्पते is fit.

15. That calm man who is the same in pain and pleasure, whom these cannot disturb, alone is able, O great amongst men, to attain to immortality.

This perfect sameness, amidst the ills of life, means full and unbroken consciousness of our oneness with the immortal Self. Thus is immortality attained.

नासतो विद्यते भावो नाभावो विद्यते सतः ।
उभयोरपि दृष्टोऽन्तस्त्वनयोस्तत्त्वदर्शिभिः ।। १६

असत: Of the unreal भाव: existence न विद्यते is not सत: of the real अपि also अभाव: non-existence न विद्यते is not तत्त्वदर्शिभि: by the knowers of the Truth तु indeed अनयो: उभयो: of these two अन्त: the final truth दृष्ट: seen.

16. The unreal never is. The Real never is not. Men possessed of the knowledge of the Truth fully know both these.

Unreal and Real: The determination of the nature of the Real is the quest of all philosophy. Śri Kṛṣṇa here states that a thing which never remains the same for any given period is unreal, and that the Real on the other hand is always the same. The whole of the phenomenal world, therefore, must be unreal, because in it no one state endures for even an infinitesimal division of time. And that which takes note of this incessant change, and is therefore itself changeless—the Ātman, Consciousness—is the Real.

अविनाशि तु तद्विद्धि येन सर्वमिदं ततम्।
विनाशमव्ययस्यास्य न कश्चित्कर्तुमर्हति ॥ १७

येन By which इदं this सर्वम् all ततम् is pervaded तत् That अविनाशि indestructible तु विद्धि know for certain कश्चित् one अस्य अव्ययस्य of this Immutable विनाशम् destruction कर्तुम् to do न अर्हति is not able.

17. That by which all this is pervaded—That know for certain to be indestructible. None has the power to destroy this Immutable.

That by which all this is pervaded: i.e. He that pervades all this *as the Witness*.

अन्तवन्त इमे देहा नित्यस्योक्ताः शरीरिणः ।
अनाशिनोऽप्रमेयस्य तस्माद्युध्यस्व भारत ॥ १८

नित्यस्य Of the ever-changeless अनाशिनः of the indestructible अप्रमेयस्य of the illimitable शरीरिणः of the Indweller इमे these देहाः bodies अन्तवन्तः having an end उक्ताः are said भारत O Bhārata तस्मात् therefore युध्यस्व fight.

18. Of this indwelling Self—the ever-changeless, the indestructible, the illimitable—these bodies are said to have an end. Fight, therefore, O descendant of Bharata.

Arjuna's grief which deters him from his duty of fighting against the Kauravas is born of ignorance as to the true nature of the soul. Hence Śri Bhagavān's strong and repeated attempts to illumine him on the subject.

य एनं वेत्ति हन्तारं यश्चैनं मन्यते हतम्।
उभौ तौ न विजानीतो नायं हन्ति न हन्यते॥ १९

यः Who एनं this (self) हन्तारं slayer वेत्ति knows यः च and who एनं this हतम् slain मन्यते thinks उभौ both तौ these न not विजानीतः know अयं this (Self) न not हन्ति slays न not हन्यते is slain.

19. He who takes the self to be the slayer, and he who takes It to be the slain, neither of these knows. It does not slay, nor is it slain.

Cf. KaṭhaUp.I. ii.19–20

न जायते म्रियते वा कदाचि-
न्नायं भूत्वा भविता वा न भूयः।
अजो नित्यः शाश्वतोऽयं पुराणो
न हन्यते हन्यमाने शरीरे॥ २०

अयं this (Self) कदाचित् ever न not जायते is born वा or म्रियते dies वा or न भूत्वा not having been भूयः again भविता comes into being (इति) न (it is) not. (Another paraphrase) वा Or भूत्वा having been भूयः again न भविता ceases to be (इति) न (it is) not. अजः unborn नित्यः eternal शाश्वतः changeless पुराणः ever Itself अयं this (Self) शरीरे the body हन्यमाने being killed न not हन्यते is killed.

20. This is never born, nor does it die. It is not that, not having been, It again comes into being. (Or according to another view: It is not that having been, It again ceases to be). This is unborn, eternal,

changeless, ever-Itself. It is not killed when the body is killed.

This śloka refers in the sense of denial to the six kinds of modification inherent in matter: birth, subsistence, growth, transformation, decay, and death.

वेदाविनाशिनं नित्यं य एनमजमव्ययम्।
कथं स पुरुषः पार्थ कं घातयति हन्ति कम्॥ २१

पार्थ O Pārtha यः who एनम् This (Self) अविनाशिनं indestructible नित्यं changeless अजम् unborn अव्ययम् immutable वेद knows सः that पुरुषः person कथं how कं whom हन्ति kills कं whom घातयति causes to slay.

21. He that knows This to be indestructible, changeless, without birth, and immutable, how is he, O son of Pṛthā, to slay or cause another to slay?

How is he to slay?—referring to Arjuna. To *cause another to slay*—referring to Kṛṣṇa's own part.

वासांसि जीर्णानि यथा विहाय
नवानि गृह्णाति नरोऽपराणि।
तथा शरीराणि विहाय जीर्णा-
न्यन्यानि संयाति नवानि देही॥ २२

नरः A man यथा as जीर्णानि worn-out वासांसि clothes विहाय casting off अपराणि others नवानि new गृह्णाति takes तथा so देही the embodied जीर्णानि worn-out शरीराणि bodies विहाय casting off अन्यानि others नवानि new संयाति enters.

22. Even as a man casts off worn-out clothes, and puts on others which are new, so the embodied casts off worn-out bodies, and enters into others which are new.

As one only puts off the old, when one already possesses the new garment, so the embodied is already entering a new body in the act of leaving this. The Upaniṣad compares this to the movement of a leech, which has already established a new foothold before leaving the old.

नैनं छिन्दन्ति शस्त्राणि नैनं दहति पावकः ।
न चैनं क्लेदयन्त्यापो न शोषयति मारुतः ॥ २३

शस्त्राणि Weapons एनं This (Self) नं छिन्दन्ति cut not पावकः fire एनं This न दहति burns not आपः waters एनं This न क्लेदयन्ति wet not च and मारुतः wind न शोषयति dries not.

23. This (Self), weapons cut not; This, fire burns not; This, water wets not; and This, wind dries not.

अच्छेद्योऽयमदाह्योऽयमक्लेद्योऽशोष्य एव च ।
नित्यः सर्वगतः स्थाणुरचलोऽयं सनातनः ॥ २४

अयम् This (Self) अच्छेद्यः cannot be cut अयम् This अदाह्यः cannot be burnt अक्लेद्यः cannot be wetted अशोष्यः च एव and cannot also be dried अयं This नित्यः changeless सर्वगतः all-pervading स्थाणुः unmoving अचलः immovable सनातनः eternal.

24. This Self cannot be cut, nor burnt, nor wetted, nor dried. Changeless, all-pervading, unmoving, immovable, the Self is eternal.

अव्यक्तोऽयमचिन्त्योऽयमविकार्योऽयमुच्यते ।
तस्मादेवं विदित्वैनं नानुशोचितुमर्हसि ॥ २५

अयम् This (Self) अव्यक्तः unmanifested अयम् This अचिन्त्यः unthinkable अयम् This अविकार्यः unchangeable उच्यते is said तस्मात् therefore एवं thus एनं This विदित्वा knowing अनुशोचितुम् to mourn न अर्हसि oughtest not.

25. This (Self) is said to be unmanifested, unthinkable, and unchangeable. Therefore, knowing This to be such, thou oughtest not to mourn.

This Self is infinite and partless, so can be neither subject nor object of any action.

अथ चैनं नित्यजातं नित्यं वा मन्यसे मृतम् ।
तथापि त्वं महाबाहो नैनं शोचितुमर्हसि ॥ २६

अथ च But if एनं This (Self) नित्यजातं constantly born वा or नित्यं constantly मृतम् dead मन्यसे thinkest तथापि even then महाबाहो mighty-armed त्वं thou एनं This शोचितुम् to mourn न अर्हसि oughtest not.

26. But if thou shouldst take This to have constant birth and death, even in that case, O mighty-armed, thou oughtest not to mourn for This.

Kṛṣṇa here, for the sake of argument, takes up the materialistic supposition, and shows that even if the Self were impermanent, sorrow ought to be destroyed, since in that case there would be no hereafter, no sin, and no hell.

जातस्य हि ध्रुवो मृत्युर्ध्रुवं जन्म मृतस्य च।
तस्मादपरिहार्येऽर्थे न त्वं शोचितुमर्हसि ॥ २७

हि For जातस्य of that which is born मृत्युः death ध्रुवः certain मृतस्य च and of that which is dead जन्म birth ध्रुवं certain तस्मात् therefore अपरिहार्ये अर्थे in an unavoidable matter त्वं thou शोचितुम् to grieve न अर्हसि oughtest not.

27. Of that which is born, death is certain; of that which is dead, birth is certain. Over the unavoidable, therefore, thou oughtest not to grieve.

This śloka concerns only those who are not yet free. So long as there is desire, birth and death are inevitable. *Therefore thou oughtest not to grieve*: Since you cannot control the inevitable and preserve the bodies of your relations, work out your own *Karma* and go beyond both birth and death.

अव्यक्तादीनि भूतानि व्यक्तमध्यानि भारत।
अव्यक्तनिधनान्येव तत्र का परिदेवना ॥ २८

भारत O Bhārata भूतानि beings अव्यक्तादीनि unmanifested in the beginning व्यक्तमध्यानि manifested in the middle state अव्यक्तनिधनानि एव unmanifested again in the end तत्र there का what परिदेवना grief.

28. All beings are unmanifested in their beginning, O Bhārata, manifested in their middle state, and unmanifested again in their end. What is there then to grieve about ?

Beings: In their relationships as sons and friends, who are mere combinations of material elements, correlated as causes and effects.

The idea here is that which has no existence in the beginning and in the end, must be merely illusory in the interim, and should not therefore be allowed to have any influence upon the mind.

आश्चर्यवत्पश्यति कश्चिदेन-
माश्चर्यवद्वदति तथैव चान्यः ।
आश्चर्यवच्चैनमन्यः शृणोति
श्रुत्वाप्येनं वेद न चैव कश्चित् ॥ २९

कश्चित् Some one एनम् This (Self) आश्चर्यवत् as a wonder पश्यति looks upon तथा एव च and so also अन्यः another आश्चर्यवत् as a wonder वदति speaks अन्यः च another again एनम् This आश्चर्यवत् as a wonder शृणोति hears कश्चित् च and yet another श्रुत्वा अपि though hearing एनं This न एव वेद knows not at all.

29. Some look upon the Self as marvellous. Others speak of It as wonderful. Others again hear of It as a wonder. And still others, though hearing, do not understand It at all.

The śloka may also be interpreted in the sense that those who see, hear, and speak of the Self are wonderful men, because their number is so small. It is not therefore remarkable that you should mourn, because the Ātman is so difficult to comprehend.

देही नित्यमवध्योऽयं देहे सर्वस्य भारत।
तस्मात्सर्वाणि भूतानि न त्वं शोचितुमर्हसि॥ ३०

भारत O Bhārata अयं this देही Indweller सर्वस्य of all देहे in the body नित्यम् ever अवध्यः indestructible तस्मात् therefore त्वं thou सर्वाणि all भूतानि beings शोचितुम् to mourn न अर्हसि oughtest not.

30. This, the Indweller in the bodies of all, is ever indestructible, O descendant of Bharata. Therefore thou oughtest not to mourn for any creature.

Kṛṣṇa here returns to His own point of view.

स्वधर्ममपि चावेक्ष्य न विकम्पितुमर्हसि।
धर्म्याद्धि युद्धाच्छ्रेयोऽन्यत्क्षत्रियस्य न विद्यते॥ ३१

स्वधर्मम् Own Dharma अपि च and also अवेक्ष्य looking at न not विकम्पितुम् to waver अर्हसि oughtest हि for धर्म्यात् युद्धात् than a righteous war क्षत्रियस्य for a Kṣatriya अन्यत् any other श्रेयः higher न विद्यते exists not.

31. Looking at thine own Dharma, also, thou oughtest not to waver, for there is nothing higher for a Kṣatriya than a righteous war.

That is to say, it is the duty of a Kṣatriya to fight in the interest of his country, people, and religion.

यदृच्छया चोपपन्नं स्वर्गद्वारमपावृतम्।
सुखिनः क्षत्रियाः पार्थ लभन्ते युद्धमीदृशम्॥ ३२

पार्थ O Partha यदृच्छया of itself उपपन्नं come च verily अपावृतम् opened स्वर्गद्वारम् the gate of heaven ईदृशम् such युद्धम् battle सुखिन: happy क्षत्रिया: Kṣatriyas लभन्ते gain.

32. Fortunate certainly are the Kṣatriyas, O son of Pṛthā, who are called to fight in such a battle that comes unsought as an open gate to heaven.

The *Śāstras* say that if a Kṣatriya, fighting for a righteous cause, falls in the battle-field, he at once goes to heaven.

अथ चेत्त्वमिमं धर्म्यं संग्रामं न करिष्यसि।
ततः स्वधर्मं कीर्तिं च हित्वा पापमवाप्स्यसि॥ ३३

अथ चेत् But if त्वम् thou इमं this धर्म्यं righteous संग्रामं warfare न करिष्यसि wouldst not do ततः then स्वधर्मं own Dharma कीर्तिं च and honour हित्वा forfeiting पापम् sin अवाप्स्यसि shalt incur.

33. But if thou refusest to engage in this righteous warfare, then forfeiting thine own Dharma and honour, thou shalt incur sin.

अकीर्तिञ्चापि भूतानि कथयिष्यन्ति तेऽव्ययाम्।
संभावितस्य चाकीर्तिर्मरणादतिरिच्यते॥ ३४

अपि च And also भूतानि beings ते of thee अव्ययाम् everlasting अकीर्तिम् dishonour कथयिष्यन्ति will tell संभावितस्य of the honoured अकीर्तिः dishonour मरणात् than death च surely अतिरिच्यते exceeds.

34. The world also will ever hold thee in reprobation. To the honoured, disrepute is surely worse than death.

The present argument—ślokas 33–36—assumes that the cause in hand is already proved to be right. Hence it could only be from cowardice that Arjuna could abandon it. Even a hero may be weakened by the stirring of his deepest emotions.

भयाद्रणादुपरतं मंस्यन्ते त्वां महारथाः ।
येषां च त्वं बहुमतो भूत्वा यास्यसि लाघवम् ।। ३५

महारथाः च And the great chariot-warriors त्वां thee भयात् from fear रणात् from battle उपरतं withdrawn मंस्यन्ते will regard येषां of those त्वं thou बहुमतः much-thought-of भूत्वा having been लाघवम् lightness यास्यसि wilt receive.

35. The great chariot-warriors* will believe that thou hast withdrawn from the battle through fear. And thou wilt be lightly esteemed by them who have thought much of thee.

---

* *Vide* commentary 1.6.

अवाच्यवादांश्च बहून्वदिष्यन्ति तवाहिताः ।
निन्दन्तस्तव सामर्थ्यं ततो दुःखतरं नु किम् ।। ३६

तव Thine अहिता: च enemies also तव thy सामर्थ्यं prowess निन्दन्त: cavilling बहून् many अवाच्यवादान् unutterable things वदिष्यन्ति will say तत: than this दु:खतरं more painful नु किम् what (could be).

36. Thine enemies also, cavilling at thy great prowess, will say of thee things that are not to be uttered. What could be more intolerable than this?

हतो वा प्राप्स्यसि स्वर्गं जित्वा वा भोक्ष्यसे महीम् ।
तस्मादुत्तिष्ठ कौन्तेय युद्धाय कृतनिश्चयः ।। ३७

हत: Slain वा or स्वर्गं heaven प्राप्स्यसि shalt gain जित्वा conquering वा or महीम् earth भोक्ष्यसे shalt enjoy तस्मात् therefore कौन्तेय O son of Kunti युद्धाय for fight कृतनिश्चय: resolved उत्तिष्ठ arise.

37. Dying thou gainest heaven; conquering thou enjoyest the earth. Therefore, O son of Kuntī, arise, resolved to fight.

सुखदुःखे समे कृत्वा लाभालाभौ जयाजयौ ।
ततो युद्धाय युज्यस्व नैवं पापमवाप्स्यसि ।। ३८

सुखदु:खे Pain and pleasure समे the same कृत्वा having made लाभालाभौ gain and loss जयाजयौ conquest and defeat तत: then युद्धाय for battle युज्यस्व be ready एवं thus पापम् sin न no अवाप्स्यसि shalt incur.

38. Having made pain and pleasure, gain and loss, conquest and defeat, the same, engage thou then in battle. So shalt thou incur no sin.

It is always the desire for one of the pairs of opposites that binds. When an act is done without attachment either for itself or its fruit, then *Karma* can be worked out without adding to its store, and this leads to Freedom.

एषा तेऽभिहिता सांख्ये बुद्धिर्योगे त्विमां शृणु।
बुद्ध्या युक्तो यया पार्थ कर्मबन्धं प्रहास्यसि ॥ ३९

सांख्ये In regard to Self-realisation एषा this बुद्धिः wisdom ते to thee अभिहिता declared योगे तु but in regard to Yoga इमां it शृणु hear पार्थ O Pārtha यया with which बुद्ध्या wisdom युक्तः endued कर्मबन्धं bondage of Karma प्रहास्यसि shalt break through.

39. The wisdom of Self-realisation has been declared unto thee. Hearken thou now to the wisdom of Yoga, endued with which, O son of Pṛthā, thou shalt break through the bonds of Karma.

Yoga: Karma-Yoga, or that plan of conduct which secures the working out of past *Karma,* non-accumulation of new and the striving for Self-realisation with the whole of the will. In this discipline, one's sole object in life is Self-realisation; hence no importance is attached to anything else. Thus all actions are performed without attachment, or care for results. So no new *Karma* is made: only the already accumulated is exhausted. And at the same time, the whole will is left free to devote itself to the achievement of Self-realisation alone.

In the preceding ślokas, 11–25, Kṛṣṇa has given the point of view of the highest knowledge, the ancient *Brahmajñāna.* In the 26th and 27th we have a purely materialistic standpoint. Ślokas 28 to 37 give the attitude of a man of the world. In the 38th we have an anticipation of the Yoga. And in what is to follow, we have Śrī Kṛṣṇa's own contribution to the philosophy of life.

नेहाभिक्रमनाशोऽस्ति प्रत्यवायो न विद्यते।
स्वल्पमप्यस्य धर्मस्य त्रायते महतो भयात्॥ ४०

इह In this अभिक्रमनाश: waste of attempt न अस्ति is not प्रत्यवाय: (च and) production of contrary results न विद्यते exists not अस्य धर्मस्य of this Dharma स्वल्पं very little अपि even महत: भयात् from great terror त्रायते protects.

40. In this, there is no waste of the unfinished attempt, nor is there production of contrary results. Even very little of this Dharma protects from the great terror.

Waste of the unfinished attempt: A religious rite or ceremony performed for a definite object, if left uncompleted, is wasted, like a house unroofed which is neither serviceable nor enduring. In Karma-Yoga, however, that is, action and worship performed without desire, this law does not apply, for every effort results in immediate purification of the heart. *Production of contrary results*: In worship for an object, any imperfection in the process produces positive loss instead of gain. As in cases of sickness, the non-use of the right medicine results in death. *The great terror*: Being caught in the wheel of birth and death.

व्यवसायात्मिका बुद्धिरेकेह कुरुनन्दन।
बहुशाखा ह्यनन्ताश्च बुद्धयोऽव्यवसायिनाम्॥ ४१

कुरुनन्दन O scion of Kuru इह in this व्यवसायात्मिका one-pointed बुद्धिः determination एका single (एव only) अव्यवसायिनाम् of the undecided बुद्धयः purposes हि indeed बहुशाखाः many-branching च and अनन्ताः innumerable.

41. In this, O scion of Kuru, there is but a single one-pointed determination. The purposes of the undecided are innumerable and many-branching.

In Karma-Yoga, the one goal is Self-realisation. *The undecided* (that is, about the highest), naturally devote themselves to lower ideals, none of which can satisfy. Thus they pass from plan to plan.

यामिमां पुष्पितां वाचं प्रवदन्त्यविपश्चितः।
वेदवादरताः पार्थ नान्यदस्तीतिवादिनः॥ ४२
कामात्मानः स्वर्गपरा जन्मकर्मफलप्रदाम्।
क्रियाविशेषबहुलां भोगैश्वर्यगतिं प्रति॥ ४३
भोगैश्वर्यप्रसक्तानां तयापहृतचेतसाम्।
व्यवसायात्मिका बुद्धिः समाधौ न विधीयते॥ ४४

पार्थ O Pārtha अविपश्चितः the unwise वेदवादरताः taking pleasure in the panegyric statements of the Vedas अन्यत् anything else न अस्ति does not exist इति this

वादिन: declaring कामात्मान: full of desires स्वर्गपरा: with heaven as their highest goal याम् which इमां this (well-known) पुष्पितां flowery जन्मकर्मफलप्रदाम् leading to (new) birth as the result of their works भोगैश्वर्यगतिं प्रति for the attainment of pleasure and power क्रियाविशेषबहुलां exuberant with various specific actions वाचं word प्रवदन्ति expatiate upon भोगैश्वर्यप्रसक्तानां of (people) deeply attached to pleasure and power तया by that अपहृतचेतसाम् with their discrimination stolen away व्यवसायात्मिका set बुद्धि: determination समाधौ in the mind न विधीयते is not formed.

42–44. O Pārtha, no set determination is formed in the minds of those that are deeply attached to pleasure and power, and whose discrimination is stolen away by the flowery words of the unwise, who are full of desires and look upon heaven as their highest goal and who, taking pleasure in the panegyric words of the Vedas, declare that there is nothing else. Their flowery words are exuberant with various specific rites as the means to pleasure and power and are the causes of (new) births as the result of their works (performed with desire).

Samādhi has been rendered into "mind" in the above. The generally accepted significance of the term (absorption in God-consciousness produced by deep meditation) would give an equally consistent and happy meaning. Persons attached to pleasure and power cannot have perfect steadiness of mind in divine meditation.

Panegyric words of the Vedas: The *Karma-Kāṇḍa* or the sacrificial portion of the Vedas which lays down specific rules for specific actions and their fruits, and extols these latter unduly. *Nothing else*: Beyond the heavenly enjoyments procurable by the sacrificial rites of the Vedas.

त्रैगुण्यविषया वेदा निस्त्रैगुण्यो भवार्जुन।
निर्द्वन्द्वो नित्यसत्त्वस्थो निर्योगक्षेम आत्मवान्॥ ४५

वेदाः The Vedas त्रैगुण्यविषयाः deal with the three *Guṇas* अर्जुन O Arjuna (त्वम् thou) निस्त्रैगुण्यः free from the triad of *Guṇas* निर्द्वन्द्वः free from the pairs of opposites नित्यसत्त्वस्थः ever-balanced निर्योगक्षेमः free from getting and keeping आत्मवान् established in the Self भव be.

45. The Vedas deal with the three *Guṇas*. Be thou free, O Arjuna, from the triad of the *Guṇas,* free from the pairs of opposites, ever-balanced, free from (the thought of) getting and keeping, and established in the Self.

The Vedas deal with etc.: That is to say, the Vedas treat of relativity. *Pairs of opposites*: *Dvandva,* all correlated ideas and sensations, e.g., good and bad, pleasure and pain, heat and cold, light and darkness, etc.

Guṇa is a technical term of the Sāṅkhya philosophy also used in the same sense by the Vedānta. *Prakṛti* or Nature is constituted of three *Guṇas; Sattva* (equilibrium), *Rajas* (attraction), *Tamas* (inertia). *Prakṛti is* the three *Guṇas, not* that she *has* them. *Guṇa* is wrongly translated as quality; it is substance as well as quality, matter, *and* force. Wherever there is name and form, there is *Guṇa*. *Guṇa* also means a rope, that which binds.

यावानर्थ उदपाने सर्वतः संप्लुतोदके।
तावान्सर्वेषु वेदेषु ब्राह्मणस्य विजानतः ।। ४६

सर्वत: Everywhere संप्लुतोदके being flooded उदपाने in a reservoir यावान् as much अर्थ: use विजानत: ब्राह्मणस्य of the knowing Brāhmaṇa सर्वेषु in all वेदेषु the Vedas तावान् so much (use).

46. To the Brāhmaṇa who has known the Self, all the Vedas are of so much use as a reservoir is, when there is a flood everywhere.

A man possessed of Self-knowledge has no need whatever of the Vedas. This does not, however, mean that the Vedas are useless; only to the knower of Brahman they have no value, as the transient pleasures derivable from them are comprehended in the infinite bliss of Self-knowledge.

कर्मण्येवाधिकारस्ते मा फलेषु कदाचन।
मा कर्मफलहेतुर्भूर्मा ते सङ्गोऽस्त्वकर्मणि ।। ४७

कर्मणि In work एव only ते thy अधिकार: right कदाचन ever फलेषु in fruits मा not कर्मफलहेतु: the producer of the results of acts मा भू: shouldst not be अकर्मणि in inaction ते thy सङ्ग: attachment मा not अस्तु let be.

47. Thy right is to work only; but never to the fruits thereof. Be thou not the producer of the fruits of (thy) actions; neither let thy attachment be towards inaction.

Be thou not the producer, etc.: That is, do not work with any desire for results, for actions produce fruits or bondage only if they are performed with desire.

Karma primarily means action, but a much profounder meaning has come to be attached to this word. It means the destiny forged by one in one's past incarnation or present: the store of tendencies, impulses, characteristics, and habits laid by, which determines the future embodiment, environment, and the whole of one's organisation.

Another meaning of *Karma* often used in reference to one's caste or position in life, is duty, the course of conduct which one ought to follow in pursuance of the tendencies which one acquired in one's past, with a view to working them out and regaining the pristine purity of the Self.

योगस्थः कुरु कर्माणि सङ्गं त्यक्त्वा धनञ्जय।
सिद्ध्यसिद्ध्योः समो भूत्वा समत्वं योग उच्यते॥ ४८

धनञ्जय O Dhanañjaya योगस्थः steadfast in Yoga सङ्गं attachment त्यक्त्वा abandoning सिद्ध्यसिद्ध्योः in regard to success and failure समः the same भूत्वा being कर्माणि actions कुरु perform समत्वं evenness of mind (in regard to success and failure) योगः Yoga उच्यते is called.

48. Being steadfast in Yoga, O Dhanañjaya, perform actions, abandoning attachment, remaining unconcerned as regards success and failure. This evenness of mind (in regard to success and failure) is known as Yoga.

दूरेण ह्यवरं कर्म बुद्धियोगाद्धनञ्जय।
बुद्धौ शरणमन्विच्छ कृपणाः फलहेतवः ॥ ४९

धनञ्जय O Dhanañjaya हि as बुद्धियोगात् than work performed with the mind undisturbed by thoughts of results दूरेण by far कर्म work अवरं inferior बुद्धौ in evenness of mind शरणम् refuge अन्विच्छ seek फलहेतवः seekers after results कृपणाः wretched.

49. Work (with desire) is verily far inferior to that performed with the mind undisturbed by thoughts of results. O Dhanañjaya, seek refuge in this evenness of mind. Wretched are they who act for results.

बुद्धियुक्तो जहातीह उभे सुकृतदुष्कृते।
तस्माद्योगाय युज्यस्व योगः कर्मसु कौशलम् ॥ ५०

बुद्धियुक्तः Endued with evenness of mind इह in this (life) उभे both सुकृतदुष्कृते virtue and vice जहाति casts off तस्मात् therefore योगाय to Yoga युज्यस्व devote thyself योगः Yoga कर्मसु in work कौशलम् dexterity.

50. Endued with this evenness of mind, one frees oneself in this life, alike from vice and virtue. Devote thyself, therefore, to this Yoga. Yoga is the very dexterity of work.

Alike from vice and virtue: A follower of Karma-Yoga can have no personal motive for any action. Our action without motive becomes colourless, and loses its character of vice or virtue.

Dexterity of work: It is the nature of work to produce bondage. Karma-Yoga is the dexterity of work, because it not only robs work of its power to bind, but also transforms it into an efficient means of freedom.

कर्मजं बुद्धियुक्ता हि फलं त्यक्त्वा मनीषिणः ।
जन्मबन्धविनिर्मुक्ताः पदं गच्छन्त्यनामयम् ।। ५१

बुद्धियुक्ता: Possessed of evenness of mind मनीषिण: the wise कर्मजं फलं the fruit of action त्यक्त्वा abandoning जन्मबन्धविनिर्मुक्ता: freed from the fetters of birth अनामयम् beyond evil पदं state हि verily गच्छन्ति go to.

51. The wise, possessed of this evenness of mind, abandoning the fruits of their actions, freed for ever from the fetters of birth, go to that state which is beyond all evil.

यदा ते मोहकलिलं बुद्धिर्व्यतितरिष्यति ।
तदा गन्तासि निर्वेदं श्रोतव्यस्य श्रुतस्य च ।। ५२

यदा When ते thy बुद्धि: intellect मोहकलिलं taint of illusion व्यतितरिष्यति crosses beyond तदा then श्रोतव्यस्य of what is to be heard श्रुतस्य च and of what is heard निर्वेदं indifference गन्तासि thou shalt attain.

52. When thy intellect crosses beyond the taint of illusion, then shalt thou attain to indifference, regarding things heard and things yet to be heard.

The taint of illusion: the identifying of the Self with the non-Self, the ego.

श्रुतिविप्रतिपन्ना ते यदा स्थास्यति निश्चला।
समाधावचला बुद्धिस्तदा योगमवाप्स्यसि।। ५३

यदा When ते thy श्रुतिविप्रतिपन्ना tossed about by the conflict of opinions बुद्धिः intellect अचला firmly established समाधौ in the Self निश्चला immovable स्थास्यति will remain तदा then योगं Self-realisation अवाप्स्यसि shalt attain.

53. When thy intellect, tossed about by the conflict of opinions, has become immovable and firmly established in the Self, then thou shalt attain Self-realisation.

अर्जुन उवाच

स्थितप्रज्ञस्य का भाषा समाधिस्थस्य केशव।
स्थितधीः किं प्रभाषेत किमासीत व्रजेत किम्।। ५४

अर्जुनः Arjuna उवाच said:

केशव O Keśava स्थितप्रज्ञस्य of the (man of) steady wisdom समाधिस्थस्य of the (man) merged in *Samādhi* का what भाषा description स्थितधीः (the man of) steady wisdom किं what प्रभाषेत speaks किम् what (how) आसीत sits किम् what (how) व्रजेत walks.

Arjuna said:

54. What, O Keśava, is the description of the man of steady wisdom, merged in *Samādhi* ? How (on the other hand) does the man of steady wisdom speak, how sit, how walk?

Arjuna is asking, (1) what is the state of the mind of the man of realisation when in *Samādhi*? and (2) how is its influence shown in his conduct when out of it ?

Steady wisdom: Settled conviction of one's identity with Brahman gained by direct realisation.

श्रीभगवानुवाच

प्रजहाति यदा कामान्सर्वान्पार्थ मनोगतान्।
आत्मन्येवात्मना तुष्टः स्थितप्रज्ञस्तदोच्यते।। ५५

श्रीभगवान् The Blessed Lord उवाच said:

पार्थ O Pārtha यदा when सर्वान् all मनोगतान् of the mind कामान् desires प्रजहाति casts off आत्मनि एव in the Self alone आत्मना by the Self तुष्टः satisfied तदा then स्थितप्रज्ञः of steady wisdom उच्यते is said.

The Blessed Lord said:

55. When a man completely casts away, O Pārtha, all the desires of the mind, satisfied in the Self alone by the Self, then is he said to be one of steady wisdom.

This answers the first part of Arjuna's question.

दुःखेष्वनुद्विग्नमनाः सुखेषु विगतस्पृहः।
वीतरागभयक्रोधः स्थितधीर्मुनिरुच्यते।। ५६

दुःखेषु In adversity अनुद्विग्नमनाः of unshaken mind सुखेषु in happiness विगतस्पृहः without hankering वीतरागभयक्रोधः free from affection, fear, and wrath मुनिः *Muni* स्थितधीः of steady wisdom उच्यते is said.

56. He whose mind is not shaken by adversity, who does not hanker after happiness, who has become free from affection, fear, and wrath, is indeed the *Muni* of steady wisdom.

This and the following two *ślokas* answer the second part of Arjuna's question, as to the conduct of one of perfect realisation.

Muni: Man of meditation.

यः सर्वत्रानभिस्नेहस्तत्तत्प्राप्य शुभाशुभम्।
नाभिनन्दति न द्वेष्टि तस्य प्रज्ञा प्रतिष्ठिता॥ ५७

यः Who सर्वत्र everywhere अनभिस्नेहः without attachment तत् तत् whatever शुभाशुभम् good and evil प्राप्य receiving न अभिनन्दति does not rejoice न द्वेष्टि is not vexed तस्य his प्रज्ञा wisdom प्रतिष्ठिता is fixed.

57. He who is everywhere unattached, not pleased at receiving good, nor vexed at evil, his wisdom is fixed.

Not pleased, etc.: consequently he does not praise or blame. This is an answer to the query: "How does he speak?"

यदा संहरते चायं कूर्मोऽङ्गानीव सर्वशः।
इन्द्रियाणीन्द्रियार्थेभ्यस्तस्य प्रज्ञा प्रतिष्ठिता॥ ५८

यदा When च also अयं this (Yogi) कूर्मः tortoise अङ्गानि limbs इव like इन्द्रियार्थेभ्यः from sense-objects इन्द्रियाणि

senses सर्वशः completely संहरते withdraws तस्य his प्रज्ञा wisdom प्रतिष्ठिता is steadied.

58. When also, like the tortoise drawing its limbs, he can completely withdraw the senses from their objects, then his wisdom becomes steady.

Withdraw the senses: bring the mind back upon the Self from all sense-objects. This is known as *Pratyāhāra* in Yoga.

To explain the *śloka* more fully: a man of the highest realisation can, at any moment, shake himself clear of all impressions of the sense-world and go into *Samādhi,* with the ease and naturalness of a tortoise drawing its limbs within itself.

विषया विनिवर्तन्ते निराहारस्य देहिनः ।
रसवर्जं रसोऽप्यस्य परं दृष्ट्वा निवर्तते ।। ५९

निराहारस्य Abstinent देहिनः of the man विषयाः objects विनिवर्तन्ते fall away रसवर्जं leaving the longing (तु but) परं the Supreme दृष्ट्वा having seen अस्य of this (man of settled wisdom) रसः longing अपि even निवर्तते falls away.

59. Objects fall away from the abstinent man, leaving the longing behind. But his longing also ceases, who sees the supreme.

Abstinent man: An unillumined person abstaining from sense-pleasure for penance, or because of physical incapacity.

यततो ह्यपि कौन्तेय पुरुषस्य विपश्चितः ।
इन्द्रियाणि प्रमाथीनि हरन्ति प्रसभं मनः ।। ६०

कौन्तेय O Kaunteya यततः striving विपश्चितः पुरुषस्य of a wise man अपि even हि indeed प्रमाथीनि turbulent इन्द्रियाणि senses प्रसभं violently मनः mind हरन्ति snatch away.

60. The turbulent senses, O son of Kuntī, do violently snatch away the mind of even a wise man, striving after perfection.

तानि सर्वाणि संयम्य युक्त आसीत मत्परः ।
वशे हि यस्येन्द्रियाणि तस्य प्रज्ञा प्रतिष्ठिता ।। ६१

युक्तः The steadfast तानि them सर्वाणि all संयम्य having controlled मत्परः focussed on Me as the Supreme आसीत sits हि verily यस्य whose इन्द्रियाणि senses वशे under control तस्य his प्रज्ञा wisdom प्रतिष्ठिता settled.

61. The steadfast, having controlled them all, sits focussed on Me as the Supreme. His wisdom is steady, whose senses are under control.

ध्यायतो विषयान्पुंसः सङ्गस्तेषूपजायते ।
सङ्गात् संजायते कामः कामात् क्रोधोऽभिजायते ।। ६२

विषयान् Objects ध्यायतः thinking पुंसः of a man तेषु in them सङ्गः attachment उपजायते is produced सङ्गात् from attachment कामः longing संजायते is born कामात् from longing क्रोधः anger अभिजायते grows.

62. Thinking of objects, attachment to them is formed in a man. From attachment longing, and from longing anger grows.

क्रोधाद्भवति सम्मोहः सम्मोहात्स्मृतिविभ्रमः ।
स्मृतिभ्रंशाद्बुद्धिनाशो बुद्धिनाशात्प्रणश्यति ॥ ६३

क्रोधात् From anger सम्मोह: delusion भवति comes सम्मोहात् from delusion स्मृतिविभ्रम: loss of memory स्मृतिभ्रंशात् from loss of memory बुद्धिनाश: the ruin of discrimination बुद्धिनाशात् from the ruin of discrimination प्रणश्यति (he) perishes.

63. From anger comes delusion, and from delusion loss of memory. From loss of memory comes the ruin of discrimination, and from the ruin of discrimination he perishes.

A beautiful image appears. The tendency of the mind is to repeat it. Then, if the image is allowed to recur, a liking grows. With the growth of liking the wish to come close, to possess, appears. Any obstacle to this produces wrath. The impulse of anger throws the mind into confusion, which casts a veil over the lessons of wisdom learnt by past experience. Thus deprived of his moral standard, he is prevented from using his discrimination. Failing in discrimination, he acts irrationally, on the impulse of passion, and paves the way to a moral death.

Thus Kṛṣṇa traces moral degradation to those first breaths of thought that come softly and almost unconsciously to the mind.

रागद्वेषवियुक्तैस्तु विषयानिन्द्रियैश्चरन्।
आत्मवश्यैर्विधेयात्मा प्रसादमधिगच्छति ।। ६४

तु But रागद्वेषवियुक्तैः free from attraction and aversion आत्मवश्यैः self-restrained इन्द्रियैः with senses विषयान् objects चरन् moving (amongst) विधेयात्मा the self-controlled प्रसादम् tranquillity अधिगच्छति attains.

64. But the self-controlled man, moving among objects with senses under restraint, and free from attraction and aversion, attains to tranquillity.

The above is in answer to Arjuna's fourth question, "How does he move?"

प्रसादे सर्वदुःखानां हानिरस्योपजायते।
प्रसन्नचेतसो ह्याशु बुद्धिः पर्यवतिष्ठते ।। ६५

प्रसादे In tranquillity अस्य of him सर्वदुःखानां of all sorrows हानिः destruction उपजायते happens प्रसन्नचेतसः of the tranquil-minded हि because आशु soon बुद्धिः intellect पर्यवतिष्ठते is established in firmness.

65. In tranquillity, all sorrow is destroyed. For the intellect of him, who is tranquil-minded, is soon established in firmness.

That is, firmly concentrates itself on the Self.

नास्ति बुद्धिरयुक्तस्य न चायुक्तस्य भावना।
न चाभावयतः शान्तिरशान्तस्य कुतः सुखम्।। ६६

अयुक्तस्य Of the unsteady बुद्धिः knowledge (of the Self) नास्ति is not अयुक्तस्य of the unsteady भावना meditation च also न not अभावयतः च and of the unmeditative शान्तिः peace न not अशान्तस्य of the peaceless सुखम् happiness कुतः whence.

66. No knowledge (of the Self) has the unsteady. Nor has he meditation. To the unmeditative there is no peace. And how can one without peace have happiness ?

इन्द्रियाणां हि चरतां यन्मनोऽनुविधीयते।
तदस्य हरति प्रज्ञां वायुर्नावमिवाम्भसि॥ ६७

हि For चरतां wandering इन्द्रियाणां of senses यत् which मनः mind अनुविधीयते follows तत् that अस्य his वायुः wind अम्भसि in water नावम् boat इव like प्रज्ञां discrimination हरति scatters.

67. For, the mind, which follows in the wake of the wandering senses, carries away his discrimination, as a wind (carries away from its course) a boat on the waters.

तस्माद्यस्य महाबाहो निगृहीतानि सर्वशः।
इन्द्रियाणीन्द्रियार्थेभ्यस्तस्य प्रज्ञा प्रतिष्ठिता॥ ६८

महाबाहो O mighty-armed तस्मात् therefore यस्य whose इन्द्रियाणि senses इन्द्रियार्थेभ्यः from sense-objects सर्वशः completely निगृहीतानि restrained तस्य his प्रज्ञा knowledge प्रतिष्ठिता (is) steady.

68. Therefore, O mighty-armed, his knowledge is steady, whose senses are completely restrained from their objects.

This does not mean that the senses remain completely estranged, but that they are all estrangeable at will.

या निशा सर्वभूतानां तस्यां जागर्ति संयमी।
यस्यां जाग्रति भूतानि सा निशा पश्यतो मुनेः ॥ ६९

सर्वभूतानां Of all beings या what निशा night संयमी the self-controlled तस्यां in that जागर्ति keeps awake यस्यां in what भूतानि all beings जाग्रति are awake पश्यत: seeing (the Self) मुने: of the *Muni* सा that निशा night.

69. That which is night to all beings, in that the self-controlled man wakes. That in which all beings wake, is night to the Self-seeing *Muni*.

Where all beings are in darkness, there the *Muni* sees, and *vice versa*. The consciousness of the man of realisation is so full of God that he cannot see anything apart from Him. The ignorant man, on the other hand, lives in the world of plurality alone and God is a non-entity to him.

It follows, that non-susceptibility to the influences of Nature, that is, perfect self-control (spoken of in the preceding *śloka*) is quite as natural a trait of the illumined soul as its opposite is of the ignorant.

आपूर्यमाणमचलप्रतिष्ठं
समुद्रमापः प्रविशन्ति यद्वत्।
तद्वत्कामा यं प्रविशन्ति सर्वे
स शान्तिमाप्नोति न कामकामी ॥ ७०

यद्वत् As आपूर्यमाणम् filled from all sides अचलप्रतिष्ठं based in stillness समुद्रम् ocean आप: waters प्रविशन्ति enter तद्वत् so सर्वे all कामा: desires यं to which (मुनि: *Muni*) प्रविशन्ति enter स: he शान्तिम् peace आप्नोति attains कामकामी desirer of desires न not.

70. As into the ocean—brimful, and still—flow the waters, even so the *Muni* into whom enter all desires, he, and not the desirer of desires, attains to peace.

The ocean is not at all affected by the waters flowing into it from all sides. Similarly, that man alone finds true peace in whom no reaction of desire is produced by the objects of enjoyment, which he happens to come across during his sojourn on earth.

विहाय कामान्यः सर्वान्पुमांश्चरति निस्पृहः ।
निर्ममो निरहङ्कारः स शान्तिमधिगच्छति ।। ७१

य: that पुमान् man सर्वान् all कामान् desires विहाय abandoning निस्पृह: devoid of longing निरहंकार: without the sense of "I" निर्मम: without the sense of "mine" चरति moves (lives) स: he शान्तिम् peace अधिगच्छति attains.

71. That man who lives devoid of longing, abandoning all desires, without the sense of "I" and "mine", he attains to peace.

The man who lives—merely to work out his past *Karma*.

एषा ब्राह्मी स्थितिः पार्थ नैनां प्राप्य विमुह्यति।
स्थित्वाऽस्यामन्तकालेऽपि ब्रह्मनिर्वाणमृच्छति ।। ७२

पार्थ O Pārtha एषा this ब्राह्मी स्थितिः (having one's) being in Brahman एनां this प्राप्य attaining न not विमुह्यति is deluded अन्तकाले at the end of life अपि even अस्याम् therein स्थित्वा having stayed ब्रह्मनिर्वाणम् oneness with Brahman ऋच्छति attains.

72. This is to have one's being in Brahman, O son of Pṛthā. None, attaining to this, becomes deluded. Being established therein, even at the end of life, a man attains to oneness with Brahman.

इति सांख्ययोगो नाम द्वितीयोऽध्यायः ।।

The end of the second chapter, designated,
The Way of Knowledge.

तृतीयोऽध्यायः
(कर्मयोगः)
THIRD CHAPTER
(The Way of Action)

अर्जुन उवाच

ज्यायसी चेत्कर्मणस्ते मता बुद्धिर्जनार्दन।
तत्किं कर्मणि घोरे मां नियोजयसि केशव॥ १

अर्जुनः Arjuna उवाच said:

जनार्दन O Janārdana केशव O Keśava चेत् if कर्मणः to action बुद्धिः knowledge ज्यायसी superior ते by Thee मता considered तत् then किं why घोरे terrible कर्मणि in action मां me नियोजयसि engagest.

Arjuna said:

1. If, O Janārdana, according to Thee, knowledge is superior to action, why then, O Keśava, dost Thou engage me in this terrible action ?

व्यामिश्रेणेव वाक्येन बुद्धिं मोहयसीव मे।
तदेकं वद निश्चित्य येन श्रेयोऽहमाप्नुयाम्॥ २

व्यामिश्रेण Conflicting वाक्येन with words इव seemingly मे my बुद्धिं understanding मोहयसि art bewildering इव as it were तत् that एकं one निश्चित्य for certain वद tell येन by which अहम् I श्रेय: highest आप्नुयाम् shall attain.

2. With these seemingly conflicting words, Thou art, as it were, bewildering my understanding. Tell me that one thing for certain, by which I can attain to the highest.

श्रीभगवानुवाच

लोकेऽस्मिन्द्विविधा निष्ठा पुरा प्रोक्ता मयाऽनघ।
ज्ञानयोगेन सांख्यानां कर्मयोगेन योगिनाम्।। ३

श्रीभगवान् The Blessed Lord उवाच said:

अनघ O sinless one! अस्मिन् in this लोके world द्विविधा twofold निष्ठा (path of) devotion मया by Me पुरा in the beginning प्रोक्ता said ज्ञानयोगेन by the path of knowledge सांख्यानां of the meditative कर्मयोगेन by the path of action योगिनाम् of the active.

The Blessed Lord said:

3. In the beginning (of creation), O sinless one, the twofold path of devotion was given by Me to this world; — the path of knowledge for the meditative, the path of work for the active.

Meditative—those who prefer meditation to external action.

Active—those who believe in external work with or without meditation.

न कर्मणामनारम्भान्नैष्कर्म्यं पुरुषोऽश्नुते ।
न च सन्न्यसनादेव सिद्धिं समधिगच्छति ।। ४

पुरुष: A person कर्मणाम् of works अनारम्भात् from non-performance नैष्कर्म्यं worklessness न not अश्नुते reaches च and सन्न्यसनात् from giving up एव merely सिद्धिं perfection न not समधिगच्छति attains.

4. By non-performance of work none reaches worklessness; by merely giving up action no one attains to perfection.

Worklessness and perfection: These are synonymous terms, meaning, becoming one with the Infinite and free from all ideas of want. A man who has reached this state can have no necessity or desire for work as a means to an end. Perfect satisfaction in the Self is his natural condition. (*Vide* III. 17).

न हि कश्चित्क्षणमपि जातु तिष्ठत्यकर्मकृत् ।
कार्यते ह्यवशः कर्म सर्वः प्रकृतिजैर्गुणैः ।। ५

जातु Ever क्षणम् for an instant अपि even कश्चित् anyone अकर्मकृत् without performing action न not हि verily तिष्ठति rests हि for प्रकृतिजै: born of *Prakṛti* गुणै: by the *Guṇas* सर्व: all अवश: helpless कर्म action कार्यते are made to do.

5. Verily none can ever rest for even an instant, without performing action; for all are made to act, helplessly indeed, by the *Guṇas* born of *Prakṛti*.

All are made to act: All men living under bondage.

कर्मेन्द्रियाणि संयम्य य आस्ते मनसा स्मरन्।
इन्द्रियार्थान्विमूढात्मा मिथ्याचारः स उच्यते॥ ६

यः Who कर्मेन्द्रियाणि organs of action संयम्य restraining मनसा by the mind इन्द्रियार्थान् sense-objects स्मरन् remembering आस्ते sits सः he विमूढात्मा of deluded understanding मिथ्याचारः hypocrite उच्यते is called.

6. He, who restraining the organs of action, sits revolving in the mind, thoughts regarding objects of sense, he, of deluded understanding, is called a hypocrite.

यस्त्विन्द्रियाणि मनसा नियम्यारभतेऽर्जुन।
कर्मेन्द्रियैः कर्मयोगमसक्तः स विशिष्यते॥ ७

अर्जुन O Arjuna यः who तु but इन्द्रियाणि senses मनसा by the mind नियम्य controlling असक्तः unattached कर्मेन्द्रियैः by the organs of action कर्मयोगम् path of work आरभते follows सः he विशिष्यते excels.

7. But, O Arjuna, he who, controlling the senses by the mind, unattached, directs his organs of action to the path of work, excels.

नियतं कुरु कर्म त्वं कर्म ज्यायो ह्यकर्मणः।
शरीरयात्रापि च ते न प्रसिध्येदकर्मणः॥ ८

त्वं Thou नियतं obligatory कर्म action कुरु perform हि for अकर्मणः to inaction कर्म action ज्यायः superior अकर्मणः (of the) inactive ते thy शरीरयात्रा maintenance of the body अपि even च and न not प्रसिध्येत् would be possible.

8. Do thou perform obligatory* action; for action is superior to inaction; and even the bare maintenance of the body would not be possible if thou art inactive.

यज्ञार्थात्कर्मणोऽन्यत्र लोकोऽयं कर्मबन्धनः ।
तदर्थं कर्म कौन्तेय मुक्तसङ्गः समाचर ।। ९

यज्ञार्थात् For the sake of *Yajña* कर्मण: of action अन्यत्र otherwise अयं this लोक: world कर्मबन्धन: bound by action कौन्तेय O Kaunteya (अत: therefore) तदर्थं for that मुक्तसङ्ग: devoid of attachment कर्म action समाचर perform.

9. The world is bound by actions other than those performed for the sake of *Yajña*; do thou, therefore, O son of Kuntī, perform action for *Yajña* alone, devoid of attachment.

Yajña: means a religious rite, sacrifice, worship: or an action done with a good or spiritual motive. It also means the Deity. The Taittirīya-Saṁhitā (I. vii. 4.) says, "*Yajña* is Viṣṇu Himself."

सहयज्ञाः प्रजाः सृष्ट्वा पुरोवाच प्रजापतिः ।
अनेन प्रसविष्यध्वमेष वोऽस्त्विष्टकामधुक् ।। १०

पुरा In the beginning प्रजापति: the Prajāpati सहयज्ञा: together with *Yajña* प्रजा: mankind सृष्ट्वा having created उवाच said अनेन by this प्रसविष्यध्वम् shall (ye) multiply एष: this व: your इष्टकामधुक् milch cow of desires अस्तु let be.

* See comment on V. 13.

10. The Prajāpati, having in the beginning created mankind together with *Yajña*, said, "By this shall ye multiply; this shall be the milch cow of your desires.

Prajāpati: the creator or Brahmā.

देवान् भावयतानेन ते देवा भावयन्तु वः ।
परस्परं भावयन्तः श्रेयः परमवाप्स्यथ ।। ११

अनेन With this देवान् the *Devas* भावयत cherish ते those देवा: *Devas* व: you भावयन्तु may cherish परस्परं one another भावयन्त: cherishing परम् highest श्रेय: good अवाप्स्यथ (ye) shall gain.

11. "Cherish the *Devas* with this, and may those *Devas* cherish you: thus cherishing one another, ye shall gain the highest good.

Devas: (lit. the shining ones) beings much higher than man in the scale of evolution, who are in charge of cosmic functions.

इष्टान्भोगान्हि वो देवा दास्यन्ते यज्ञभाविताः ।
तैर्दत्तानप्रदायैभ्यो यो भुङ्क्ते स्तेन एव सः ।। १२

देवा: The *Devas* यज्ञभाविता: cherished by *Yajña* इष्टान् desired-for भोगान् objects व: to you दास्यन्ते will give हि so तै: by them दत्तान् given एभ्य: to them अप्रदाय without offering य: who भुङ्क्ते enjoys स: he स्तेन: thief एव verily.

12. "The *Devas*, cherished by *Yajña*, will give you desired-for objects." So, he who enjoys objects given by the *Devas* without offering (in return) to them, is verily a thief.

यज्ञशिष्टाशिनः सन्तो मुच्यन्ते सर्वकिल्बिषैः ।
भुञ्जते ते त्वघं पापा ये पचन्त्यात्मकारणात् ।। १३

यज्ञशिष्टाशिन: Eating the remnants of *Yajña* सन्त: the good सर्वकिल्बिषै: from all sins मुच्यन्ते are freed ये who तु but आत्मकारणात् for themselves पचन्ति cook ते they पापा: sinful ones अघं sin भुञ्जते eat.

13. The good, eating the remnants of *Yajña*, are freed from all sins: but who cook food (only) for themselves, those sinful ones eat sin.

Deva-Yajña: offering sacrifices to the gods, *Brahma-Yajña*: teaching and reciting the scriptures, *Pitṛ-Yajña*: offering libations of water etc. to one's ancestors, *Nṛ-Yajña*: the feeding of the hungry, and *Bhūta-Yajña*: the feeding of the lower animals—these are the five daily duties enjoined on householders. The performance of these duties frees them from the fivefold sin, inevitable to a householder's life, due to the killing of life, from the use of, (1) the pestle and mortar, (2) the grinding-stone, (3) the oven, (4) the water-jar, and (5) the broom.

अन्नाद्भवन्ति भूतानि पर्जन्यादन्नसम्भवः ।
यज्ञाद्भवति पर्जन्यो यज्ञः कर्मसमुद्भवः ।। १४

भूतानि Beings अन्नात् from food भवन्ति come forth पर्जन्यात् from rain अन्नसम्भवः production of food पर्जन्यः rain यज्ञात् from *Yajña* भवति arises यज्ञः *Yajña* कर्मसमुद्भवः born of *Karma*.

14. From food come forth beings: from rain food is produced: from *Yajña* arises rain; and *Yajña* is born of *Karma*.

Yajña: Here it denotes not the sacrificial deeds themselves but the subtle principle into which they are converted, after they have been performed, to appear, later on, as their fruits.This is technically known as *Apūrva*.

Karma or sacrificial deeds prescribed in the Vedas.

कर्म ब्रह्मोद्भवं विद्धि ब्रह्माक्षरसमुद्भवम्।
तस्मात्सर्वगतं ब्रह्म नित्यं यज्ञे प्रतिष्ठितम्।। १५

कर्म *Karma* ब्रह्मोद्भवं risen from the Veda ब्रह्म Veda अक्षरसमुद्भवम् risen from the Imperishable विद्धि know तस्मात् therefore सर्वगतं all-pervading ब्रह्म Veda नित्यं ever यज्ञे in *Yajña* प्रतिष्ठितम् centred.

15. Know *Karma* to have risen from the Veda, and the Veda from the Imperishable. Therefore the all-pervading Veda is ever centred in *Yajña*.

All-pervading Veda: because it illumines all subjects and is the store of all knowledge, being the out-breathing of the Omniscient. It is said to be ever centred in *Yajña*, because it deals chiefly with *Yajña*, as the means of achieving the end, either of prosperity or final liberation, according as it is performed with or without desire.

एवं प्रवर्तितं चक्रं नानुवर्तयतीह यः।
अघायुरिन्द्रियारामो मोघं पार्थ स जीवति॥ १६

यः Who इह here एवं thus प्रवर्तितं set revolving चक्रं wheel न not अनुवर्तयति follows पार्थ O Pārtha अघायुः living in sin इन्द्रियारामः satisfied in the senses सः he मोघं in vain जीवति lives.

16. He who here follows not the wheel thus set revolving, living in sin, and satisfied in the senses, O son of Pṛthā—he lives in vain.

The *wheel* of action started by Prajāpati on the basis of Veda and sacrifice.

यस्त्वात्मरतिरेव स्यादात्मतृप्तश्च मानवः।
आत्मन्येव च सन्तुष्टस्तस्य कार्यं न विद्यते॥ १७

तु But यः मानवः that man आत्मरतिः devoted to the Self एव alone च and आत्मतृप्तः satisfied with the Self च and आत्मनि in the Self एव alone सन्तुष्टः content स्यात् may be तस्य his कार्यं work to be done (i.e., duty) न not विद्यते exists.

17. But the man who is devoted to the Self, and is satisfied with the Self, and content in the Self alone, has no obligatory duty.

नैव तस्य कृतेनार्थो नाकृतेनेह कश्चन।
न चास्य सर्वभूतेषु कश्चिदर्थव्यपाश्रयः ।। १८

तस्य Of that man इह in this world कृतेन by action done अर्थः object न not एव surely (अस्ति is) अकृतेन by action not done कश्चन any (loss) न not (अस्ति is) च and अस्य of this man सर्वभूतेषु among all beings कश्चित् any अर्थव्यपाश्रयः depending for any object न not.

18. He has no object in this world (to gain) by doing (an action), nor (does he incur any loss) by non-performance of action—nor has he (need of) depending on any being for any object.

तस्मादसक्तः सततं कार्यं कर्म समाचर।
असक्तो ह्याचरन् कर्म परमाप्नोति पूरुषः ।। १९

तस्मात् Therefore असक्तः without attachment सततं always कार्यं which should be done, i.e. obligatory कर्म action समाचर perform हि because असक्तः without attachment कर्म action आचरन् performing पूरुषः man परम् the highest आप्नोति attains.

19. Therefore, do thou always perform actions which are obligatory, without attachment; by performing action without attachment, one attains to the highest.

कर्मणैव हि संसिद्धिमास्थिता जनकादयः।
लोकसंग्रहमेवापि संपश्यन् कर्तुमर्हसि ।। २०

हि Verily जनकादय: Janaka and others कर्मणा by action एव alone संसिद्धिम् perfection आस्थिता: attained अपि also लोकसंग्रहम् guidance of men एव only संपश्यन् having in view कर्तुम् to perform (action) अर्हसि thou shouldst.

20. Verily by action alone, Janaka and others attained perfection; also, simply with the view for the guidance of men, thou shouldst perform action.

Guidance of men: the Sanskrit word means, gathering of men—that is, into the right path.

यद्यदाचरति श्रेष्ठस्तत्तदेवेतरो जनः ।
स यत्प्रमाणं कुरुते लोकस्तदनुवर्तते ।। २१

श्रेष्ठ: The superior यत् यत् whatsoever आचरति does इतर: inferior जन: man तत् तत् that एव only (does) स: that (superior) man यत् what प्रमाणं demonstration कुरुते does तत् that लोक: the world (people) अनुवर्तते follows.

21. Whatsoever the superior person does, that is followed by others. What he demonstrates by action, that people follow.

न मे पार्थास्ति कर्तव्यं त्रिषु लोकेषु किञ्चन ।
नानवाप्तमवाप्तव्यं वर्त एव च कर्मणि ।। २२

पार्थ O Pārtha! मे My कर्तव्यं duty न not अस्ति is त्रिषु in the three लोकेषु worlds अनवाप्तम् unattained अवाप्तव्यं to be gained किञ्चन anything न not च yet कर्मणि in action एव verily वर्ते am.

22. I have, O son of Pṛthā, no duty, nothing that I have not gained; and nothing that I have to gain, in the three worlds; yet, I continue in action.

यदि ह्यहं न वर्तेयं जातु कर्मण्यतन्द्रितः ।
मम वर्त्मानुवर्तन्ते मनुष्याः पार्थ सर्वशः ।। २३

पार्थ O Pārtha! यदि if अहं I जातु ever अतन्द्रितः without relaxation कर्मणि in action न not वर्तेयं should be (तदा then) हि surely मनुष्याः men मम My वर्त्म path सर्वशः in every way अनुवर्तन्ते (would) follow.

23. If ever I did not continue in work without relaxation, O son of Pṛthā, men would, in every way follow in My wake.

उत्सीदेयुरिमे लोका न कुर्यां कर्म चेदहम् ।
सङ्करस्य च कर्ता स्यामुपहन्यामिमाः प्रजाः ।। २४

चेत् If अहम् I कर्म action न not कुर्यां would do इमे these लोकाः worlds उत्सीदेयुः would perish च and संकरस्य of the admixture (of races) कर्ता author स्याम् would be इमाः these प्रजाः beings उपहन्याम् would ruin.

24. If I do not perform action, these worlds would perish. I would be the cause of the admixture of races, and I would ruin these beings.

सक्ताः कर्मण्यविद्वांसो यथा कुर्वन्ति भारत ।
कुर्याद्विद्वांस्तथाऽसक्तश्चिकीर्षुर्लोकसंग्रहम् ।। २५

भारत O Bhārata! कर्मणि to action सक्ता: attached अविद्वांस: the unwise यथा as कुर्वन्ति act असक्त: unattached लोकसंग्रहम् guidance of the world चिकीर्षु: desirous of विद्वान् the wise तथा so कुर्यात् should act.

25. As do the unwise, attached to work, act, so should the wise act, O descendant of Bharata, (but) without attachment, desirous of the guidance of the world.

न बुद्धिभेदं जनयेदज्ञानां कर्मसङ्गिनाम्।
योजयेत्सर्वकर्माणि विद्वान्युक्तः समाचरन्॥ २६

कर्मसङ्गिनाम् Of the persons attached to action अज्ञानां the ignorant बुद्धिभेदं unsettlement of the understanding न not जनयेत् should create विद्वान् the wise one युक्त: steady सर्वकर्माणि all actions समाचरन् acting योजयेत् should engage.

26. One should not unsettle the understanding of the ignorant, attached to action; the wise one, (himself) steadily acting, should engage (the ignorant) in all work.

प्रकृतेः क्रियमाणानि गुणैः कर्माणि सर्वशः।
अहङ्कारविमूढात्मा कर्ताहमिति मन्यते॥ २७

प्रकृते: Of the *Prakṛti* गुणै: by the *Guṇas* सर्वश: everywhere कर्माणि works क्रियमाणानि are performed अहंकारविमूढात्मा one whose understanding is deluded by egoism अहम् I कर्ता doer इति thus मन्यते thinks.

27. The *Guṇas* of *Prakṛti* perform all action. With the understanding deluded by egoism, man thinks, "I am the doer."

तत्त्ववित्तु महाबाहो गुणकर्मविभागयोः।
गुणा गुणेषु वर्तन्त इति मत्वा न सज्जते॥ २८

तु But महाबाहो O mighty-armcd! गुणकर्मविभागयोः of the divisions of *Guṇa* and *Karma* तत्त्ववित् knower of truth गुणाः *Guṇas* (in the shape of the senses) गुणेषु amidst the *Guṇas* (in the shape of the objects) वर्तन्ते remain इति this मत्वा knowing न not सज्जते becomes attached.

28. But, O mighty-armed, one, with true insight into the domains of *Guṇa* and *Karma*, knowing that *Guṇas* as senses merely rest on *Guṇas* as objects, does not become attached.

With true insight etc.: Knowing the truth that the Self is distinct from all *Guṇas* and actions.

प्रकृतेर्गुणसंमूढाः सज्जन्ते गुणकर्मसु।
तानकृत्स्नविदो मन्दान् कृत्स्नविन्न विचालयेत्॥ २९

प्रकृतेः Of the *Prakṛti* गुणसंमूढाः persons deluded by *Guṇas* गुणकर्मसु in the functions of the *Guṇas* सज्जन्ते become attached तान् those अकृत्स्नविदः of imperfect knowledge मन्दान् the dull-witted कृत्स्नवित् man of perfect knowledge न not विचालयेत् should unsettle (the understanding).

29. Men of perfect knowledge should not unsettle (the understanding of) people of dull wit and imperfect knowledge, who, deluded by the *Guṇas* of *Prakṛti*, attach (themselves) to the functions of the *Guṇas*.

Those of imperfect knowledge—those who can only see as far as the immediate effect of actions.

मयि सर्वाणि कर्माणि सन्न्यस्याध्यात्मचेतसा ।
निराशीर्निर्ममो भूत्वा युध्यस्व विगतज्वरः ॥ ३०

सर्वाणि All कर्माणि actions मयि to Me सन्न्यस्य renouncing अध्यात्मचेतसा with mind centred on the Self निराशीः devoid of hope निर्ममः devoid of egoism भूत्वा being विगतज्वरः free from (mental) fever युध्यस्व fight.

30. Renouncing all actions to Me, with mind centred on the Self, getting rid of hope and selfishness, fight—free from (mental) fever.

ये मे मतमिदं नित्यमनुतिष्ठन्ति मानवाः ।
श्रद्धावन्तोऽनसूयन्तो मुच्यन्ते तेऽपि कर्मभिः ॥ ३१

श्रद्धावन्तः Full of *Śraddhā* अनसूयन्तः not cavilling ये those who मानवाः men मे My इदं this मतम् teaching नित्यम् constantly अनुतिष्ठन्ति practise ते they अपि even कर्मभिः from action मुच्यन्ते are freed.

31. Those men who constantly practise this teaching of Mine, full of *Śraddhā* and without cavilling, they too, are freed from work.

Śraddhā: is a mental attitude constituted primarily of sincerity of purpose, humility, reverence, and faith. You have *Śraddhā* for your Guru—it is sincere reverence. You have *Śraddhā* for the Gītā—it is admiration for those of its teachings you understand and faith in those that you do not. You give alms to a beggar with *Śraddhā*—it is a sense of humility combined with the hope that what you give will be acceptable and serviceable.

ये त्वेतदभ्यसूयन्तो नानुतिष्ठन्ति मे मतम्।
सर्वज्ञानविमूढांस्तान्विद्धि नष्टानचेतसः ॥ ३२

तु But ये those who एतत् this मे My मतम् teaching अभ्यसूयन्तः decrying न not अनुतिष्ठन्ति practise सर्वज्ञानविमूढान् deluded in all knowledge अचेतसः devoid of discrimination तान् them नष्टान् ruined विद्धि know.

32. But those who decrying this teaching of Mine, do not practise (it), deluded in all knowledge, and devoid of discrimination, know them to be ruined.

सदृशं चेष्टते स्वस्याः प्रकृतेर्ज्ञानवानपि।
प्रकृतिं यान्ति भूतानि निग्रहः किं करिष्यति ॥ ३३

ज्ञानवान् A wise man अपि even स्वस्याः of his own प्रकृतेः nature सदृशं in accordance with चेष्टते acts भूतानि being प्रकृतिं nature यान्ति follow निग्रहः restraint किं what करिष्यति will do.

33. Even a wise man acts in accordance with his own nature; beings follow nature; what can restraint do ?

The reason why some people do not follow the teaching of the Lord is explained here: Their (lower) nature proves too strong for them.

इन्द्रियस्येन्द्रियस्यार्थे रागद्वेषौ व्यवस्थितौ ।
तयोर्न वशमागच्छेत्तौ ह्यस्य परिपन्थिनौ ।। ३४

इन्द्रियस्य Of the senses इन्द्रियस्य अर्थे in the object of the senses रागद्वेषौ attachment and aversion व्यवस्थितौ ordained by nature तयो: of those two वशम् sway न not आगच्छेत् should come under तौ those two हि verily अस्य his परिपन्थिनौ foes.

34. Attachment and aversion of the senses for their respective objects are natural; let none come under their sway; they are his foes.

His: or the seeker after truth.

Though, as has been said in the foregoing *Śloka*, some are so completely under the sway of their natural propensities, that restraint is of no avail to them, yet the seeker after truth should never think of following their example, but should always exert himself to overrule all attachment and aversion of the senses for their objects.

श्रेयान् स्वधर्मो विगुणः परधर्मात् स्वनुष्ठितात् ।
स्वधर्मे निधनं श्रेयः परधर्मो भयावहः ।। ३५

स्वनुष्ठितात् From the well-performed परधर्मात् Dharma of another विगुण: imperfect स्वधर्म: one's own Dharma श्रेयान् better स्वधर्मे in one's own Dharma निधनं death श्रेय: better परधर्म: Dharma of another भयावह: fraught with fear.

35. Better is one's own Dharma, (though) imperfect, than the Dharma of another well-performed. Better is death in one's own Dharma: the Dharma of another is fraught with fear.

The implication is that Arjuna's thought of desisting from fight and going in for the calm and peaceful life of the Brāhmaṇa, is prompted by man's natural desire to shun what is disagreeable and embrace what is agreeable to the senses. He should on no account yield to this weakness.

अर्जुन उवाच

अथ केन प्रयुक्तोऽयं पापं चरति पूरुषः ।
अनिच्छन्नपि वार्ष्णेय बलादिव नियोजितः ।। ३६

अर्जुनः Arjuna उवाच said:
वार्ष्णेय O Vārṣṇeya! अथ now अनिच्छन् not wishing अपि even अयं this पूरुषः Puruṣa केन by what प्रयुक्तः impelled बलात् by force इव as it were नियोजितः constrained पापं sin चरति commits.

Arjuna said:
36. But impelled by what does man commit sin, though against his wishes, O Vārṣṇeya, constrained as it were by force ?

Vārṣṇeya: a descendant of the race of Vṛṣṇi.

श्रीभगवानुवाच

काम एष क्रोध एष रजोगुणसमुद्भवः ।
महाशनो महापाप्मा विद्ध्येनमिह वैरिणम् ।। ३७

श्रीभगवान् The Blessed Lord उवाच said:

रजोगुणसमुद्भवः Born of the *Rajo-guṇa* महाशनः of great craving महापाप्मा of great sin एषः this कामः desire

एषः this क्रोधः anger इह in this world एनम् this वैरिणम् foe विद्धि know.

The Blessed Lord said:

37. It is desire—it is anger, born of the *Rajo-guṇa*; of great craving, and of great sin; know this as the foe here (in this world).

It is desire, etc.: anger is only another form of desire—desire obstructed. (See Note, II. 62–63).

धूमेनाव्रियते वह्निर्यथाऽदर्शो मलेन च ।
यथोल्बेनावृतो गर्भस्तथा तेनेदमावृतम् ।। ३८

यथा As वह्निः fire धूमेन by smoke आव्रियते is enveloped (यथा as) आदर्शः mirror मलेन by dust च and यथा as गर्भः embryo उल्बेन by the secundine आवृतः covered तथा so तेन by that इदम् this आवृतम् covered.

38. As fire is enveloped by smoke, as a mirror by dust, as an embryo by the secundine, so is it covered by that.

"*It*" is knowledge, and "*that*" is desire, as explained in the following *Śloka*.

Three stages of the overclouding of knowledge or Self by desire are described by the three illustrations given here. The first stage is *Sāttvika*—"fire enveloped by smoke"—the rise of a slight wind of discrimination dispels the smoke of desire in a *Sāttvika* heart. The second, the *Rājasika*—the removal of "the dust on a mirror" requires some time and preparation. While the third—the *Tāmasika*, takes a much longer time like the release of "the embryo" from the afterbirth.

आवृतं ज्ञानमेतेन ज्ञानिनो नित्यवैरिणा।
कामरूपेण कौन्तेय दुष्पूरेणानलेन च॥ ३९

कौन्तेय O Kaunteya ज्ञानिन: of the wise नित्यवैरिणा by the constant foe कामरूपेण whose form is desire च and दुष्पूरेण unappeasable एतेन अनलेन by this fire ज्ञानम् knowledge आवृतं covered.

39. Knowledge is covered by this, the constant foe of the wise, O son of Kuntī, the unappeasable fire of desire.

Desire is undoubtedly the foe of all mankind. Why it is said to be the constant foe of the wise, is that they *feel* it to be so even when not under its sway. Fools are awakened for a moment only, when they suffer from its painful reactions.

इन्द्रियाणि मनो बुद्धिरस्याधिष्ठानमुच्यते।
एतैर्विमोहयत्येष ज्ञानमावृत्य देहिनम्॥ ४०

इन्द्रियाणि Senses मन: mind बुद्धि: intellect अस्य its अधिष्ठानम् abode उच्यते is said एष: this एतै: by these ज्ञानम् knowledge आवृत्य covering देहिनम् the embodied विमोहयति deludes.

40. The senses, the mind, and the intellect are said to be its abode: through these, it deludes the embodied by veiling his wisdom.

Like a wise general, Kṛṣṇa points out the fortress of the enemy, by conquering which the enemy is easily defeated.

Through these: by vitiating the senses, mind, and the intellect.

तस्मात्त्वमिन्द्रियाण्यादौ नियम्य भरतर्षभ।
पाप्मानं प्रजहि ह्येनं ज्ञानविज्ञाननाशनम्॥ ४१

भरतर्षभ O Bull of the Bharata race! तस्मात् therefore त्वम् you आदौ at the outset इन्द्रियाणि senses नियम्य controlling ज्ञानविज्ञाननाशनम् the destroyer of knowledge and realisation पाप्मानं the sinful हि surely एनं this प्रजहि kill.

41. Therefore, O Bull of the Bharata race, controlling the senses at the outset, kill it—the sinful, the destroyer of knowledge and realisation.

इन्द्रियाणि पराण्याहुरिन्द्रियेभ्यः परं मनः।
मनसस्तु परा बुद्धिर्यो बुद्धेः परतस्तु सः॥ ४२

इन्द्रियाणि Senses पराणि superior आहुः (they) say इन्द्रियेभ्यः to the senses मनः mind परं superior मनसः to mind तु but बुद्धि intellect परा superior यः who तु but बुद्धेः to the intellect परतः superior सः He (the Ātman).

42. The senses are said to be superior (to the body); the mind is superior to the senses; the intellect is superior to the mind; and that which is superior to the intellect is He (the Ātman).

एवं बुद्धेः परं बुद्ध्वा संस्तभ्यात्मानमात्मना।
जहि शत्रुं महाबाहो कामरूपं दुरासदम्॥ ४३

महाबाहो O mighty-armed! एवं thus बुद्धेः to the intellect परं superior बुद्ध्वा knowing आत्मना by the Self आत्मानम् self संस्तभ्य restraining कामरूपं whose form is desire दुरासदम् unseizable शत्रुं enemy जहि destroy.

43. Thus, knowing Him who is superior to the intellect, and restraining the self by the Self, destroy, O mighty-armed, that enemy, the unseizable foe, desire.

इति कर्मयोगो नाम तृतीयोऽध्यायः॥

The end of the third chapter, designated,
The Way of Action.

चतुर्थोऽध्यायः
(ज्ञानकर्मसन्न्यासयोगः)

FOURTH CHAPTER
(The Way of Renunciation of Action in Knowledge)

श्रीभगवानुवाच

इमं विवस्वते योगं प्रोक्तवानहमव्ययम्।
विवस्वान्मनवे प्राह मनुरिक्ष्वाकवेऽब्रवीत्॥ १

श्रीभगवान् The Blessed Lord उवाच said:

अहम् I विवस्वते to Vivasvat इमं this अव्ययम् imperishable योगं Yoga प्रोक्तवान् told विवस्वान् Vivasvān मनवे to Manu प्राह told मनुः Manu इक्ष्वाकवे to Ikṣvāku अब्रवीत् told.

The Blessed Lord said:

1. I told this imperishable Yoga to Vivasvat; Vivasvat told it to Manu; (and) Manu told it to Ikṣvāku.

Vivasvat: the Sun. *Manu*: the law-giver. Ikṣvāku was the famous ancestor of the Solar dynasty of Kṣatriyas.

This Yoga is said to be imperishable, because the end attainable through it is imperishable.

एवं परम्पराप्राप्तमिमं राजर्षयो विदुः ।
स कालेनेह महता योगो नष्टः परन्तप ।। २

एवं Thus परम्पराप्राप्तम् handed down in regular succession इमं it राजर्षयः the royal sages विदुः knew परन्तप O scorcher of foes! इह in this world सः that योगः Yoga महता by long कालेन lapse of time नष्टः declined.

2. Thus handed down in regular succession, the royal sages knew it. This Yoga, by long lapse of time, declined in this world, O scorcher of foes.

स एवायं मया तेऽद्य योगः प्रोक्तः पुरातनः ।
भक्तोऽसि मे सखा चेति रहस्यं ह्येतदुत्तमम् ।। ३

मे My भक्तः devotee सखा friend च and असि (thou) art इति for this reason सः एव even that पुरातनः ancient योगः Yoga अयं this अद्य this day मया by Me ते to thee प्रोक्तः has been told हि for एतत् this उत्तमम् profound रहस्यं secret.

3. I have this day told thee that same ancient Yoga, (for) thou art My devotee, and My friend, and this secret is profound indeed.

Secret: Not as the privilege of an individual or a sect, but because of its profundity. It is a secret to the unworthy only.

अर्जुन उवाच

अपरं भवतो जन्म परं जन्म विवस्वतः ।
कथमेतद्विजानीयां त्वमादौ प्रोक्तवानिति ।। ४

अर्जुनः Arjuna उवाच said:

भवतः Thy जन्म birth अपरं later विवस्वतः of Vivasvat जन्म birth परं prior एतम् this कथम् how विजानीयां should (I) know त्वम् Thou आदौ in the beginning प्रोक्तवान् told इति this.

Arjuna said:

4. Later was Thy birth, and that of Vivasvat prior; how then should I understand that Thou toldest this in the beginning ?

श्रीभगवानुवाच

बहूनि मे व्यतीतानि जन्मानि तव चार्जुन।
तान्यहं वेद सर्वाणि न त्वं वेत्थ परन्तप।। ५

श्रीभगवान् The Blessed Lord उवाच said:

परन्तप O scorcher of foes अर्जुन Arjuna मे My तव thy च and बहूनि many जन्मानि births व्यतीतानि have passed away अहं I तानि them सर्वाणि all वेद know त्वं thou न not वेत्थ knowest.

The Blessed Lord said:

5. Many are the births that have been passed by Me and thee, O Arjuna. I know them all, whilst thou knowest not, O scorcher of foes.

अजोऽपि सन्नव्ययात्मा भूतानामीश्वरोऽपि सन्।
प्रकृतिं स्वामधिष्ठाय सम्भवाम्यात्ममायया।। ६

अजः Unborn सन् being अपि even अव्ययात्मा of changeless nature भूतानाम् of beings ईश्वरः Lord अपि even सन् being स्वाम् of one's own प्रकृतिं *Prakṛti* अधिष्ठाय subjugating आत्ममायया by My own Māyā सम्भवामि come into being.

6. Though I am unborn, of changeless nature and Lord of beings, yet subjugating My *Prakṛti,* I come into being by My own Māyā.

Subjugating My Prakṛti: He does not come into being as others do, bound by *Karma,* under the thraldom *of Prakṛti* (Nature). He is not tied by the fetters of the *Guṇas*— because He is the Lord of Māyā.

By My own Māyā: My embodiment is only apparent and does not touch My true nature.

यदा यदा हि धर्मस्य ग्लानिर्भवति भारत।
अभ्युत्थानमधर्मस्य तदात्मानं सृजाम्यहम्॥ ७

भारत O Bhārata यदा यदा whenever हि surely धर्मस्य of *Dharma* ग्लानिः decline अधर्मस्य of *Adharma* अभ्युत्थानम् rise भवति is तदा then अहम् I आत्मानं Myself सृजामि embody.

7. Whenever, O descendant of Bharata, there is decline of *Dharma,* and rise of *Adharma,* then I embody Myself.

The *Dharma* and its opposite *Adharma* imply all the duties (and their opposites) as ordained for men in different stations by the definite scheme of their life and salvation.

परित्राणाय साधूनां विनाशाय च दुष्कृताम्।
धर्मसंस्थापनार्थाय संभवामि युगे युगे।। ८

साधूनां Of the good परित्राणाय for the protection च and दुष्कृताम् of the wicked विनाशाय for the destruction धर्मसंस्थापनार्थाय for the establishment of *Dharma* युगे युगे in every age संभवामि I come into being.

8. For the protection of the good, for the destruction of the wicked, and for the establishment of *Dharma,* I come into being in every age.

Destruction of the wicked: in order to destroy their wickedness, and give them life eternal.

जन्म कर्म च मे दिव्यमेवं यो वेत्ति तत्त्वतः।
त्यक्त्वा देहं पुनर्जन्म नैति मामेति सोऽर्जुन।। ९

अर्जुन O Arjuna यः who मे My एवं thus दिव्यम् divine जन्म birth च and कर्म action तत्त्वतः in true light वेत्ति knows सः he देहं body त्यक्त्वा leaving पुनः again जन्म birth न not एति gets माम् Me एति attains.

9. He who thus knows, in true light, My divine birth and action, leaving the body, is not born again: he attains to Me, O Arjuna.

He who knows etc.: He who knows the great truth—that the Lord though apparently born is ever beyond birth and death, apparently active in the cause of righteousness, is ever beyond all action—becomes illumined with Self-knowledge. Such a man is never born again.

**वीतरागभयक्रोधा मन्मया मामुपाश्रिताः ।
बहवो ज्ञानतपसा पूता मद्भावमागताः ।। १०**

वीतरागभयक्रोधाः Freed from attachment, fear, and anger मन्मयाः absorbed in Me माम् Me उपाश्रिताः taking refuge in ज्ञानतपसा by the fire of knowledge पूताः purified बहवः many मद्भावम् My Being आगताः have attained.

10. Freed from attachment, fear, and anger, absorbed in Me, taking refuge in Me, purified by the fire of knowledge, many have attained My Being.

Many have attained: The import is that the path of liberation here taught by Śrī Kṛṣṇa is not of recent origin, nor is it dependent upon His present manifestation, but has been handed down from time immemorial.

**ये यथा मां प्रपद्यन्ते तांस्तथैव भजाम्यहम् ।
मम वर्त्मानुवर्तन्ते मनुष्याः पार्थ सर्वशः ।। ११**

ये Who यथा whatever way मां Me प्रपद्यन्ते worship तान् them अहम् I तथा in the same way एव verily भजामि bestow (their desires) पार्थ O Pārtha मनुष्याः men सर्वशः in all ways मम My वर्त्म path अनुवर्तन्ते follow.

11. In whatever way men worship Me, in the same way do I fulfil their desires; (it is) My path, O son of Pṛthā, (that) men tread, in all ways.

In this *śloka* Śrī Kṛṣṇa anticipates the objection that God is partial to some and unkind to others, since He blesses some with Self-knowledge and leaves the rest in darkness and misery. This difference is not due to any difference in His attitude towards them, but is of their own choice.

My path: In the whole region of thought and action, wherever there is fulfilment of object, no matter what, the same is due to the Lord. As the Self within, He brings to fruition all wishes, when the necessary conditions are fulfilled.

काङ्क्षन्तः कर्मणां सिद्धिं यजन्त इह देवताः ।
क्षिप्रं हि मानुषे लोके सिद्धिर्भवति कर्मजा ।। १२

कर्मणां Of actions सिद्धिं success काङ्क्षन्तः longing for इह in this world देवताः gods यजन्ते worship हि because मानुषे in the human लोके world क्षिप्रं quickly कर्मजा born of action सिद्धिः success भवति is attained.

12. Longing for success in action, in this world, (men) worship the gods. Because success resulting from action, is quickly attained in the human world.

Because success....human world: Wordly success is much easier of attainment than Self-Knowledge. Hence it is that the ignorant do not go in for the latter.

चातुर्वर्ण्यं मया सृष्टं गुणकर्मविभागशः ।
तस्य कर्तारमपि मां विद्ध्यकर्तारमव्ययम् ।। १३

मया By Me गुणकर्मविभागशः by the differentiation of *Guṇa* and *Karma* चातुर्वर्ण्यं fourfold caste सृष्टं was created तस्य thereof कर्तारम् author अपि even मां Me अव्ययम् changeless अकर्तारम् non-doer विद्धि know.

13. The fourfold caste was created by Me, by the differentiation of *Guṇa* and *Karma*. Though I am the author thereof, know Me to be the non-doer, and changeless.

This *śloka* is intended to explain the diversity of human temperaments and tendencies. All men are not of the same nature, because of the preponderance of the different *Guṇas* in them.

The caste system was originally meant to make perfect the growth of humanity, by the special culture of certain features through the process of discriminate selection.

Though I am the author etc.: The Lord, though the author of the caste system, is yet not the author. The same dread of being taken as a doer or an agent crops up again and again. The paradox is explained in Chap. IX. 5-10. Māyā is the real author, but He is taken as such, because it is His light which gives existence, not only to all actions, but to Māyā herself.

न मां कर्माणि लिम्पन्ति न मे कर्मफले स्पृहा।
इति मां योऽभिजानाति कर्मभिर्न स बध्यते॥ १४

कर्माणि Actions मां Me न not लिम्पन्ति taint मे My कर्मफले in the result of action स्पृहा desire न not इति thus य: who मां Me अभिजानाति knows स: he कर्मभि: by actions न not बध्यते is fettered.

14. Actions do not taint Me, nor have I any thirst for the result of action. He who knows Me thus is not fettered by action.

Actions do not taint Me: *Karma* cannot introduce into Me anything foreign. I never depart from My true self, which is All-fullness.

एवं ज्ञात्वा कृतं कर्म पूर्वैरपि मुमुक्षुभिः ।
कुरु कर्मैव तस्मात्त्वं पूर्वैः पूर्वतरं कृतम् ।। १५

एवं Thus ज्ञात्वा knowing पूर्वै: by the ancient मुमुक्षुभि: seekers after freedom अपि even कर्म action कृतं was done तस्मात् therefore त्वं thou पूर्वै: by the ancients पूर्वतरं in olden times कृतम् done कर्म action एव verily कुरु perform.

15. Knowing thus, the ancient seekers after freedom also performed action. Do thou, therefore, perform action, as did the ancients in olden times.

Knowing thus: Taking this point of view, that is, that the Self can have no desire for the fruits of action and cannot be soiled by action.

किं कर्म किमकर्मेति कवयोऽप्यत्र मोहिताः ।
तत्ते कर्म प्रवक्ष्यामि यज्ज्ञात्वा मोक्ष्यसेऽशुभात् ।। १६

किं What कर्म action किम् what अकर्म inaction इति thus अत्र in this कवय: sages अपि even मोहिता: bewildered (अत: therefore) यत् which ज्ञात्वा knowing अशुभात् from evil मोक्ष्यसे you will be freed तत् that ते to you कर्म action प्रवक्ष्यामि (I) shall tell.

16. Even sages are bewildered, as to what is action and what is inaction. I shall, therefore, tell you what action is, by knowing which you will be freed from evil.

Evil: the evil of existence, the wheel of birth and death.

कर्मणो ह्यपि बोद्धव्यं बोद्धव्यञ्च विकर्मणः ।
अकर्मणश्च बोद्धव्यं गहना कर्मणो गतिः ॥ १७

हि Because कर्मण: of actions अपि even (तत्त्वम् the true nature) बोद्धव्यं has to be understood विकर्मण: of the forbidden action च and (अपि even) बोद्धव्यम् has to be understood अकर्मण: of inaction च and (अपि even) बोद्धव्यं has to be understood कर्मण: of *Karma* गति: nature गहना impenetrable.

17. For verily, (the true nature) even of action (enjoined by the *Śāstras*) should be known, as also, (that) of forbidden action, and of inaction: the nature of *Karma* is impenetrable.

कर्मण्यकर्म यः पश्येदकर्मणि च कर्म यः ।
स बुद्धिमान्मनुष्येषु स युक्तः कृत्स्नकर्मकृत् ॥ १८

य: Who कर्मणि in action अकर्म inaction पश्येत् would see य: who अकर्मणि in inaction च and कर्म action पश्येत् would see स: he मनुष्येषु among men बुद्धिमान् intelligent स: he युक्त: Yogi कृत्स्नकर्मकृत् doer of all action.

18. He who sees inaction in action, and action in inaction is intelligent among men, he is a Yogi and a doer of all action.

An action is an action so long as the idea of actorship of the Self holds good. Directly as the idea of actorship disappears, no matter what or how much is done, action has lost its nature. It has become harmless: it can no longer bind. On the other hand, how much soever inactive an ignorant person may remain, so long as there is the idea of actorship in him he is constantly doing action. Action equals to belief in the actorship of oneself and inaction its reverse.

He is the doer of all action: He has achieved the end of all action, which is freedom.

यस्य सर्वे समारम्भाः कामसङ्कल्पवर्जिताः ।
ज्ञानाग्निदग्धकर्माणं तमाहुः पण्डितं बुधाः ।। १९

यस्य Whose सर्वे all समारम्भा: undertakings कामसङ्कल्पवर्जिता: devoid of plan and desire for results बुधा: the sages ज्ञानाग्निदग्धकर्माणं whose actions are burnt by the fire of knowledge तम् him पण्डितं wise आहु: call.

19. Whose undertakings are all devoid of plan and desire for results, and whose actions are burnt by the fire of knowledge, him, the sages call wise.

Whose undertakings etc.: Who is devoid of egoism.

त्यक्त्वा कर्मफलासङ्गं नित्यतृप्तो निराश्रयः ।
कर्मण्यभिप्रवृत्तोऽपि नैव किञ्चित्करोति सः ।। २०

स: He कर्मफलासङ्गं clinging to the fruits of action त्यक्त्वा forsaking नित्यतृप्त: ever satisfied निराश्रय: depending on nothing कर्मणि in action अभिप्रवृत्त: engaged अपि even किञ्चित् anything एव verily न not करोति does.

20. Forsaking the clinging to fruits of action, ever satisfied, depending on nothing, though engaged in action, he does not do anything.

निराशीर्यतचित्तात्मा त्यक्तसर्वपरिग्रहः ।
शारीरं केवलं कर्म कुर्वन्नाप्नोति किल्बिषम् ।। २१

निराशी: Without hope यतचित्तात्मा one whose mind and body have been controlled त्यक्तसर्वपरिग्रह: one who has relinquished all possessions केवलं merely शारीरं bodily कर्म action कुर्वन् doing किल्बिषम् evil न not आप्नोति incurs.

21. Without hope, the body and mind controlled, and all possessions relinquished, he does not suffer any evil consequences, by doing mere bodily action.

Evil consequences: resulting from good and bad actions, for both lead to bondage.

यदृच्छालाभसन्तुष्टो द्वन्द्वातीतो विमत्सरः ।
समः सिद्धावसिद्धौ च कृत्वापि न निबध्यते ।। २२

यदृच्छालाभसन्तुष्ट: Content with what comes to him without effort द्वन्द्वातीत: unaffected by the pairs of opposites विमत्सर: free from envy सिद्धौ in success असिद्धौ in failure च and सम: even-minded कृत्वा acting अपि even न not निबध्यते is bound.

22. Content with what comes to him without effort, unaffected by the pairs of opposites, free from envy, even-minded in success and failure, though acting, he is not bound.

गतसङ्गस्य मुक्तस्य ज्ञानावस्थितचेतसः ।
यज्ञायाचरतः कर्म समग्रं प्रविलीयते ।। २३

गतसङ्गस्य Of one who is devoid of attachment मुक्तस्य the liberated ज्ञानावस्थितचेतस: whose mind is centred in knowledge यज्ञाय for *Yajña* आचरत: performing समग्रं whole कर्म *Karma* प्रविलीयते dissolves away.

23. Devoid of attachment, liberated, with mind centred in knowledge, performing work for *Yajña* alone, his whole *Karma* dissolves away.

ब्रह्मार्पणं ब्रह्म हविर्ब्रह्माग्नौ ब्रह्मणा हुतम् ।
ब्रह्मैव तेन गन्तव्यं ब्रह्मकर्मसमाधिना ।। २४

अर्पणं Process of offering ब्रह्म Brahman हवि: oblation as clarified butter ब्रह्म Brahman ब्रह्माग्नौ in the fire of Brahman ब्रह्मणा by Brahman हुतम् is offered ब्रह्मकर्मसमाधिना by the man who is absorbed in action which is Brahman तेन by him ब्रह्म Brahman एव verily गन्तव्यं should be reached.

24. The process of offering is Brahman, the clarified butter is Brahman, offered by Brahman in the fire of Brahman; by seeing Brahman in action, he reaches Brahman alone.

How can the whole *Karma* of a person, engaged in work, melt away as stated here ? Because after knowledge, his whole life becomes one act of *Yajña,* in which the process of oblation, the offering, the fire, the doer of the sacrifice, the work, and the goal, are all Brahman. Since his *Karma* produces no other result than the attainment of Brahman, his *Karma* is said to melt away.

दैवमेवापरे यज्ञं योगिनः पर्युपासते।
ब्रह्माग्नावपरे यज्ञं यज्ञेनैवोपजुह्वति ।। २५

अपरे Other योगिन: Yogis दैवम् pertaining to *Devas* एव verily यज्ञं sacrifice पर्युपासते perform अपरे others ब्रह्माग्नौ in the fire of Brahman यज्ञेन by self एव verily यज्ञं the self उपजुह्वति offer as sacrifice.

25. Some Yogis perform sacrifices to *Devas* alone, while others offer the self as sacrifice by the self in the fire of Brahman alone.

Others offer etc.: The sacrifice referred to here is divesting the Self of Its *Upādhis* (limiting adjuncts), so that It is found to be the Self.

श्रोत्रादीनीन्द्रियाण्यन्ये संयमाग्निषु जुह्वति।
शब्दादीन्विषयानन्य इन्द्रियाग्निषु जुह्वति ।। २६

अन्ये Others संयमाग्निषु in the fire of control श्रोत्रादीनि organ of hearing, etc. इन्द्रियाणि senses जुह्वति offer as sacrifice अन्ये others शब्दादीन् sound, etc. विषयान् sense-objects इन्द्रियाग्निषु in the fire of the senses जुह्वति offer as sacrifice.

26. Some again offer hearing and other senses as sacrifice in the fire of control, while others offer sound and other sense-objects as sacrifice in the fire of the senses.

Others offer sound etc.: Others direct their senses towards pure and unforbidden objects, and in so doing regard themselves as performing acts of sacrifice.

सर्वाणीन्द्रियकर्माणि प्राणकर्माणि चापरे।
आत्मसंयमयोगाग्नौ जुह्वति ज्ञानदीपिते।। २७

अपरे Others ज्ञानदीपिते kindled by knowledge आत्मसंयम-योगाग्नौ in the fire of control in Self सर्वाणि all इन्द्रियकर्माणि actions of the senses प्राणकर्माणि functions of the vital energy च and जुह्वति offer as sacrifice.

27. Some again offer all the actions of senses and the functions of the vital energy, as sacrifice in the fire of control in Self, kindled by knowledge.

द्रव्ययज्ञास्तपोयज्ञा योगयज्ञास्तथाऽपरे।
स्वाध्यायज्ञानयज्ञाश्च यतयः संशितव्रताः।। २८

तथा Again अपरे others द्रव्ययज्ञाः those who offer wealth as sacrifice तपोयज्ञाः those who offer austerity as sacrifice योगयज्ञाः those who offer Yoga as sacrifice संशितव्रताः persons of rigid vows यतयः persons of self-restraint स्वाध्यायज्ञानयज्ञाः those who offer study and knowledge as sacrifice च and.

28. Others again offer wealth, austerity, and Yoga, as sacrifice, while still others, of self-restraint and rigid vows, offer study of the scriptures and knowledge, as sacrifice.

Offer Yoga as sacrifice: Practise the eightfold Yoga as an act of sacrifice.

अपाने जुह्वति प्राणं प्राणेऽपानं तथाऽपरे।
प्राणापानगती रुद्ध्वा प्राणायामपरायणाः॥ २९
अपरे नियताहाराः प्राणान्प्राणेषु जुह्वति।

तथा Yet अपरे others अपाने into the *Apāna* प्राणं the *Prāṇa* प्राणे into the *Prāṇa* अपानं the *Apāna* जुह्वति sacrifice प्राणापानगती courses of the outgoing and incoming breaths रुद्ध्वा stopping प्राणायामपरायणाः constantly practising the regulation of the vital energy अपरे others नियताहाराः persons of regulated food प्राणान् functions of the *Prāṇas* प्राणेषु in the *Prāṇas* जुह्वति sacrifice.

29. Yet some offer as sacrifice, the outgoing into the incoming breath, and the incoming into the outgoing, stopping the courses of the incoming and outgoing breaths, constantly practising the regulation of the vital energy; while others of regulated food, offer in the *Prāṇas* the functions thereof.

Offer in the Prāṇas the functions thereof: Whatever *Prāṇas* has been controlled, into it they sacrifice all other *Prāṇas;* these latter become, as it were, merged in the former. Or, in another way: They control the different *Prāṇas* and unify them by the foregoing method; the senses are thus attenuated and are merged in the unified *Prāṇa,* as an act of sacrifice.

All the various acts described in verses 25 to 29, as offerings of sacrifice, are only conceived as such, the study of the scriptures is regarded as an act of sacrifice, and so on.

सर्वेऽप्येते यज्ञविदो यज्ञक्षपितकल्मषाः ।। ३ ०
यज्ञशिष्टामृतभुजो यान्ति ब्रह्म सनातनम् ।
नायं लोकोऽस्त्ययज्ञस्य कुतोऽन्यः कुरुसत्तम ।। ३ १

सर्वे All अपि even एते these यज्ञविद: knowers of *Yajña* यज्ञक्षपितकल्मषा: persons having their sins consumed by *Yajña* कुरुसत्तम O best of the Kurus यज्ञशिष्टामृतभुज: persons eating of the nectar—the remnant of *Yajña* सनातनम् eternal ब्रह्म Brahman यान्ति go अयं this लोक: world अयज्ञस्य of the non-performer of *Yajña* न not अस्ति is अन्य: another कुत: how.

30–31. All of these are knowers of *Yajña,* having their sins consumed by *Yajña,* and eating of the nectar—the remnant of *Yajña*—they go to the Eternal Brahman. (Even) this world is not for the non-performer of *Yajña,* how then another, O best of the Kurus ?

They go to the Eternal Brahman: in course of time, after attaining knowledge through purification of heart.

Even this world is not for the non-performer of Yajña: this means—He that does not perform any of the *Yajñas* mentioned above is not fit even for this wretched human world—how then could he hope to gain a better world than this?

एवं बहुविधा यज्ञा वितता ब्रह्मणो मुखे ।
कर्मजान्विद्धि तान्सर्वानेवं ज्ञात्वा विमोक्ष्यसे ।। ३ २

ब्रह्मण: Of the Veda मुखे (lit. mouth), in the storehouse एवं thus बहुविधा: various यज्ञा: *Yajñas* वितता: are strewn तान् them सर्वान् all कर्मजान् born of action विद्धि know एवं thus ज्ञात्वा knowing विमोक्ष्यसे (thou) shalt be free.

32. Various *Yajñas,* like the above, are strewn in the storehouse of the Veda. Know them all to be born of action; and thus knowing, thou shalt be free.

Strewn in the storehouse of the Veda: inculcated by or known through the Veda.

श्रेयान्द्रव्यमयाद्यज्ञाज्ज्ञानयज्ञः परन्तप ।
सर्वं कर्माखिलं पार्थ ज्ञाने परिसमाप्यते ।। ३३

परन्तप O scorcher of foes यज्ञात् to sacrifice द्रव्यमयात् with (material) objects ज्ञानयज्ञ: knowledge-sacrifice श्रेयान् superior पार्थ O Pārtha सर्वं all अखिलं in its entirety कर्म action ज्ञाने in knowledge परिसमाप्यते culminates.

33. Knowledge-sacrifice, O scorcher of foes, is superior to sacrifice (performed) with (material) objects. All action in its entirety, O Pārtha, attains its consummation in knowledge.

तद्विद्धि प्रणिपातेन परिप्रश्नेन सेवया ।
उपदेक्ष्यन्ति ते ज्ञानं ज्ञानिनस्तत्त्वदर्शिनः ।। ३४

प्रणिपातेन By prostrating thyself परिप्रश्नेन by question सेवया by service तत् that (ज्ञानम् knowledge) विद्धि know ज्ञानिन: the wise तत्त्वदर्शिन: those who have realised the Truth ते thee ज्ञानं knowledge उपदेक्ष्यन्ति will instruct.

34. Know that, by prostrating thyself, by questions, and by service; the wise, those who have realised the Truth, will instruct thee in that knowledge.

Prostration before the Guru, questions and personal services to him, constitute discipleship.

Those who have realised the Truth: mere theoretical knowledge, however perfect, does not qualify a person to be a Guru: the Truth, or Brahman, must be realised, before one can claim that most elevated position.

यज्ज्ञात्वा न पुनर्मोहमेवं यास्यसि पाण्डव ।
येन भूतान्यशेषेण द्रक्ष्यस्यात्मन्यथो मयि ।। ३५

पाण्डव O Pāṇḍava यत् which ज्ञात्वा knowing पुनः again एवं like this मोहम् delusion न not यास्यसि will get येन by which अशेषेण all भूतानि beings आत्मनि in (thy) self अथो and मयि in Me (i e., highest Self) द्रक्ष्यसि (thou) shalt see.

35. Knowing which, thou shalt not, O Pāṇḍava, again get deluded like this, and by which thou shalt see the whole of creation in (thy) Self and in Me.

Which: the knowledge referred to in the preceeding *śloka* to be learnt from the Guru.

अपि चेदसि पापेभ्यः सर्वेभ्यः पापकृत्तमः ।
सर्वं ज्ञानप्लवेनैव वृजिनं सन्तरिष्यसि ।। ३६

सर्वेभ्यः Among all अपि even पापेभ्यः most sinful चेत् (even) if पापकृत्तमः most sinful असि (thou) be सर्वं all वृजिनं sin ज्ञानप्लवेन by the raft of knowledge एव alone सन्तरिष्यसि shalt go across.

36. Even if thou be the most sinful among all the sinful, yet by the raft of knowledge alone thou shalt go across all sin.

यथैधांसि समिद्धोऽग्निर्भस्मसात्कुरुतेऽर्जुन ।
ज्ञानाग्निः सर्वकर्माणि भस्मसात्कुरुते तथा ।। ३७

अर्जुन O Arjuna यथा as समिद्धः blazing अग्निः fire एधांसि wood भस्मसात् reduced to ashes कुरुते makes तथा so ज्ञानाग्निः fire of knowledge सर्वकर्माणि all *Karma* भस्मसात् reduced to ashes कुरुते makes.

37. As blazing fire reduces wood into ashes, so, O Arjuna, does the fire of knowledge reduce all *Karma* to ashes.

Excepting of course the *Prārabdha,* or *Karma* which, after causing the present body, has begun to bear fruits.

न हि ज्ञानेन सदृशं पवित्रमिह विद्यते ।
तत्स्वयं योगसंसिद्धः कालेनात्मनि विन्दति ।। ३८

हि Verily इह in this world ज्ञानेन knowledge सदृशं like पवित्रम् purifying न not विद्यते exists कालेन in time योगसंसिद्धः reaching perfection by Yoga आत्मनि in one's own heart स्वयं oneself तत् that (knowledge) विन्दति realises.

38. Verily there exists nothing in this world purifying like knowledge. In good time, having reached perfection in Yoga, one realises that oneself in one's own heart.

श्रद्धावाँल्लभते ज्ञानं तत्परः संयतेन्द्रियः।
ज्ञानं लब्ध्वा परां शान्तिमचिरेणाधिगच्छति ॥ ३९

श्रद्धावान् The man of *śraddhā* तत्पर: devoted संयतेन्द्रिय: the master of one's senses ज्ञानं knowledge लभते attains ज्ञानं knowledge लब्ध्वा having attained अचिरेण at once परां supreme शान्तिम् to peace अधिगच्छति goes.

39. The man with *Śraddhā,* the devoted, the master of one's senses, attains (this) knowledge. Having attained knowledge one goes at once to the Supreme Peace.

अज्ञश्चाश्रद्दधानश्च संशयात्मा विनश्यति।
नायं लोकोऽस्ति न परो न सुखं संशयात्मनः ॥ ४०

अज्ञ: The ignorant अश्रद्दधान: the man without *Śraddhā* संशयात्मा the doubting self विनश्यति goes to destruction संशयात्मन: of the doubting self अयं this लोक: world न not अस्ति is न not च and पर: the next न not च and सुखं happiness.

40. The ignorant, the man without *Śraddhā,* the doubting self, goes to destruction. The doubting self has neither this world, nor the next, nor happiness.

The ignorant: one who knows not the Self.

The man without Śraddhā: one who has no faith in the words and teachings of his Guru.

The doubting self has etc.: One of a doubting disposition fails to enjoy this world, owing to his constantly rising suspicion about the people, and things around him, and is also full of doubt as regards the next world; so do the ignorant and the man without *Śraddhā*.

योगसन्न्यस्तकर्माणं ज्ञानसंछिन्नसंशयम् ।
आत्मवन्तं न कर्माणि निबध्नन्ति धनञ्जय ।। ४१

धनञ्जय O Dhanañjaya योगसन्न्यस्तकर्माणं one who has renounced work by Yoga ज्ञानसंछिन्नसंशयम् one whose doubts are rent asunder by knowledge आत्मवन्तं poised in the Self कर्माणि action न not निबध्नन्ति bind.

41. With work renounced by Yoga and doubts rent asunder by knowledge, O Dhanañjaya, actions do not bind him who is poised in the Self.

तस्मादज्ञानसंभूतं हृत्स्थं ज्ञानासिनात्मनः ।
छित्त्वैनं संशयं योगमातिष्ठोत्तिष्ठ भारत ।। ४२

तस्मात् Therefore आत्मन: of the Self अज्ञानसंभूतं born of ignorance हृत्स्थं residing in the heart एनं this संशयं doubt ज्ञानासिना by the sword of knowledge छित्त्वा cutting योगम् Yoga आतिष्ठ take refuge in भारत O Bhārata उत्तिष्ठ arise.

42. Therefore cutting with the sword of knowledge, this doubt about the Self, born of ignorance, residing in thy heart, take refuge in Yoga. Arise, O Bhārata!

इति ज्ञानकर्मसन्न्यासयोगो नाम चतुर्थोऽध्यायः ।।

The end of fourth chapter, designated,
The Way of Renunciation of Action in Knowledge.

पञ्चमोऽध्यायः
(सन्न्यासयोगः)
FIFTH CHAPTER
(The Way of Renunciation)

अर्जुन उवाच

सन्न्यासं कर्मणां कृष्ण पुनर्योगं च शंससि।
यच्छ्रेय एतयोरेकं तन्मे ब्रूहि सुनिश्चितम्॥ १

अर्जुन: Arjuna उवाच said:

कृष्ण O Kṛṣṇa कर्मणां of actions सन्न्यासं renunciation पुन: again योगं performance च and शंससि commendest एतयो: of these two यत् which श्रेय: the better एकं one तत् that (एकं one) सुनिश्चितम् decisively मे to me ब्रूहि tell.

Arjuna said:

1. Renunciation of action, O Kṛṣṇa, thou commendest, and again, its performance. Which is the better one of these? Do thou tell me decisively.

In IV. 18, 19, 21, 22, 24, 32, 33, 37, and 41, the Lord has spoken of the renunciation of all actions; and in IV.42, He has exhorted Arjuna to engage in Yoga, in performance of action. Owing to the mutual opposition between the two, which makes it impossible for one man to resort to both of them at the same time, doubt arises in the mind of Arjuna, and hence the question as above.

Its Performance—"Yoga" in the text: Yoga here and in the following verses means Karma-Yoga.

श्रीभगवानुवाच

सन्न्यासः कर्मयोगश्च निःश्रेयसकरावुभौ।
तयोस्तु कर्मसन्न्यासात्कर्मयोगो विशिष्यते॥ २

श्रीभगवान् The Blessed Lord उवाच said:

सन्न्यास: Renunciation कर्मयोग: performance of action च and उभौ both निःश्रेयसकरौ leading to freedom तयो: of those two तु but कर्मसन्न्यासात् than renunciation of action कर्मयोग: performance of action विशिष्यते is superior.

The Blessed Lord said:

2. Both renunciation and performance of action lead to freedom: of these, performance of action is superior to the renunciation of action.

Performance of action—is superior to mere renunciation (that is unaccompanied with knowledge) in the case of the novice in the path of spirituality. See the sixth *śloka* of this chapter.

ज्ञेयः स नित्यसन्न्यासी यो न द्वेष्टि न काङ्क्षति।
निर्द्वन्द्वो हि महाबाहो सुखं बन्धात्प्रमुच्यते॥ ३

य: Who न not द्वेष्टि dislikes न not काङ्क्षति likes स: he नित्यसन्न्यासी constant *Sannyāsī* ज्ञेय: should be known महाबाहो O mighty-armed हि verily निर्द्वन्द्व: one free from the pairs of opposites बन्धात् from bondage सुखं easily प्रमुच्यते is set free.

3. He should be known a constant *Sannyāsī*, who neither likes nor dislikes: for, free from the pairs of opposites, O mighty-armed, he is easily set free from bondage.

Constant Sannyāsī: he need not have taken *Sannyāsa* formally, but if he has the above frame of mind, he is a *Sannyāsī* for ever and aye.

Neither likes nor dislikes: Neither hates pain and the objects causing pain, nor desires pleasure and the objects causing pleasure, though engaged in action.

सांख्ययोगौ पृथग्बालाः प्रवदन्ति न पण्डिताः ।
एकमप्यास्थितः सम्यगुभयोर्विन्दते फलम् ।। ४

बालाः Children सांख्ययोगौ *Sāṅkhya* (knowledge) and performance of actions पृथक् distinct (इति this) प्रवदन्ति speak न not पण्डिताः the wise एकम् one अपि even सम्यक् truly आस्थितः established in उभयोः of both फलम् fruit विन्दते gains.

4. Children, not the wise, speak of knowledge and performance of action, as distinct. He who truly lives in one, gains the fruits of both.

Children: the ignorant people devoid of insight into the purpose of the *Śāstra*.

यत्सांख्यैः प्राप्यते स्थानं तद्योगैरपि गम्यते ।
एकं सांख्यं च योगं च यः पश्यति स पश्यति ।। ५

सांख्यैः By the *Jñānis* यत् which स्थानं plane प्राप्यते is reached योगैः by the *Karma-yogis* अपि even तत् that गम्यते is reached यः who सांख्यं knowledge च and योगं performance of action च and एकं one पश्यति sees सः he पश्यति sees.

5. The plane which is reached by the *Jñānis* is also reached by the *Karma-yogis*. He who sees knowledge and performance of actions as one, alone sees.

सन्न्यासस्तु महाबाहो दुःखमाप्तुमयोगतः ।
योगयुक्तो मुनिर्ब्रह्म न चिरेणाधिगच्छति ।। ६

महाबाहो O mighty-armed अयोगतः without performance of action सन्न्यासः renunciation of action आप्तुम् to attain दुःखम् hard तु but योगयुक्तः devoted to the path of action मुनिः a man of meditation न चिरेण quickly ब्रह्म to Brahman अधिगच्छति goes.

6. Renunciation of action, O mighty-armed, is hard to attain to without performance of action; the man of meditation, purified by devotion to action, quickly goes to Brahman.

It is not that renunciation of action based on knowledge is not superior to performance of action, but that the latter method is easier for a beginner, and qualifies him for the higher path, by purifying his mind. Hence it is the proper, and therefore the superior course, in *his* case.

योगयुक्तो विशुद्धात्मा विजितात्मा जितेन्द्रियः ।
सर्वभूतात्मभूतात्मा कुर्वन्नपि न लिप्यते ।। ७

योगयुक्तः Devoted to the path of action विशुद्धात्मा a man of purified mind विजितात्मा one with the body conquered जितेन्द्रियः one whose senses are subdued सर्वभूतात्मभूतात्मा one who realises his self as the self in all beings कुर्वन् acting अपि though न not लिप्यते is tainted.

7. With the mind purified by devotion to performance of action, and the body conquered, and senses subdued, one who realises one's self, as the self in all beings, though acting, is not tainted.

नैव किञ्चित्करोमीति युक्तो मन्येत तत्त्ववित् ।
पश्यञ्छृण्वन्स्पृशञ्जिघ्रन्नश्नन्गच्छन्स्वपञ्छ्वसन् ।। ८
प्रलपन्विसृजन्गृह्णन्नुन्मिषन्निमिषन्नपि ।
इन्द्रियाणीन्द्रियार्थेषु वर्तन्त इति धारयन् ।। ९

युक्तः Centred (in the Self) तत्त्ववित् the knower of truth पश्यन् seeing शृण्वन् hearing स्पृशन् touching जिघ्रन् smelling अश्नन् eating गच्छन् going स्वपन् sleeping श्वसन् breathing प्रलपन् speaking विसृजन् letting go गृह्णन् holding उन्मिषन् opening (the eyes) निमिषन् closing (the eyes) अपि though इन्द्रियाणि senses इन्द्रियार्थेषु amongst sense-objects वर्तन्ते move इति this धारयन् being convinced किञ्चित् anything एव at all न not करोमि (I) do इति this मन्येत should think.

8-9. The knower of Truth, (being) centred (in the Self) should think, "I do nothing at all"—though seeing, hearing, touching, smelling, eating, going, sleeping, breathing, speaking, letting go, holding, opening, and closing the eyes—convinced that it is the senses that move among sense objects.

ब्रह्मण्याधाय कर्माणि सङ्गं त्यक्त्वा करोति यः ।
लिप्यते न स पापेन पद्मपत्रमिवाम्भसा ॥ १०

यः Who ब्रह्मणि in Brahman आधाय resigning सङ्गं attachment त्यक्त्वा forsaking कर्माणि actions करोति does सः he अम्भसा by water पद्मपत्रम् lotus-leaf इव like पापेन by evil न not लिप्यते soiled.

10. He who does actions forsaking attachment, resigning them to Brahman, is not soiled by evil, like unto a lotus-leaf by water.

Evil: the results, good and bad, producing bondage.

कायेन मनसा बुद्ध्या केवलैरिन्द्रियैरपि ।
योगिनः कर्म कुर्वन्ति सङ्गं त्यक्त्वात्मशुद्धये ॥ ११

योगिनः Devotees in the path of work सङ्गं attachment त्यक्त्वा forsaking आत्मशुद्धये for the purification of the heart केवलैः only कायेन by body मनसा by mind बुद्ध्या by intellect इन्द्रियैः by senses अपि even कर्म action कुर्वन्ति perform.

11. Devotees in the path of work perform action, only with body, mind, senses, and intellect, forsaking attachment, for the purification of the heart.

Only with etc.—without egotism or selfishness: it applies *to* body, mind, senses, and intellect.

युक्तः कर्मफलं त्यक्त्वा शान्तिमाप्नोति नैष्ठिकीम्।
अयुक्तः कामकारेण फले सक्तो निबध्यते ॥ १२

युक्त: The well-poised कर्मफलं fruit of action त्यक्त्वा forsaking नैष्ठिकीम् born of steadfastness शान्तिम् peace आप्नोति attains अयुक्त: the unbalanced कामकारेण led by desire फले in the fruit (of action) सक्त: (being) attached निबध्यते is bound.

12. The well-poised, forsaking the fruit of action, attains peace, born of steadfastness; the unbalanced one, led by desire, is bound by being attached to the fruit (of action).

Born of steadfastness: Śaṅkara explains *Naiṣṭhikīm* as gradual perfection in the path of knowledge, having the following stages of development: (1) purity of heart, (2) gaining of knowledge, (3) renunciation of action, (4) steadiness in knowledge.

सर्वकर्माणि मनसा सन्न्यस्यास्ते सुखं वशी।
नवद्वारे पुरे देही नैव कुर्वन्न कारयन् ॥ १३

वशी Subduer (of the senses) देही embodied soul मनसा by discrimination सर्वकर्माणि all actions सन्न्यस्य having renounced सुखं happily नवद्वारे in the nine-gated पुरे city न not एव verily कुर्वन् acting न not (एव verily) कारयन् causing (others) to act आस्ते rests.

13. The subduer (of the senses), having renounced all actions by discrimination rests happily in the city of the nine gates, neither acting, nor causing (others) to act.

All actions: 1. *Nitya* or obligatory—the performance of which does not produce any merit while the non-performance produces demerit. 2. *Naimittika*—those arising on the occurrence of some special events, as the birth of a son: these also are customary. 3. *Kāmya*—those intended for securing some special ends: these are only optional. 4. *Niṣiddha*—forbidden. He rests happily in the body (of nine organic openings), seeing inaction in action: just exhausting his *Prārabdha*-not relating or identifying himself with anything of the dual universe.

न कर्तृत्वं न कर्माणि लोकस्य सृजति प्रभुः ।
न कर्मफलसंयोगं स्वभावस्तु प्रवर्तते ।। १४

प्रभु: The Lord लोकस्य for the world न neither कर्तृत्वं agency न nor कर्माणि actions न not कर्मफलसंयोगं union with the fruits of action सृजति creates तु but स्वभाव: (Nature) universal ignorance प्रवर्तते leads to action.

14. Neither agency, nor actions does the Lord create for the world, nor (does He bring about) the union with the fruit of action. It is universal ignorance that does (it all).

नादत्ते कस्यचित् पापं न चैव सुकृतं विभुः ।
अज्ञानेनावृतं ज्ञानं तेन मुह्यन्ति जन्तवः ।। १५

विभु: Omnipresent कस्यचित् of anyone पापं demerit न not आदत्ते takes सुकृतं merit च एव and न not अज्ञानेन by ignorance ज्ञानं knowledge आवृतं enveloped तेन hence जन्तव: beings मुह्यन्ति get deluded.

15. The Omnipresent takes note of the merit or demerit of none. Knowledge is enveloped in ignorance, hence do beings get deluded.

In unmistakable words, Kṛṣṇa describes the position of *Īśvara*, or the Lord, in relation to the Universe, in these two verses.

He is all-blissful, all-perfect; even the shadow of a motive or relation in Him, would be contradictory to His nature. His mere proximity to *Prakṛti* or Nature endues the latter with power and potency of causing all that is. *Jīva* is bound so long as it relates itself to, and identifies itself with, this Nature. When it ceases to do so, it attains freedom. The whole teaching of the Gītā, and therefore of all the Hindu scriptures, on this subject, is condensed in the above.

ज्ञानेन तु तदज्ञानं येषां नाशितमात्मनः ।
तेषामादित्यवज्ज्ञानं प्रकाशयति तत्परम् ।। १६

तु But आत्मन: of Self ज्ञानेन by knowledge येषां whose तत् that अज्ञानं ignorance नाशितम् is destroyed तेषाम् their तत् that ज्ञानं knowledge परम् the Supreme (Brahman) आदित्यवत् like the sun प्रकाशयति reveals.

16. But whose ignorance is destroyed by the knowledge of Self—that knowledge of theirs, like the sun, reveals the Supreme (Brahman).

तद्बुद्धयस्तदात्मानस्तन्निष्ठास्तत्परायणाः ।
गच्छन्त्यपुनरावृत्तिं ज्ञाननिर्धूतकल्मषाः ।। १७

तद्बुद्धयः Those who have their intellect absorbed in That तदात्मानः those whose self is That तन्निष्ठाः those who are steadfast in That तत्परायणाः those whose consummation is That ज्ञाननिर्धूतकल्मषाः those whose impurities have been shaken off by knowledge अपुनरावृत्तिं non-return गच्छन्ति attain.

17. Those who have their intellect absorbed in That, whose self is That, whose steadfastness is in That, whose consummation is That, their impurities cleansed by knowledge, they attain to non-return (*Mokṣa*).

विद्याविनयसंपन्ने ब्राह्मणे गवि हस्तिनि ।
शुनि चैव श्वपाके च पण्डिताः समदर्शिनः ।। १८

पण्डिताः The knowers of the Self एव verily विद्याविनयसंपन्ने in one endowed with learning and humility ब्राह्मणे in a Brāhmaṇa गवि in a cow हस्तिनि in an elephant शुनि in a dog च and श्वपाके in a pariah (lit. one who cooks or eats a dog) च and समदर्शिनः lookers with an equal eye (भवन्ति become).

18. The knowers of the Self look with an equal eye on a Brāhmaṇa endowed with learning and humility, a cow, an elephant, a dog, and a pariah.

Because they can see nothing but the Self. It makes no difference to the sun whether it be reflected in the Gangā, in wine, in a small pool, or in any unclean liquid; the same is the case with the Self. No *Upādhi* (or limiting adjunct) can attach to it.

इहैव तैर्जितः सर्गो येषां साम्ये स्थितं मनः ।
निर्दोषं हि समं ब्रह्म तस्माद् ब्रह्मणि ते स्थिताः ॥ १९

येषां Whose मनः mind साम्ये in evenness स्थितं fixed इह in this world एव verily तैः by them सर्गः (relative) existence जितः is conquered हि indeed ब्रह्म Brahman समं even निर्दोषं without imperfection तस्मात् therefore ते they ब्रह्मणि in Brahman स्थिताः are established.

19. (Relative) existence has been conquered by them, even in this world, whose mind rests in evenness, since Brahman is even and is without imperfection; therefore they indeed rest in Brahman.

Relative existence: All bondage as of birth, death, etc. All possibility of bondage is destroyed when the mind attains perfect evenness, which in other words means—becoming Brahman.

न प्रहृष्येत् प्रियं प्राप्य नोद्विजेत्प्राप्य चाप्रियम् ।
स्थिरबुद्धिरसंमूढो ब्रह्मविद् ब्रह्मणि स्थितः ॥ २०

ब्रह्मवित् Knower of Brahman ब्रह्मणि in Brahman स्थितः established स्थिरबुद्धिः one with intellect steady असंमूढः undeluded प्रियं the pleasant प्राप्य receiving न not प्रहृष्येत् should rejoice अप्रियम् the unpleasant च and प्राप्य receiving न not उद्विजेत् should be troubled.

20. Resting in Brahman, with intellect steady, and without delusion, the knower of Brahman neither rejoiceth on receiving what is pleasant, nor grieveth on receiving what is unpleasant.

बाह्यस्पर्शेष्वसक्तात्मा विन्दत्यात्मनि यत्सुखम् ।
स ब्रह्मयोगयुक्तात्मा सुखमक्षयमश्नुते ।। २१

बाह्यस्पर्शेषु In the contacts (of the senses) with the external objects असक्तात्मा one whose heart is unattached आत्मनि in the Self यत् what सुखम् joy विन्दति realises सः he ब्रह्मयोगयुक्तात्मा heart devoted to the meditation of Brahman अक्षयम् undecaying सुखम् happiness अश्नुते attains.

21. With the heart unattached to external objects, he realises the joy that is in the Self. With the heart devoted to the meditation of Brahman, he attains undecaying happiness.

Heart—Antaḥ-karaṇa.

ये हि संस्पर्शजा भोगा दुःखयोनय एव ते ।
आद्यन्तवन्तः कौन्तेय न तेषु रमते बुधः ।। २२

कौन्तेय O Kaunteya ये which हि verily संस्पर्शजाः contact-born भोगाः enjoyments ते they दुःखयोनयः generators of misery एव only आद्यन्तवन्तः with beginning and end बुधः the wise man तेषु in them न not रमते seeks pleasure.

22. Since enjoyments that are contact-born are parents of misery alone, and with beginning and

end, O son of Kuntī, a wise man does not seek pleasure in them.

शक्नोतीहैव यः सोढुं प्राक् शरीरविमोक्षणात् ।
कामक्रोधोद्भवं वेगं स युक्तः स सुखी नरः ॥ २३

यः Who शरीरविमोक्षणात् liberation from the body प्राक् before कामक्रोधोद्भवं born of lust and anger वेगम् impulse इह in this world एव verily सोढुं to withstand शक्नोति is able सः he युक्तः steadfast in Yoga सः he सुखी happy नरः man.

23. He who can withstand in this world, before the liberation from the body, the impulse arising from lust and anger, he is steadfast (in Yoga), he is a happy man.

योऽन्तःसुखोऽन्तरारामस्तथाऽन्तर्ज्योतिरेव यः ।
स योगी ब्रह्मनिर्वाणं ब्रह्मभूतोऽधिगच्छति ॥ २४

यः Who अन्तःसुखः one whose happiness is within अन्तरारामः one whose relaxation is within तथा again यः who अन्तर्ज्योतिः one whose light is within सः that योगी Yogī एव alone ब्रह्मभूतः becoming Brahman ब्रह्मनिर्वाणं bliss in Brahman, i.e., absolute freedom अधिगच्छति gains.

24. Whose happiness is within, whose relaxation is within, whose light is within, that Yogī alone, becoming Brahman, gains absolute freedom.

Within: In the Self.

Absolute Freedom: *Brahma-Nirvāṇa*. He attains *Mokṣa* while still living in the body.

लभन्ते ब्रह्मनिर्वाणमृषयः क्षीणकल्मषाः ।
छिन्नद्वैधा यतात्मानः सर्वभूतहिते रताः ॥ २५

क्षीणकल्मषाः Those whose imperfections are exhausted छिन्नद्वैधाः those whose doubts are dispelled यतात्मानः those whose senses are controlled सर्वभूतहिते in the good of all beings रताः engaged ऋषयः *Ṛṣis* ब्रह्मनिर्वाणम् absolute freedom लभन्ते obtain.

25. With imperfections exhausted, doubts dispelled, senses controlled, engaged in the good of all beings, the *Ṛṣis* obtain absolute freedom.

Ṛṣis: Men of right vision and renunciation.

कामक्रोधवियुक्तानां यतीनां यतचेतसाम् ।
अभितो ब्रह्मनिर्वाणं वर्तते विदितात्मनाम् ॥ २६

कामक्रोधवियुक्तानां Of those who have been released from lust and anger यतचेतसाम् of those whose heart is controlled विदितात्मनाम् of those who have realised the Self यतीनाम् of the *Sannyāsins* अभितः both here and hereafter ब्रह्मनिर्वाणम् absolute freedom वर्तते exists.

26. Released from lust and anger, the heart controlled, the Self realised, absolute freedom is for such *Sannyāsins*, both here and hereafter.

स्पर्शान् कृत्वा बहिर्बाह्यांश्चक्षुश्चैवान्तरे भ्रुवोः ।
प्राणापानौ समौ कृत्वा नासाभ्यन्तरचारिणौ ॥ २७

यतेन्द्रियमनोबुद्धिर्मुनिर्मोक्षपरायणः ।
विगतेच्छाभयक्रोधो यः सदा मुक्त एव सः ॥ २८

बाह्यान् External स्पर्शान् (contacts) objects बहि: outside कृत्वा shutting out चक्षु: eye च and भ्रुवो: of the (two) eyebrows अन्तरे in the middle एव thus नासाभ्यन्तरचारिणौ moving inside the nostrils प्राणापानौ currents of *Prāṇa* and *Apāna* समौ even कृत्वा having made यतेन्द्रियमनोबुद्धि: one who has controlled one's senses, mind, and intellect मोक्षपरायण: one to whom *Mokṣa* is the supreme goal विगतेच्छाभयक्रोध: freed from desire, fear, and anger य: who मुनि: man of meditation स: he सदा for ever मुक्त: free एव verily.

27-28. Shutting out external objects; steadying the eyes between the eyebrows; restricting the even currents of *Prāṇa* and *Apāna* inside the nostrils; the senses, mind, and intellect controlled; with *Mokṣa* as the supreme goal; freed from desire, fear, and anger: such a man of meditation is verily free for ever.

External objects: Sound and other sense-objects. External objects are shut out from the mind by not thinking of them. When the eyes are half-closed in meditation, the eye-balls remain fixed, and their gaze converges, as it were, between the eyerbows. Prāṇa is the outgoing breath, Apāna the incoming; the restriction described is effected by Prāṇāyāma.

These two verses are the aphorisms of which the following chapter is the commentary.

भोक्तारं यज्ञतपसां सर्वलोकमहेश्वरम्।
सुहृदं सर्वभूतानां ज्ञात्वा मां शान्तिमृच्छति ।। २९

यज्ञतपसां Of Yajñas and asceticisms भोक्तारं dispenser सर्वलोकमहेश्वरम् Great Lord of all the worlds सर्वभूतानां of all beings सुहृदं friend मां Me ज्ञात्वा knowing शान्तिम् peace ऋच्छति attains.

29. Knowing Me as the dispenser of Yajñas and asceticisms, as the Great Lord of all worlds, as the friend of all beings, he attains Peace.

Dispenser: Both as author and goal, the Lord is the dispenser of the fruit of all actions.

Friend: Doer of good without expecting any return.

इति सन्न्यासयोगो नाम पञ्चमोऽध्यायः ।।

The end of the fifth chapter, designated,
The Way of Renunciation.

षष्ठोऽध्यायः
(ध्यानयोगः)

SIXTH CHAPTER
(The Way of Meditation)

श्रीभगवानुवाच

अनाश्रितः कर्मफलं कार्यं कर्म करोति यः ।
स सन्न्यासी च योगी च न निरग्निर्न चाक्रियः ॥ १

श्रीभगवान् The Blessed Lord उवाच said:

यः Who कर्मफलं fruit of action अनाश्रितः not leaning to कार्यम् bounden कर्म duty करोति performs सः he सन्न्यासी renouncer of action च and योगी of steadfast mind च and न not निरग्निः one without fire न not च and अक्रियः one without action.

The Blessed Lord said:

1. He who performs his bounden duty without leaning to the fruit of action—he is a renouncer of action as well as of steadfast mind: not he who is without fire, nor he who is without action.

Bounden duty: *Nityakarma*.

Renouncer of action as well as of steadfast mind: *Sannyāsī* and *Yogī*.

Without fire: He that has renounced actions enjoined by the Vedas, requiring fire as adjunct, e.g. *Agnihotra*.

Without action: He who has renounced actions which do not require fire as adjunct, such as austerities and meritorious acts like digging wells etc.

यं सन्न्यासमिति प्राहुर्योगं तं विद्धि पाण्डव।
न ह्यसन्न्यस्तसङ्कल्पो योगी भवति कश्चन॥ २

पाण्डव O Pāṇḍava यम् which सन्न्यासम् renunciation इति this प्राहु: said तं that योगम् devotion to action विद्धि know हि for असन्न्यस्तसङ्कल्प: one who has not forsaken *Saṅkalpa* कश्चन anyone योगी a devotee to action न not भवति becomes.

2. Know that to be devotion to action, which is called renunciation, O Pāṇḍava, for none becomes a devotee to action without forsaking *Saṅkalpa*.

Saṅkalpa—is the working of the imaging faculty, forming fancies, making plans, and again brushing them aside conceiving future results, starting afresh on a new line, leading to different issues, and so on and so forth. No one can be a *Karma-Yogī* or a devotee to action, who makes plans and wishes for the fruit of action.

आरुरुक्षोर्मुनेर्योगं कर्म कारणमुच्यते।
योगारूढस्य तस्यैव शमः कारणमुच्यते॥ ३

योगं Concentration आरुरुक्षो: wishing to climb (i.e. to attain) मुने: of the man of meditation कर्म work कारणम् means उच्यते is said योगारूढस्य of one who has attained concentration तस्य his शम: inaction एव verily कारणम् way उच्यते is said.

3. For the man of meditation wishing to attain purification of heart leading to concentration, work is said to be the way: For him, when he has attained such (concentration), inaction is said to be the way.

Purification of the heart leading to concentration—Yoga. "For a *Brāhmaṇa* there is no wealth like unto (the eye of) oneness, (and) evenness, truth, refinement, steadiness, harmlessness, straightforwardness, *and gradual withdrawal from all action*"—*Mahābhārata*, Śānti-Parva, 175.38.

यदा हि नेन्द्रियार्थेषु न कर्मस्वनुषज्जते ।
सर्वसंकल्पसन्न्यासी योगारूढस्तदोच्यते ।। ४

यदा When हि verily न neither इन्द्रियार्थेषु in sense-objects न not कर्मसु in actions अनुषज्जते is attached तदा then सर्वसङ्कल्पसन्न्यासी renouncer of all *Saṅkalpas* योगारूढ: to have attained concentration उच्यते is said.

4. Verily, when there is no attachment, either to sense-objects, or to actions, having renounced all *Saṅkalpas*, then is one said to have attained concentration.

Attained concentration: *Yogārūḍha*.

Renouncer of all Saṅkalpas: "O desire, I know where thy root lies: thou art born of *Saṅkalpa*. I shall not think of thee, and thou shalt cease to exist, together with thy root."—*Mahābhārala*, Śānti-Parva, 177.25.

उद्धरेदात्मनात्मानं नात्मानमवसादयेत्।
आत्मैव ह्यात्मनो बन्धुरात्मैव रिपुरात्मनः ॥ ५

आत्मना By self आत्मानं oneself उद्धरेत् should uplift न not (तु but) आत्मानम् oneself अवसादयेत् should drag down हि verily आत्मा self एव alone आत्मन: of onself बन्धु: friend आत्मा self एव verily आत्मन: of oneself रिपु: enemy.

5. A man should uplift himself by his own self, so let him not weaken this self. For this self is the friend of oneself, and this self is the enemy of oneself.

The self-conscious nature of man is here considered in two aspects as being both the object of spiritual uplift and the subject of spiritual uplift, the ego acted upon and the ego acting upon the former. This latter active principle or ego should be kept strong in its uplifting function, for it is apt to turn an enemy if it is not a friend; and the next verse explains the reason.

बन्धुरात्मात्मनस्तस्य येनात्मैवात्मना जितः।
अनात्मनस्तु शत्रुत्वे वर्तेतात्मैव शत्रुवत् ॥ ६

येन By whom आत्मना by oneself एव verily आत्मा self जित: is conquered तस्य his आत्मा self आत्मन: of oneself बन्धु: friend तु but अनात्मन: of unconquered self आत्मा self एव verily शत्रुवत् like foe शत्रुत्वे in the position of a foe वर्तेत would remain.

6. The self (the active part of our nature) is the friend of the self, for him who has conquered

himself by this self. But to the unconquered self, this self is inimical, (and behaves) like (an external) foe.

The self is the friend of one, in whom the aggregate of the body and the senses has been brought under control, and an enemy when such is not the case.

जितात्मनः प्रशान्तस्य परमात्मा समाहितः ।
शीतोष्णसुखदुःखेषु तथा मानापमानयोः ॥ ७

जितात्मन: Of the self-controlled प्रशान्तस्य the serene one परमात्मा the Supreme Self शीतोष्णसुखदुःखेषु in cold and heat, pleasure and pain तथा as also मानापमानयो: in honour and dishonour समाहित: is steadfast.

7. To the self-controlled and serene, the Supreme Self is the object of constant realisation, in cold and heat, pleasure and pain, as well as in honour and dishonour.

Hence he remains unruffled in pleasant and adverse environments.

ज्ञानविज्ञानतृप्तात्मा कूटस्थो विजितेन्द्रियः ।
युक्त इत्युच्यते योगी समलोष्टाश्मकाञ्चनः ॥ ८

ज्ञानविज्ञानतृप्तात्मा One whose heart is satisfied by wisdom and realisation कूटस्थ: unshaken विजितेन्द्रिय: who has conquered his senses समलोष्टाश्मकाञ्चन: one to whom a lump of earth, stone, and gold are the same योगी Yogī युक्त: steadfast इति this उच्यते is said.

8. Whose heart is filled with satisfaction by wisdom and realisation, and is changeless, whose senses are conquered, and to whom a lump of earth, stone, and gold are the same — that Yogī is called steadfast.

Wisdom—Jñāna: knowledge of *Śāstras*.

Realisation—Vijñāna: onc's own experience of the teachings of *Śāstras*.

Changeless—like the anvil. Things are hammered and shaped on the anvil, but the anvil remains unchanged: in the same manner he is called *Kūṭastha*—whose heart remains unchanged though objects are present.

सुहृन्मित्रार्युदासीनमध्यस्थद्वेष्यबन्धुषु ।
साधुष्वपि च पापेषु समबुद्धिर्विशिष्यते ।। ९

सुहृत् Well-wisher मित्रम् friend अरि: foe उदासीन: the neutral मध्यस्थ: the arbiter द्वेष्य: the hateful बन्धु: relative (सुहृन्मित्रार्युदासीनमध्यस्थद्वेष्यबन्धुषु in well-wishers etc.) साधुषु in the righteous अपि even च and पापेषु in the unrighteous समबुद्धि: one whose mind is even विशिष्यते attains excellence.

9. He attains excellence who looks with equal regard upon well-wishers, friends, foes, neutrals, arbiters, the hateful, the relatives, and upon the righteous and the unrighteous alike.

योगी युञ्जीत सततमात्मानं रहसि स्थितः ।
एकाकी यतचित्तात्मा निराशीरपरिग्रहः ।। १०

योगी Yogī सततम् constantly रहसि in solitude स्थित: remaining एकाकी alone यतचित्तात्मा one with body and mind controlled निराशी: free from hope अपरिग्रह: free from possession आत्मानं युञ्जीत should practise concentration of the heart.

10. The Yogī should constantly practise concentration of the heart, retiring into solitude, alone, with the mind and body subdued, and free from hope and possession.

शुचौ देशे प्रतिष्ठाप्य स्थिरमासनमात्मनः ।
नात्युच्छ्रितं नातिनीचं चैलाजिनकुशोत्तरम् ।। ११

शुचौ In a clean देशे spot आत्मन: one's own स्थिरम् firm न not अत्युच्छ्रितम् too high न not अतिनीचम् too low चैलाजिनकुशोत्तरम् a cloth, a skin, and Kuśa-grass, arranged in consecution आसनम् seat प्रतिष्ठाप्य having established.

11. Having established in a clean spot his seat, firm, neither too high nor too low, made of a cloth, a skin, and *Kuśa*-grass, arranged in consecution.

Arranged in consecution: that is—the *Kuśa*-grass arranged on the ground; above that, a tiger or a deer skin, covered by a cloth.

तत्रैकाग्रं मनः कृत्वा यतचित्तेन्द्रियक्रियः ।
उपविश्यासने युञ्ज्याद्योगमात्मविशुद्धये ।। १२

तत्र There आसने on the seat उपविश्य sitting मन: mind एकाग्रं one-pointed कृत्वा making यतचित्तेन्द्रियक्रिय: one who has subdued the action of mind and senses आत्मविशुद्धये for the purification of the heart योगम् Yoga युञ्ज्यात् should practise.

12. There, seated on that seat, making the mind one-pointed and subduing the action of the mind and the senses, let him practise Yoga for the purification of the heart.

समं कायशिरोग्रीवं धारयन्नचलं स्थिरः।
संप्रेक्ष्य नासिकाग्रं स्वं दिशश्चानवलोकयन्॥ १३

कायशिरोग्रीवं Body, head, and neck समं erect अचलं still धारयन् holding स्थिर: (being) firm स्वं one's own नासिकाग्रं tip of the nose संप्रेक्ष्य gazing at दिश: directions च and अनवलोकयन् not looking.

13. Let him firmly hold his body, head, and neck erect and still, (with the eye-balls fixed, as if) gazing at the tip of his nose, and not looking around.

Gazing at the tip of his nose—could not be literally meant here, because then the mind would be fixed only there, and not on the Self: when the eyes are half-closed in meditation, and the eyeballs are still, the gaze is directed, *as it were*, on the tip of the nose.

प्रशान्तात्मा विगतभीर्ब्रह्मचारिव्रते स्थितः ।
मनः संयम्य मच्चित्तो युक्त आसीत मत्परः ॥ १४

प्रशान्तात्मा Serene-hearted विगतभी: fearless ब्रह्मचारिव्रते in the vow of a *Brahmacārī* स्थित: established मन: mind संयम्य controlling मच्चित्त: thinking of Me मत्पर: having Me as the supreme goal युक्त: steadfast आसीत should sit.

14. With the heart serene and fearless, firm in the vow of a *Brahmacārī*, with the mind controlled, and ever thinking of Me, let him sit (in Yoga) having Me as his supreme goal.

युञ्जन्नेवं सदात्मानं योगी नियतमानसः ।
शान्तिं निर्वाणपरमां मत्संस्थामधिगच्छति ॥ १५

एवं Thus सदा always आत्मानं mind युञ्जन् keeping steadfast नियतमानस: one with subdued mind योगी Yogī निर्वाणपरमां that which culminates in *Nirvāṇa* (*Mokṣa*) मत्संस्थाम् residing in Me शान्तिं peace अधिगच्छति attains.

15. Thus always keeping the mind steadfast, the Yogī of subdued mind attains the peace residing in Me—the peace which culminates in *Nirvāṇa* (*Mokṣa*).

नात्यश्नतस्तु योगोऽस्ति न चैकान्तमनश्नतः ।
न चातिस्वप्नशीलस्य जाग्रतो नैव चार्जुन ॥ १६

अर्जुन O Arjuna अत्यश्नत: of one who eats too much तु indeed न not योग: Yoga अस्ति is न not च and एकान्तम् at all अनश्नत: of one who does not eat न not च and अतिस्वप्नशीलस्य of one who sleeps too much न not च and एव verily जाग्रत: of the wakeful.

16. (Success in) Yoga is not for him who eats too much or too little—nor, O Arjuna, for him who sleeps too much or too little.

The Yoga-*śāstra* prescribes: "Half (the stomach) for food and condiments, the third (quarter) for water, and the fourth should be reserved for free motion of air".

युक्ताहारविहारस्य युक्तचेष्टस्य कर्मसु।
युक्तस्वप्नावबोधस्य योगो भवति दुःखहा॥ १७

युक्ताहारविहारस्य Of one who is moderate in eating and recreation (such as walking, etc.) कर्मसु in actions युक्तचेष्टस्य of one who is moderate in effort (for work) युक्तस्वप्नावबोधस्य of one who is moderate in sleep and wakefulness दु:खहा destructive of misery योग: Yoga भवति becomes.

17. To him who is temperate in eating and recreation, in his effort for work, and in sleep and wakefulness, Yoga becomes the destroyer of misery.

यदा विनियतं चित्तमात्मन्येवावतिष्ठते।
निःस्पृहः सर्वकामेभ्यो युक्त इत्युच्यते तदा॥ १८

यदा When विनियतं completely controlled चित्तम् mind आत्मनि in the Self एव verily अवतिष्ठते rests तदा then सर्वकामेभ्य: from all desires नि:स्पृह: free from longing युक्त: steadfast इति this उच्यते is said.

18. When the completely controlled mind rests serenely in the Self alone, free from longing after all desires, then is one called steadfast (in the Self).

यथा दीपो निवातस्थो नेङ्गते सोपमा स्मृता ।
योगिनो यतचित्तस्य युञ्जतो योगमात्मनः ।। १९

यथा As निवातस्थ: placed in a windless spot दीप: lamp न not इङ्गते flickers आत्मन: of the Self योगम् concentration युञ्जत: of the practising one यतचित्तस्य of one with subdued mind योगिन: of the Yogī सा that उपमा simile स्मृता is thought.

19. "As a lamp in a spot sheltered from the wind does not flicker"—even such has been the simile used for a Yogī of subdued mind, practising concentration in the Self.

यत्रोपरमते चित्तं निरुद्धं योगसेवया ।
यत्र चैवात्मनात्मानं पश्यन्नात्मनि तुष्यति ।। २०
सुखमात्यन्तिकं यत्तद्बुद्धिग्राह्यमतीन्द्रियम् ।
वेत्ति यत्र न चैवायं स्थितश्चलति तत्त्वतः ।। २१
यं लब्ध्वा चापरं लाभं मन्यते नाधिकं ततः ।
यस्मिन्स्थितो न दुःखेन गुरुणापि विचाल्यते ।। २२

तं विद्याद्दुःखसंयोगवियोगं योगसंज्ञितम् ।
स निश्चयेन योक्तव्यो योगोऽनिर्विण्णचेतसा ॥ २३

यत्र In which state योगसेवया by the practice of concentration निरुद्धं absolutely restrained चित्तं mind उपरमते attains quietude यत्र in which state च and आत्मना by self आत्मानं the Self पश्यन् seeing आत्मनि in the Self एव alone तुष्यति is satisfied.

(यत्र Where) अयं this यत्तत् that which आत्यन्तिकम् infinite बुद्धिग्राह्यम् perceived by the intellect अतीन्द्रियम् transcending the senses सुखम् bliss वेत्ति knows यत्र where च and स्थितः established तत्त्वतः from one's real state न एव never चलति departs.

यं Which च and लब्ध्वा having obtained ततः from that अधिकं superior अपरं other लाभं acquisition न not मन्यते regards यस्मिन् in which स्थितः established गुरुणा by great दुःखेन sorrow अपि even न not विचाल्यते is moved.

तं That दुःखसंयोगवियोगं a state of severance from the contact of pain योगसंज्ञितम् called by the name of Yoga विद्यात् should know अनिर्विण्णचेतसा with undepressed heart सः that योगः Yoga निश्चयेन with perseverance योक्तव्यः should be practised.

20–23. When the mind, absolutely restrained by the practice of concentration, attains quietude, and when seeing the Self by the self, one is satisfied in his own Self; when he feels that infinite bliss—which is perceived by the (purified) intellect and which transcends the senses, and established wherein he never departs from his real state; and having obtained which, regards no other acquisition superior to that, and where established, he is not moved even by heavy sorrow; let that be known as the state, called by the name of Yoga—a state of severance from the contact of pain. This Yoga should be practised with perseverance, undisturbed by depression of heart.

Which is perceived . . . intellect: Which the purified intellect can grasp independently of the senses. When in meditation the mind is deeply concentrated, the senses do not function and are resolved into their cause—that is, the mind; and when the latter is steady, so that there is only the intellect functioning, or in other words, cognition only exists, the indescribable Self is realised.

सङ्कल्पप्रभवान्कामांस्त्यक्त्वा सर्वानशेषतः ।
मनसैवेन्द्रियग्रामं विनियम्य समन्ततः ।। २४

संकल्पप्रभवान् Born of *Saṅkalpa* सर्वान् all कामान् desires अशेषत: without reserve त्यक्त्वा abandoning मनसा by the mind एव alone समन्तत: from all sides इन्द्रियग्रामं group of senses विनियम्य completely restraining.

24. Abandoning without reserve all desires born of *Saṅkalpa*, and completely restraining, by the mind alone, the whole group of senses from their objects in all directions;

शनैः शनैरुपरमेद्बुद्ध्या धृतिगृहीतया ।
आत्मसंस्थं मनः कृत्वा न किञ्चिदपि चिन्तयेत् ।। २५

धृतिगृहीतया Set in patience बुद्ध्या by the intellect मनः mind आत्मसंस्थं placed in the Self कृत्वा making शनैः शनैः by degrees उपरमेत् should attain quietude न not किञ्चित् anything अपि even चिन्तयेत् should think.

25. With the intellect set in patience, with the mind fastened on the Self, let him attain quietude by degrees: let him not think of anything.

यतो यतो निश्चरति मनश्चञ्चलमस्थिरम्।
ततस्ततो नियम्यैतदात्मन्येव वशं नयेत्॥ २६

चञ्चलम् Restless अस्थिरम् unsteady मनः mind यतः यतः from whatever (reason) निश्चरति wanders away ततः ततः from that एतत् this (मनः mind) नियम्य curbing आत्मनि in the Self एव alone वशं subjugation नयेत् should bring.

26. Through whatever reason the restless, unsteady mind wanders away, let him, curbing it from that, bring it under the subjugation of the Self alone.

प्रशान्तमनसं ह्येनं योगिनं सुखमुत्तमम्।
उपैति शान्तरजसं ब्रह्मभूतमकल्मषम्॥ २७

प्रशान्तमनसं One of perfectly tranquil mind शान्तरजसं one whose passions are quieted अकल्मषम् one who is free from taint ब्रह्मभूतम् Brahman-become एनं this योगिनं Yogī हि verily उत्तमम् supreme सुखम् bliss उपैति comes.

27. Verily, the supreme bliss comes to that Yogī of perfectly tranquil mind, with passions quieted, Brahman-become, and freed from taint.

Brahman-become: i.e., one who has realised that all is Brahman.

Taint—of good and evil.

युञ्जन्नेवं सदात्मानं योगी विगतकल्मषः ।
सुखेन ब्रह्मसंस्पर्शमत्यन्तं सुखमश्नुते ॥ २८

एवं Thus सदा constantly आत्मानं mind युञ्जन् engaging विगतकल्मषः free from taint योगी Yogī सुखेन easily ब्रह्मसंस्पर्शम् generated by the contact with Brahman अत्यन्तं intense सुखम् bliss अश्नुते attains.

28. The Yogī, freed from taint (of good and evil), constantly engaging the mind thus, with ease attains the infinite bliss of contact with Brahman.

सर्वभूतस्थमात्मानं सर्वभूतानि चात्मनि ।
ईक्षते योगयुक्तात्मा सर्वत्र समदर्शनः ॥ २९

योगयुक्तात्मा One whose heart is steadfast in Yoga सर्वत्र everywhere समदर्शनः one who sees the same आत्मानं Self सर्वभूतस्थम् abiding in all beings सर्वभूतानि all beings च and आत्मनि in the Self ईक्षते sees.

29. With the heart concentrated by Yoga, with the eye of evenness for all things, he beholds the Self in all beings and all beings in the Self.

यो मां पश्यति सर्वत्र सर्वं च मयि पश्यति।
तस्याहं न प्रणश्यामि स च मे न प्रणश्यति ।। ३०

यः Who मां Me सर्वत्र everywhere पश्यति sees मयि in Me च and सर्वं everything पश्यति sees तस्य his (to him) अहं I न not प्रणश्यामि vanish सः he च and मे My (to Me) न not प्रणश्यति vanishes.

30. He who sees Me in all things and sees all things in Me, he never becomes separated from Me, nor do I become separated from him.

Separated: i.e., by time, space, or anything intervening.

सर्वभूतस्थितं यो मां भजत्येकत्वमास्थितः।
सर्वथा वर्तमानोऽपि स योगी मयि वर्तते ।। ३१

यः Who सर्वभूतस्थितं dwelling in all beings मां Me एकत्वम् unity आस्थितः established भजति worships सर्वथा in every way वर्तमानः remaining अपि even सः that योगी Yogī मयि in Me वर्तते abides.

31. He who being established in unity, worships me, who am dwelling in all beings, whatever his mode of life, that Yogī abides in Me.

Worships Me: Realises Me as the Self of all.
Established in unity: i.e., having resolved all duality in the underlying unity.

आत्मौपम्येन सर्वत्र समं पश्यति योऽर्जुन।
सुखं वा यदि वा दुःखं स योगी परमो मतः ।। ३२

अर्जुन O Arjuna य: who सर्वत्र everywhere सुखं pleasure वा or यदि if वा or दु:खं pain आत्मौपम्येन by comparison with himself समं the same पश्यति sees स: that योगी Yogī परम: highest मत: is regarded.

32. He who judges of pleasure or pain everywhere, by the same standard as he applies to himself, that Yogī, O Arjuna, is regarded as the highest.

Seeing that whatever is pleasure or pain to himself, is alike pleasure or pain to all beings, he, the highest of Yogīs, wishes good to all and evil to none—he is always harmless and compassionate to all creatures.

अर्जुन उवाच

योऽयं योगस्त्वया प्रोक्तः साम्येन मधुसूदन।
एतस्याहं न पश्यामि चञ्चलत्वात् स्थितिं स्थिराम्।। ३३

अर्जुन: Arjuna उवाच said:
मधुसूदन O slayer of Madhu त्वया by Thee साम्येन by unity or evenness य: which अयं this योग: Yoga प्रोक्त: said एतस्य its स्थिराम् lasting स्थितिं endurance चञ्चलत्वात् from restlessness अहं I न not पश्यामि see.

Arjuna said:
33. This Yoga which has been taught by thee, O slayer of Madhu, as characterised by evenness, I do not see (the possibility of) its lasting endurance, owing to restlessness (of the mind).

चञ्चलं हि मनः कृष्ण प्रमाथि बलवद्दृढम् ।
तस्याहं निग्रहं मन्ये वायोरिव सुदुष्करम् ।। ३४

कृष्ण O Kṛṣṇa हि verily मन: mind चञ्चलं restless प्रमाथि turbulent बलवद् strong दृढम् unyielding अहं I तस्य of that निग्रहं control वायो: of the wind इव like सुदुष्करम् difficult to do मन्ये regard.

34. Verily, the mind, O Kṛṣṇa, is restless, turbulent, strong, and unyielding; I regard it quite as hard to achieve its control, as that of the wind.

"*Kṛṣṇa*", is derived from "Kṛṣ", to scrape: Kṛṣna is so called because He scrapes or draws away all sins and other evils from His devotees.

श्रीभगवानुवाच

असंशयं महाबाहो मनो दुर्निग्रहं चलम् ।
अभ्यासेन तु कौन्तेय वैराग्येण च गृह्यते ।। ३५

श्रीभगवान् The Blessed Lord उवाच said:
महाबाहो O mighty-armed मन: mind दुर्निग्रहं difficult of control चलम् restless असंशयं undoubtedly तु but कौन्तेय O son of Kuntī अभ्यासेन by practice वैराग्येण by renunciation च and गृह्यते is restrained.

The Blessed Lord said:

35. Without doubt, O mighty-armed, the mind is restless, and difficult to control; but through practice and renunciation, O son of Kuntī, it may be governed.

Cf. Patañjali's *Yoga-Sūtras*, I. 12.

Practice: Earnest and repeated attempt to make the mind steady in its unmodified state of Pure Intelligence, by means of constant meditation upon the Chosen Ideal.

Renunciation: Freedom from desire for any pleasures, seen or unseen, achieved by a constant perception of evil in them.

असंयतात्मना योगो दुष्प्राप इति मे मतिः ।
वश्यात्मना तु यतता शक्योऽवाप्तुमुपायतः ॥ ३६

असंयतात्मना By a man of uncontrolled self योग: Yoga दुष्प्राप: hard to attain इति this मे My मति: conviction वश्यात्मना by the self-controlled one तु but उपायत: by right means यतता by the striving one अवाप्तुम् to obtain शक्य: possible.

36. Yoga is hard to attain by one of uncontrolled self: such is my conviction; but the self-controlled, striving by right means, can obtain it.

अर्जुन उवाच

अयतिः श्रद्धयोपेतो योगाच्चलितमानसः ।
अप्राप्य योगसंसिद्धिं कां गतिं कृष्ण गच्छति ॥ ३७

अर्जुन: Arjuna उवाच said:

कृष्ण Kṛṣṇa श्रद्धया by *Śraddhā* उपेत: possessed अयति: uncontrolled योगात् from Yoga चलितमानस: one whose mind wanders away योगसंसिद्धिं perfection in Yoga अप्राप्य not gaining कां which गतिं end गच्छति meets.

Arjuna said:

37. Though possessed of *Śraddhā* but unable to control oneself, with the mind wandering away from Yoga, what end does one, failing to gain perfection in Yoga, meet, O Kṛṣṇa?

कच्चिन्नोभयविभ्रष्टश्छिन्नाभ्रमिव नश्यति।
अप्रतिष्ठो महाबाहो विमूढो ब्रह्मणः पथि॥ ३८

महाबाहो O mighty-armed ब्रह्मण: of Brahmaṇ पथि in the path विमूढ: deluded अप्रतिष्ठ: supportless उभयविभ्रष्ट: fallen from both छिन्न- rent अभ्रम् cloud इव like न not नश्यति perishes कच्चित् particle implying question.

38. Does he not, fallen from both, perish, without support, like a rent cloud, O mighty-armed, deluded in the path of Brahman?

Fallen from both: That is, from both the paths of knowledge and action.

एतन्मे संशयं कृष्ण छेत्तुमर्हस्यशेषतः।
त्वदन्यः संशयस्यास्य छेत्ता न ह्युपपद्यते॥ ३९

कृष्ण O Kṛṣṇa मे my एतत् this संशयं doubt अशेषत: completely छेत्तुम् to dispel अर्हसि art justified त्वदन्य: but Thee अस्य of this संशयस्य doubt छेत्ता dispeller न not हि verily उपपद्यते is fit.

39. This doubt of mine, O Kṛṣṇa, Thou shouldst completely dispel; for it is not possible for any but Thee to dispel this doubt.

Since there can be no better teacher than the Omniscient Lord.

श्रीभगवानुवाच

पार्थ नैवेह नामुत्र विनाशस्तस्य विद्यते।
नहि कल्याणकृत्कश्चिद्दुर्गतिं तात गच्छति ॥ ४०

श्रीभगवान् The Blessed Lord उवाच said:

पार्थ O son of Pṛthā न not एव verily इह here न not अमुत्र hereafter तस्य his विनाशः destruction विद्यते is तात O my son हि verily कल्याणकृत् doer of good कश्चित् any दुर्गतिं bad state, hence grief न not गच्छति goes.

The Blessed Lord said:

40. Verily, O son of Pṛthā, there is destruction for him, neither here nor hereafter for, the doer of good, O my son, never comes to grief.

Tāta—son. A disciple is looked upon as a son; Arjuna is thus addressed as he had placed himself in the position of a disciple to Kṛṣṇa.

प्राप्य पुण्यकृतां लोकानुषित्वा शाश्वतीः समाः।
शुचीनां श्रीमतां गेहे योगभ्रष्टोऽभिजायते ॥ ४१

योगभ्रष्टः One fallen from Yoga पुण्यकृतां of the righteous लोकान् worlds प्राप्य having attained शाश्वतीः eternal समाः years उषित्वा having dwelt शुचीनां of the pure श्रीमतां of the prosperous गेहे in the home अभिजायते reincarnates.

41. Having attained to the worlds of the righteous, and dwelling there for everlasting years, one fallen from Yoga reincarnates in the home of the pure and the prosperous.

Everlasting years—meaning not absolutely, but a very long period.

अथवा योगिनामेव कुले भवति धीमताम्।
एतद्धि दुर्लभतरं लोके जन्म यदीदृशम्॥ ४२

अथवा Or धीमताम् of the wise योगिनाम् of the Yogis एव verily कुले in the family भवति is born ईदृशम् such यत् which जन्म birth एतत् this हि verily लोके in the world दुर्लभतरं very rare to obtain.

42. Or else he is born into a family of wise Yogis only; verily, a birth such as that is very rare to obtain in this world.

Very rare—more difficult than the one mentioned in the preceding *Śloka*.

तत्र तं बुद्धिसंयोगं लभते पौर्वदेहिकम्।
यतते च ततो भूयः संसिद्धौ कुरुनन्दन॥ ४३

तत्र There पौर्वदेहिकम् acquired in his former body तं that बुद्धिसंयोगं union with intelligence लभते gains कुरुनन्दन O son of the Kurus च and ततः than that भूयः more संसिद्धौ for perfection यतते strives.

43. There he is united with the intelligence acquired in his former body, and strives more than before, for perfection, O son of the Kurus.

Intelligence—Saṁskāra: store of experience in the shape of impressions and habits.

Strives... perfection: Strives more strenuously to attain to higher planes of realisation than those acquired in his former birth.

पूर्वाभ्यासेन तेनैव ह्रियते ह्यवशोऽपि सः ।
जिज्ञासुरपि योगस्य शब्दब्रह्मातिवर्तते ॥ ४४

तेन By that एव verily पूर्वाभ्यासेन previous practice अवशः helpless अपि even सः he ह्रियते is borne योगस्य of Yoga जिज्ञासुः enquirer अपि even शब्दब्रह्म Word-Brahman अतिवर्तते goes beyond.

44. By that previous practice alone, he is borne on in spite of himself. Even the enquirer after Yoga rises superior to the performer of Vedic actions.

Borne on in spite of himself: carried to the goal of the course which he marked out for himself in his last incarnation, by the force of his former *Saṁskāras*, though he might be unconscious of them—or even unwilling to pursue it, owing to the interference of some untoward *Karma*.

Rises, etc.: lit. goes beyond the Word-Brahman, i.e. the Vedas.

प्रयत्नाद्यतमानस्तु योगी संशुद्धकिल्बिषः ।
अनेकजन्मसंसिद्धस्ततो याति परां गतिम् ।। ४५

तु But प्रयत्नाद् with assiduity यतमान: striving योगी Yogī संशुद्धकिल्बिष: purified of taint अनेकजन्मसंसिद्धः perfected through many births ततः then परां supreme गतिम् goal याति attains.

45. The Yogī, striving assiduously, purified of taint, gradually gaining perfection through many births, then reaches the highest goal.

तपस्विभ्योऽधिको योगी ज्ञानिभ्योऽपि मतोऽधिकः ।
कर्मिभ्यश्चाधिको योगी तस्माद्योगी भवार्जुन ।। ४६

योगी Yogi तपस्विभ्य: than ascetics अधिक: superior ज्ञानिभ्य: than the learned अपि even अधिक: superior कर्मिभ्य: than the performers of action च and योगी Yogī अधिक: superior मत: deemed तस्माद् therefore अर्जुन O Arjuna योगी Yogī भव be.

46. The Yogī is regarded as superior to those who practise asceticism, also to those who have obtained wisdom (through the *Śāstras*). He is also superior to the performers of action (enjoined in the Vedas). Therefore, be thou a Yogī, O Arjuna!

Wisdom: Knowledge from precepts, but not direct insight into the Divine Truth.

योगिनामपि सर्वेषां मद्गतेनान्तरात्मना ।
श्रद्धावान्भजते यो मां स मे युक्ततमो मतः ॥ ४७

यः Who श्रद्धावान् endued with *Śraddhā* मद्गतेन absorbed in Me अन्तरात्मना with inner self मां Me भजते worships सः he मे by Me सर्वेषां of all योगिनाम् Yogīs अपि even युक्ततमः most steadfast मतः regarded.

47. And of all Yogīs, he who with the inner self merged in Me, with *Śraddhā* devotes himself to Me, is considered by Me the most steadfast.

Of all Yogīs, etc.: Of all Yogīs he who devotes himself to the All-pervading Infinite, is superior to those who devote themselves to the lesser ideals, or gods, such as Vasu, Rudra, Āditya, etc.

इति ध्यानयोगो नाम षष्ठोऽध्यायः ॥

The end of the sixth chapter, designated
The Way of Meditation.

सप्तमोऽध्यायः

(ज्ञानविज्ञानयोगः)

SEVENTH CHAPTER

(The Way of Knowledge with Realisation)

श्रीभगवानुवाच

मय्यासक्तमनाः पार्थ योगं युञ्जन्मदाश्रयः ।
असंशयं समग्रं मां यथा ज्ञास्यसि तच्छृणु ।। १

श्रीभगवान् The Blessed Lord उवाच said:

पार्थ O son of Pṛthā मयि on Me आसक्तमनाः with mind intent मदाश्रयः taking refuge in Me योगं Yoga युञ्जन् practising समग्रं wholly मां Me असंशयं doubtless यथा how ज्ञास्यसि shalt know तत् that शृणु hear.

The Blessed Lord said:

1. With the mind intent on Me, O son of Pṛthā, taking refuge in Me, and practising Yoga, how thou shalt without doubt know Me fully, that do thou hear.

Fully: i.e., possessed of infinite greatness, strength, power, grace, and other infinite attributes.

ज्ञानं तेऽहं सविज्ञानमिदं वक्ष्याम्यशेषतः ।
यज्ज्ञात्वा नेह भूयोऽन्यज्ज्ञातव्यमवशिष्यते ।। २

अहं I ते to thee सविज्ञानम् combined with realisation इदं this ज्ञानं knowledge अशेषत: in full वक्ष्यामि shall tell यत् which ज्ञात्वा having known इह here भूय: more अन्यत् anything else ज्ञातव्यम् what ought to be known न not अवशिष्यते remains.

2. I shall tell you in full, of knowledge, speculative and practical, knowing which, nothing more here remains to be known.

मनुष्याणां सहस्रेषु कश्चिद्यतति सिद्धये।
यततामपि सिद्धानां कश्चिन्मां वेत्ति तत्त्वत: ॥ ३

मनुष्याणां Of men सहस्रेषु among thousands कश्चित् some one सिद्धये for perfection यतति strives यतताम् of the striving ones सिद्धानां of the blessed ones अपि even कश्चित् some one मां Me तत्त्वत: in reality वेत्ति knows.

3. One, perchance, in thousands of men, strives for perfection; and one perchance, among the blessed ones, striving thus, knows Me in reality.

The Blessed: *Siddhānām*—this word literally means the perfected ones—but here it means only those who having acquired good *Karma* in a past incarnation, strive for freedom in this life.

भूमिरापोऽनलो वायु: खं मनो बुद्धिरेव च।
अहंकार इतीयं मे भिन्ना प्रकृतिरष्टधा ॥ ४

भूमि: Earth आप: water अनल: fire वायु: air खं ether मन: mind बुद्धि: intellect एव verily अहंकार: egoism च and इति

thus इयं this मे My अष्टधा eightfold भिन्ना divided प्रकृतिः *Prakṛti* the Māyā belonging to the *Īśvara.*

4. *Bhūmi* (earth), *Ap* (water), *Anala* (fire), *Vāyu* (air), *Kha* (ether), mind, intellect, and egoism: thus is My *Prakṛti* divided eightfold.

The *raison d'ētre* of this reduction of matter into five elements is quite different from that conceived by modern science. Man has five senses only, just five ways in which he can be affected by matter; therefore his perception of matter cannot be divided further. The five elements are two kinds, subtle and gross. The gross state is said to be formed by taking half of a subtle element, and adding ⅛th to it, of each of the rest: e.g., gross *Ākāśa* = ½ subtle *Ākāśa* + ⅛ subtle *Vāyu* + ⅛ subtle *Tejas* + ⅛ subtle *Ap* + ⅛ subtle *Bhūmi.* Then again, the ether, air, light, water, and earth of modern science do not answer to the five elements of Hindu philosophy. *Ākāśa* is just the sound-producing agency. From *Ākāśa* rises *Vāyu,* having the properties of sound and touch. From *Vāyu* springs *Tejas,* possessing the property of visibility, as well as those of its predecessors. From *Tejas* rises *Ap,* combining with the above properties its distinctive feature—flavour. *Bhūmi* comes from *Ap,* bringing the additional property of smell to its inheritance.

अपरेयमितस्त्वन्यां प्रकृतिं विद्धि मे पराम्।
जीवभूतां महाबाहो ययेदं धार्यते जगत्॥ ५

तु But इयं this अपरा lower इतः from this अन्यां different जीवभूतां the very life-element मे My पराम् higher प्रकृतिं *Prakṛti* विद्धि know महाबाहो O mighty-armed यया by which इदं this जगत् universe धार्यते is sustained.

5. This is the lower (*Prakṛti*). But different from it, know thou, O mighty-armed, My higher *Prakṛti*—the principle of self-consciousness, by which this universe is sustained.

एतद्योनीनि भूतानि सर्वाणीत्युपधारय।
अहं कृत्स्नस्य जगतः प्रभवः प्रलयस्तथा ॥ ६

सर्वाणि All भूतानि beings एतद्योनीनि those of which these two (*Prakṛtis*) are the womb इति this उपधारय know अहं I कृत्स्नस्य of the whole जगतः universe प्रभवः source तथा and also प्रलयः dissolution.

6. Know that these (two *Prakṛtis*) are the womb of all beings; I am the origin and dissolution of the whole universe.

I am the origin, etc.: In Me the whole universe originates and dissolves, as everything springs from My *Prakṛti*.

मत्तः परतरं नान्यत्किञ्चिदस्ति धनञ्जय।
मयि सर्वमिदं प्रोतं सूत्रे मणिगणा इव ॥ ७

धनञ्जय O Dhanañjaya मत्तः than Me परतरं higher अन्यत् else किञ्चित् aught न not अस्ति is सूत्रे on a thread मणिगणाः a row of jewels इव like इदं this सर्वम् all मयि in Me प्रोतं is strung.

7. Beyond me, O Dhanañjaya, there is naught. All this is strung in Me, as a row of jewels on a thread.

Beyond Me: there is no other cause of the universe but Me.

रसोऽहमप्सु कौन्तेय प्रभाऽस्मि शशिसूर्ययोः ।
प्रणवः सर्ववेदेषु शब्दः खे पौरुषं नृषु ॥ ८

कौन्तेय O son of Kuntī अहम् I अप्सु in waters रसः sapidity शशिसूर्ययोः in the moon and the sun प्रभा radiance सर्ववेदेषु in all the Vedas प्रणवः that syllable Om खे in *Ākāśa* शब्दः sound नृषु in men पौरुषं manhood अस्मि am.

8. I am the sapidity in water, O son of Kuntī; I, the radiance in the moon and the sun; I am the Om in all the Vedas, sound in *Ākāśa*, and manhood in men.

In Me as essence, all these are woven, as being My manifestations.

पुण्यो गन्धः पृथिव्यां च तेजश्चास्मि विभावसौ ।
जीवनं सर्वभूतेषु तपश्चास्मि तपस्विषु ॥ ९

च And पृथिव्या in earth पुण्यः sweet गन्धः fragrance च and विभावसौ in fire तेजः brilliancy अस्मि (I) am सर्वभूतेषु in all beings जीवनं life च and तपस्विषु in ascetics तपः austerity अस्मि (I) am.

9. I am the sweet fragrance in earth, and the brilliance in fire am I; the life in all beings, and the austerity am I in ascetics.

बीजं मां सर्वभूतानां विद्धि पार्थ सनातनम्।
बुद्धिर्बुद्धिमतामस्मि तेजस्तेजस्विनामहम्॥ १०

पार्थ O son of Pṛthā मां Me सर्वभूतानां of all beings सनातनम् eternal बीजं seed विद्धि know बुद्धिमताम् of all the intelligent बुद्धि: intellect तेजस्विनाम् of the heroic तेज: heroism अहम् I अस्मि am.

10. Know Me, O son of Pṛthā, as the eternal seed of all beings. I am the intellect of the intelligent, and the heroism of the heroic.

बलं बलवतामस्मि कामरागविवर्जितम्।
धर्माविरुद्धो भूतेषु कामोऽस्मि भरतर्षभ॥ ११

भरतर्षभ O bull among the Bhāratas (अहम् I) बलवताम् of the strong कामरागविवर्जितम् devoid of desire and attachment बलं strength अस्मि am भूतेषु in beings धर्माविरुद्ध: unopposed to Dharma काम: desire अस्मि (I) am.

11. Of the strong, I am the strength devoid of desire and attachment. I am, O bull among the Bhāratas, desire in beings, unopposed to Dharma.

Desire: *Kāma*—thirst for objects not present to the senses.

Attachment: *Rāga*—for those presented to the senses.

Unopposed to Dharma: the desire which moves in harmony with the ordained duties of life.

ये चैव सात्त्विका भावा राजसास्तामसाश्च ये।
मत्त एवेति तान्विद्धि न त्वहं तेषु ते मयि॥ १२

ये Whatever च and एव verily सात्त्विका: belonging to *Sattva* भावा: states च and ये whatever राजसा: belonging to *Rajas* तामसा: belonging to *Tamas* तान् them मत्त: proceeding from Me एव verily इति this विद्धि know तु but अहं I तेषु in them न not ते they मयि in Me.

12. And whatever states pertaining to *Sattva,* and those pertaining to *Rajas,* and to *Tamas,* know them to proceed from Me alone; still I am not in them, but they are in Me.

All things are in Him, yet not He in them. Logically, this can only happen in superimposition through illusion: as that of a ghost seen in the stump of a tree; the ghost is in the stump, from the point of view of the man in the dark, but the stump is never in the ghost. Similarly the universe is superimposed on the Lord, seen in His place through Māyā, but He is not in it. The Lord returns to the same teaching in Chap. IX. 4, 5.

त्रिभिर्गुणमयैर्भावैरेभिः सर्वमिदं जगत्।
मोहितं नाभिजानाति मामेभ्यः परमव्ययम्॥ १३

एभि: By these त्रिभि: three गुणमयै: composed of *Guṇas* भावै: states मोहितं deluded इदं this सर्वम् all जगत् world एभ्य: from them परम् distinct अव्ययम् immutable माम् Me न not अभिजानाति knows.

13. Deluded by these states, the modifications of the three *Guṇas* (of *Prakṛti*), all this world does not know Me who is beyond them, and immutable.

दैवी ह्येषा गुणमयी मम माया दुरत्यया।
मामेव ये प्रपद्यन्ते मायामेतां तरन्ति ते॥ १४

हि Verily एषा this गुणमयी constituted of *Guṇas* दैवी divine मम My माया illusion दुरत्यया difficult to cross over ये who माम् एव Me only प्रपद्यन्ते take refuge (in) ते they एतां this मायाम् illusion तरन्ति get across.

14. Verily, this divine illusion of Mine, constituted of the *Guṇas,* is difficult to cross over; those who devote themselves to Me alone, cross over this illusion.

Divine: transcending human perception.
Devotee ... alone: Abandoning all formal religion (Dharma) completely take refuge in Me, their own Self, the Lord of illusion.

न मां दुष्कृतिनो मूढाः प्रपद्यन्ते नराधमाः।
माययाऽपहृतज्ञाना आसुरं भावमाश्रिताः॥ १५

दुष्कृतिनः Evil-doers मूढाः deluded नराधमाः the lowest of men मायया by Māyā अपहृतज्ञानाः deprived of discrimination आसुरं belonging to *Asuras* भावम् way आश्रिताः having taken to मां Me न not प्रपद्यन्ते devote themselves.

15. They do not devote themselves to Me—the evil-doers, the deluded, the lowest of men, deprived of discrimination by Māyā, and following the way of the *Asuras.*

Way of the Asuras: i.e., cruelty, untruth, and the like.

चतुर्विधा भजन्ते मां जनाः सुकृतिनोऽर्जुन।
आर्तो जिज्ञासुरर्थार्थी ज्ञानी च भरतर्षभ॥ १६

भरतर्षभ O bull among the Bhāratas अर्जुन O Arjuna चतुर्विधाः four kinds सुकृतिनः virtuous जनाः people आर्तः the distressed जिज्ञासुः the seeker of knowledge अर्थार्थी the seeker of enjoyment च and ज्ञानी the wise मां Me भजन्ते worship.

16. Four kinds of virtuous men worship Me, O Arjuna—the distressed, the seeker of knowledge, the seeker of enjoyment, and the wise, O bull among the Bhāratas.

Seeker of enjoyment: One who wishes for objects of enjoyment, both here and hereafter.

The wise: One who has forsaken all desires, knowing them to arise from Māyā.

तेषां ज्ञानी नित्ययुक्त एकभक्तिर्विशिष्यते।
प्रियो हि ज्ञानिनोऽत्यर्थमहं स च मम प्रियः॥ १७

तेषां Of them नित्ययुक्तः ever-steadfast एकभक्तिः whose devotion is to the one ज्ञानी the wise विशिष्यते excels हि verily अहं I ज्ञानिनः of the wise अत्यर्थम् supremely प्रियः dear सः च he and मम My प्रियः dear.

17. Of them, the wise man, ever-steadfast, (and fired) with devotion to the One, excels; for supremely dear am I to the wise, and he is dear to Me.

उदाराः सर्व एवैते ज्ञानी त्वात्मैव मे मतम्।
आस्थितः स हि युक्तात्मा मामेवानुत्तमां गतिम्।। १८

एते These सर्वे all एव surely उदाराः noble तु but ज्ञानी the wise आत्मा Self एव very मे My मतम् conviction हि verily युक्तात्मा steadfast-minded सः he अनुत्तमां the supreme गतिम् goal माम् Me एव verily आस्थितः is established.

18. Noble indeed are they all, but the wise man I regard as My very Self; for with the mind steadfast, he is established in Me alone, as the supreme goal.

बहूनां जन्मनामन्ते ज्ञानवान्मां प्रपद्यते।
वासुदेवः सर्वमिति स महात्मा सुदुर्लभः।। १९

बहूनां Of many जन्मनाम् (of) births अन्ते at the end ज्ञानवान् the wise मां Me वासुदेवः Vāsudeva सर्वम् all इति thus प्रपद्यते resorts सः that महात्मा the great soul सुदुर्लभः (is) very rare.

19. At the end of many births, the man of wisdom takes refuge in Me, realising that all this is Vāsudeva (the innermost Self). Very rare is that great soul.

कामैस्तैस्तैर्हृतज्ञानाः प्रपद्यन्तेऽन्यदेवताः।
तं तं नियममास्थाय प्रकृत्या नियताः स्वया।। २०

तैः तैः By this or that कामैः (by) desires हृतज्ञानाः those deprived of discrimination तं तं this or that नियमम् rite

आस्थाय having followed स्वया प्रकृत्या by their own nature नियता: led अन्यदेवता: other gods प्रपद्यन्ते worship.

20. Others again, deprived of discrimination by this or that desire, following this or that rite, devote themselves to other gods, led by their own natures.

Own natures: *Saṁskāras* acquired in previous lives.

यो यो यां यां तनुं भक्तः श्रद्धयाऽर्चितुमिच्छति।
तस्य तस्याचलां श्रद्धां तामेव विदधाम्यहम्॥ २१

य: य: whatever भक्त: devotee यां यां whatsoever तनुं form श्रद्धया with *Śraddhā* अर्चितुम् to worship इच्छति desires तस्य तस्य of him ताम् that एव surely श्रद्धां *Śraddhā* अहम् I अचलाम् unflinching विदधामि make.

21. Whatsoever form any devotee seeks to worship with *Śraddhā*—that *Śraddhā* of his do I make unwavering.

स तया श्रद्धया युक्तस्तस्याराधनमीहते।
लभते च ततः कामान्मयैव विहितान्हि तान्॥ २२

स: He तया with that श्रद्धया (by) *Śraddhā* युक्त: endued तस्य of it आराधनम् worship ईहते engages in च and तत: from that मया by Me एव surely विहितान् dispensed तान् those कामान् desires हि verily लभते gains.

22. Endued with that *Śraddhā,* he e
the worship of that, and from it, gains hi
these being verily dispensed by Me alon

अन्तवत्तु फलं तेषां तद्भवत्यल्पमेधसाम्।
देवान्देवयजो यान्ति मद्भक्ता यान्ति मामपि॥ २३

तु But अल्पमेधसाम् तेषां of those of little understanding तत् that फलं fruit अन्तवत् limited भवति becomes देवयजः the worshippers of the *Devas* देवान् the Devas यान्ति go to मद्भक्ताः My devotees माम् Me अपि too यान्ति attain.

23. But the fruit (accruing) to these men of little understanding is limited. The worshippers of the *Devas* go to the *Devas*; My devotees too come to Me.

These men of little understanding: Though the amount of exertion is the same (in the two kinds of worship), these people do not take refuge in Me, by doing which they may attain infinite results.

अव्यक्तं व्यक्तिमापन्नं मन्यन्ते मामबुद्धयः।
परं भावमजानन्तो ममाव्ययमनुत्तमम्॥ २४

अबुद्धयः The foolish मम My अव्ययम् immutable अनुत्तमम् unsurpassed परं supreme भावम् nature अजानन्तः not knowing अव्यक्तं the unmanifested माम् Me व्यक्तिम् manifestation आपन्नं come to मन्यन्ते regard.

24. The foolish regard Me, the unmanifested, as come into manifestation, not knowing My supreme state—immutable and transcendental.

The ignorant take Me as an ordinary mortal, assuming embodiment from the unmanifested state, like all other men, being impelled by the force of past *Karma*. This is due to their ignorance of my real nature; hence they do not worship Me, the One without a second.

नाहं प्रकाशः सर्वस्य योगमायासमावृतः ।
मूढोऽयं नाभिजानाति लोको मामजमव्ययम् ।। २५

अहं I योगमायासमावृत: veiled by *Yoga-Māyā,* i.e., illusion born of Yoga or the union of the three *Guṇas* सर्वस्य to all प्रकाश: manifest न not मूढ: the deluded अयं this लोक: world अजम् the Unborn अव्ययम् the Immutable माम् Me न not अभिजानाति knows.

25. Veiled by the illusion born of the congress of the *Guṇas,* I am not manifest to all. This deluded world knows Me not—the Unborn, the Immutable.

This *Yoga-Māyā* spread over the Lord, which veils the understanding of others in recognising Him, does not obscure His own knowledge, as it is His, and He is the wielder of it— just as the glamour (Māyā) caused by juggler (*Māyāvī*) does not obstruct his own knowledge. This illusion which binds others, cannot dim His vision.

वेदाहं समतीतानि वर्तमानानि चार्जुन ।
भविष्याणि च भूतानि मां तु वेद न कश्चन ।। २६

अर्जुन O Arjuna समतीतानि the past च and वर्तमानानि the present भविष्याणि the future च and भूतानि beings अहं I वेद know तु but मां Me कश्चन any one न not वेद knows.

26. I know, O Arjuna, the beings of the whole past, and the present, and the future, but Me none knoweth.

इच्छाद्वेषसमुत्थेन द्वन्द्वमोहेन भारत।
सर्वभूतानि संमोहं सर्गे यान्ति परन्तप ।। २७

परन्तप O scorcher of foes भारत O descendant of Bharata सर्गे at birth इच्छाद्वेषसमुत्थेन arisen from desire and aversion द्वन्द्वमोहेन by the delusion of the pairs of opposites सर्वभूतानि all beings संमोहं delusion यान्ति go to.

27. By the delusion of the pairs of opposites, arising from desire and aversion, O descendant of Bharata, all beings fall into delusion at birth, O scorcher of foes.

To one whose mind is subject to the dualistic delusion, caused by the passions of desire and aversion, there cannot indeed arise a knowledge of things as they are, even of the external world; far less can such an intellect grasp the transcendental knowledge of the innermost Self.

येषां त्वन्तगतं पापं जनानां पुण्यकर्मणाम्।
ते द्वन्द्वमोहनिर्मुक्ता भजन्ते मां दृढव्रताः ।। २८

तु But पुण्यकर्मणाम् of men of virtuous deeds येषां whose जनानां of men पापं sin अन्तगतं is at an end द्वन्द्वमोहनिर्मुक्ताः freed from the delusion of the pairs of opposites ते they दृढव्रताः men of firm resolve मां Me भजन्ते worship.

28. Those men of virtuous deeds, whose sin has come to an end—they, freed from the delusion of the pairs of opposites, worship Me with firm resolve.

जरामरणमोक्षाय मामाश्रित्य यतन्ति ये ।
ते ब्रह्म तद्विदुः कृत्स्नमध्यात्मं कर्म चाखिलम् ।। २९

जरामरणमोक्षाय For freedom from old age and death माम् in Me आश्रित्य having taken refuge ये who यतन्ति strive ते they तत् that ब्रह्म Brahman कृत्स्नम् the whole अध्यात्मं *Adhyātma* अखिलम् the entire कर्म *Karma* च and विदुः know.

29. Those who strive for freedom from old age and death, taking refuge in Me—they know Brahman, the whole of *Adhyātma*, and *Karma* in its entirety.

(*They know*) *the whole of Adhyātma*: They realise in full the Reality underlying the innermost individual Self.

साधिभूताधिदैवं मां साधियज्ञं च ये विदुः ।
प्रयाणकालेऽपि च मां ते विदुर्युक्तचेतसः ।। ३०

ये Who च and मां Me साधिभूतं साधिदैवं साधियज्ञं च with *Adhibhūta, Adhidaiva,* and *Adhiyajña* विदुः know ते they

युक्तचेतस: steadfast in mind प्रयाणकाले at the time of death अपि even मां Me विदु: know.

30. Those who know Me with the *Adhibhūta,* the *Adhidaiva,* and the *Adhiyajña,* (continue to) know Me even at the time of death, steadfast in mind.

Their consciousness of Me continues as ever, unaffected by the change of approaching death.

इति ज्ञानविज्ञानयोगो नाम सप्तमोऽध्याय: ॥

The end of the seventh chapter, designated,
The Way of Knowledge with Realisation.

अष्टमोऽध्यायः
(अक्षर-ब्रह्मयोगः)

EIGHTH CHAPTER
(The Way to Imperishable Brahman)

अर्जुन उवाच

किं तदब्रह्म किमध्यात्मं किं कर्म पुरुषोत्तम।
अधिभूतं च किं प्रोक्तमधिदैवं किमुच्यते ॥ १

अर्जुनः Arjuna उवाच said:

पुरुषोत्तम O best of *Puruṣas* तत् that ब्रह्म Brahman किं what अध्यात्मं *Adhyātma* किम् what कर्म *Karma* (च and) किं what अधिभूतं *Adhibhūta* किं what प्रोक्तम् called किम् what च and अधिदैवं *Adhidaiva* उच्यते is said:

Arjuna said:

1. What is the Brahman, what is *Adhyātma*, what is *Karma*, O best of *Puruṣas*? What is called *Adhibhūta*, and what *Adhidaiva*?

अधियज्ञः कथं कोऽत्र देहेऽस्मिन् मधुसूदन।
प्रयाणकाले च कथं ज्ञेयोऽसि नियतात्मभिः ॥ २

मधुसूदन O destroyer of Madhu अत्र here अस्मिन् in this देहे body कः who कथं how अधियज्ञः *Adhiyajña* च and प्रयाणकाले at the time of death नियतात्मभिः by the self-controlled कथं how ज्ञेयः knowable असि art.

2. Who, and in what way, is *Adhiyajña* here in this body, O destroyer of Madhu? And how art Thou known at the time of death, by the self-controlled?

श्रीभगवानुवाच

अक्षरं ब्रह्म परमं स्वभावोऽध्यात्ममुच्यते ।
भूतभावोद्भवकरो विसर्गः कर्मसंज्ञितः ।। ३

श्रीभगवान् The Blessed Lord उवाच said:
अक्षरं The Imperishable परमं Supreme ब्रह्म Brahman स्वभावः (His) nature, the dwelling of Brahman in each individual body अध्यात्मम् *Adhyātma* उच्यते is said भूतभावोद्भवकरः that which causes the existence and genesis of beings विसर्गः offering (to gods) कर्मसंज्ञितः is called *Karma*.

The Blessed Lord said:
3. The Imperishable is the Supreme Brahman. Its dwelling in each individual body is called *Adhyātma*; the offering in sacrifice which causes the genesis and support of beings, is called *Karma*.

Offering in sacrifice—includes here all virtuous works.
Karma: Cf. III. 14, 15.

अधिभूतं क्षरो भावः पुरुषश्चाधिदैवतम्।
अधियज्ञोऽहमेवात्र देहे देहभृतां वर ॥ ४

देहभृतां Of the embodied वर O the best क्षर: perishable भाव: existence अधिभूतं *Adhibhūta* पुरुष: Indweller अधिदैवतम् *Adhidaivata* च and अत्र here देहे in the body अहम् I एव verily अधियज्ञ: *Adhiyajña*.

4. The perishable adjunct is the *Adhibhūta*, and the Indweller is the *Adhidaivata*; I alone am the *Adhiyajña* here in this body, O best of the embodied.

Adhibhūta: that perishable adjunct which is different from, and yet depends for its existence on the self-conscious principle, i.e., everything material, everything that has birth.

Adhidaivata: The universal Self in Its subtle aspect: the Centre from which all living beings have their sense-power.

Adhiyajña: the presiding deity of sacrifice—Viṣṇu.

अन्तकाले च मामेव स्मरन्मुक्त्वा कलेवरम्।
यः प्रयाति स मद्भावं याति नास्त्यत्र संशयः ॥ ५

च and अन्तकाले at the time of death माम् Me एव only स्मरन् remembering कलेवरम् body मुक्त्वा leaving य: who प्रयाति goes forth स: he मद्भावं My being याति attains अत्र here संशय: doubt न not अस्ति is.

5. And he who at the time of death, meditating on Me alone, goes forth, leaving the body, attains My Being: there is no doubt about this.

यं यं वापि स्मरन् भावं त्यजत्यन्ते कलेवरम्।
तं तमेवैति कौन्तेय सदा तद्भावभावित: ॥ ६

अन्ते At the end यं यं whatever भावं idea (object) वा or अपि even स्मरन् remembering कलेवरम् body त्यजति leaves कौन्तेय O son of Kuntī सदा constantly तद्भावभावित: devoted to the thought of that object तं तम् that एव alone एति attains.

6. Remembering whatever object, at the end, he leaves the body, that alone is reached by him, O son of Kuntī, (because) of his constant thought of that object.

Constant thought: the idea is, that the most prominent thought of one's life occupies the mind at the time of death. One cannot get rid of it, even as one cannot get rid of a disagreeable thought-image in a dream; so the character of the body to be next attained by one is determined accordingly, i.e., by the final thought.

तस्मात् सर्वेषु कालेषु मामनुस्मर युध्य च।
मय्यर्पितमनोबुद्धिर्मामेवैष्यस्यसंशय: ॥ ७

तस्मात् Therefore सर्वेषु कालेषु at all times माम् Me अनुस्मर remember युध्य fight च and मय्यर्पितमनोबुद्धि: with mind and intellect devoted to Me असंशय: without doubt माम् Me एव verily एष्यसि shalt come to.

7. Therefore, at all times, constantly remember Me, and fight. With mind and intellect absorbed in Me, thou shalt doubtless come to Me.

Remember Me and fight: Do thou constantly keep thy mind fixed on Me and at the same time perform thy *Svadharma*, as befits a Kṣatriya: and thus thou shalt attain purification of the heart.

अभ्यासयोगयुक्तेन चेतसा नान्यगामिना ।
परमं पुरुषं दिव्यं याति पार्थानुचिन्तयन् ॥ ८

पार्थ O son of Pṛthā अभ्यासयोगयुक्तेन (with the mind made) steadfast by the method of habitual meditation नान्यगामिना not moving towards any other thing चेतसा with mind परमं Supreme दिव्यं Resplendent पुरुषं *Puruṣa* अनुचिन्तयन् meditating याति goes to.

8. With the mind not moving towards anything else, made steadfast by the method of habitual meditation, and dwelling on the Supreme, Resplendent *Puruṣa*, O son of Pṛthā, one goes to him.

Method—Yoga.

Resplendent—the Being in the solar orb, same as *Adhidaivata* of the fourth *śloka*.

कविं पुराणमनुशासितार-
मणोरणीयांसमनुस्मरेद्यः ।
सर्वस्य धातारमचिन्त्यरूप-
मादित्यवर्णं तमसः परस्तात् ॥ ९
प्रयाणकाले मनसाऽचलेन
भक्त्या युक्तो योगबलेन चैव ।
भ्रुवोर्मध्ये प्राणमावेश्य सम्यक्
स तं परं पुरुषमुपैति दिव्यम् ॥ १०

कविं Omniscient पुराणम् Ancient अनुशासितारम् Overruler अणोः than atom अणीयांसम् minuter सर्वस्य of all धातारम् Sustainer अचिन्त्यरूपम् one whose form is inconceivable आदित्यवर्णं self-luminous like the sun तमसः of the darkness (of ignorance) परस्तात् beyond प्रयाणकाले at the time of death भक्त्या with devotion युक्तः endued अचलेन unmoving मनसा with mind योगबलेन with the power of Yoga च and एव verily भ्रुवोः of the two eyebrows मध्ये betwixt प्राणम् *Prāṇa* सम्यक् thoroughly आवेश्य placing यः who अनुस्मरेत् remembers सः he तं that परं Supreme दिव्यम् Resplendent पुरुषम् *Puruṣa* उपैति reaches.

9–10. The Omniscient, the Ancient, the Overruler, minuter than an atom, the Sustainer of all, of form inconceivable, self-luminous like the sun, and beyond the darkness of Māyā—he who meditates on Him thus, at the time of death, full of devotion, with the mind unmoving, and also by the Power of Yoga, fixing the whole *Prāṇa* betwixt the eyebrows, he goes to that Supreme, Resplendent *Puruṣa*.

Self-luminous: Known by no agency like the understanding, the mind or the senses, but by Self alone.

Power of Yoga—which comes by the constant practice of *Samādhi*.

Prāṇa: the vital current.

Fixing the whole Prāṇa—means, concentrating the whole will and self-consciousness.

यदक्षरं वेदविदो वदन्ति
विशन्ति यद्यतयो वीतरागाः।
यदिच्छन्तो ब्रह्मचर्यं चरन्ति
तत्ते पदं संग्रहेण प्रवक्ष्ये ॥ ११

वेदविदः Knowers of the Veda यत् which अक्षरं imperishable वदन्ति speak वीतरागाः freed from attachment यतयः self-controlled (*Sannyāsis*) यत् which विशन्ति enter यत् which इच्छन्तः desiring ब्रह्मचर्यं *Brahmacarya* चरन्ति practise ते to thee तत् that पदं state to be obtained संग्रहेण in brief प्रवक्ष्ये (I) shall tell.

11. What the knowers of the Veda speak of as Imperishable, what the self-controlled (*Sannyāsis*), freed from attachment enter, and to gain which goal they live the life of a *Brahmacārī*, that I shall declare unto thee in brief.

Brahmacārī —a religious student who takes the vow of continence, etc.; every moment of this stage is one of hard discipline and asceticism.

Cf. Kaṭhopaniṣad, II. 14.

सर्वद्वाराणि संयम्य मनो हृदि निरुध्य च।
मूर्ध्न्याधायात्मनः प्राणमास्थितो योगधारणाम्॥ १२
ओमित्येकाक्षरं ब्रह्म व्याहरन्मामनुस्मरन्।
यः प्रयाति त्यजन्देहं स याति परमां गतिम्॥ १३

सर्वद्वाराणि All inlets (senses) संयम्य having controlled मनः mind हृदि in the heart निरुध्य having confined च and

प्राणम् *Prāṇa* मूर्ध्नि in the head आधाय having placed आत्मनः of one's self योगधारणाम् practice of concentration आस्थितः established (in) ओम् Om इति this एकाक्षरं one-syllabled ब्रह्म Brahman व्याहरन् uttering माम् Me अनुस्मरन् remembering देहं body त्यजन् leaving यः who प्रयाति departs सः he परमां Supreme गतिम् Goal याति attains.

12–13. Controlling all the senses, confining the mind in the heart, drawing the *Prāṇa* into the head, occupied in the practice of concentration, uttering the one-syllabled "*Om*"—the Brahman, and meditating on Me—he who so departs, leaving the body, attains the Supreme Goal.

अनन्यचेताः सततं यो मां स्मरति नित्यशः ।
तस्याहं सुलभः पार्थ नित्ययुक्तस्य योगिनः ॥ १४

अनन्यचेताः with the mind not thinking of any other object (undistracted) यः who मां Me नित्यशः daily सततं constantly स्मरति remembers पार्थ O son of Pṛthā अहं I तस्य of that नित्ययुक्तस्य ever-steadfast योगिनः Yogi सुलभः easily attainable.

14. I am easily attainable by that ever-steadfast Yogī who remembers Me constantly and daily, with an undistracted mind, O son of Pṛthā.

मामुपेत्य पुनर्जन्म दुःखालयमशाश्वतम् ।
नाप्नुवन्ति महात्मानः संसिद्धिं परमां गताः ॥ १५

परमां Highest संसिद्धिं perfection गताः reaching महात्मानः the great-souled ones माम् Me उपेत्य having attained दुःखालयम् home of pain अशाश्वतम् ephemeral (च and) पुनर्जन्म rebirth न not आप्नुवन्ति get.

15. Reaching the highest perfection and having attained Me, the great-souled ones are no more subject to rebirth—which is the home of pain, and ephemeral.

Ephemeral: non-eternal, of an ever-changing nature.

आब्रह्मभुवनाल्लोकाः पुनरावर्तिनोऽर्जुन ।
मामुपेत्य तु कौन्तेय पुनर्जन्म न विद्यते ।। १६

अर्जुन O Arjuna आब्रह्मभुवनात् up to (i.e. including) the realm of Brahmā लोकाः worlds पुनरावर्तिनः subject to return तु but कौन्तेय O Kaunteya माम् Me उपेत्य having attained पुनर्जन्म rebirth न not विद्यते is.

16. All the worlds, O Arjuna, including the realm of Brahmā, are subject to return, but after attaining Me, O son of Kuntī, there is no rebirth.

Subject to return: because limited by time.

सहस्रयुगपर्यन्तमहर्यद्ब्रह्मणो विदुः ।
रात्रिं युगसहस्रान्तां तेऽहोरात्रविदो जनाः ।। १७

सहस्रयुगपर्यन्तम् Ending in a thousand Yugas ब्रह्मणः of Brahmā यत् which अहः day युगसहस्रान्तां ending in a thousand Yugas रात्रिं night (ये who) विदुः know ते those जनाः men अहोरात्रविदः knowers of day and night.

17. They who know (the true measure of) day and night, know the day of Brahmā, which ends in a thousand Yugas, and the night which (also) ends in a thousand Yugas.

Day and night: mean evolution and involution of the whole universe respectively.

अव्यक्ताद्व्यक्तयः सर्वाः प्रभवन्त्यहरागमे ।
रात्र्यागमे प्रलीयन्ते तत्रैवाव्यक्तसंज्ञके ॥ १८

अहरागमे At the approach of day अव्यक्तात् from the unmanifested सर्वाः all व्यक्तयः manifestations प्रभवन्ति proceed रात्र्यागमे at the approach of night तत्र into that एव verily अव्यक्तसंज्ञके in that which is called the unmanifested प्रलीयन्ते merge.

18. At the approach of (Brahmā's) day, all manifestations proceed from the unmanifested state; at the approach of night, they merge verily into that alone, which is called the unmanifested.

भूतग्रामः स एवायं भूत्वा भूत्वा प्रलीयते ।
रात्र्यागमेऽवशः पार्थ प्रभवत्यहरागमे ॥ १९

पार्थ O son of Pṛthā सः that एव verily अयं this भूतग्रामः multitude of beings भूत्वा भूत्वा being born again and again रात्र्यागमे at the approach of night प्रलीयते merge अहरागमे at the approach of day अवशः helpless प्रभवति re-manifest.

19. The very same multitude of beings (that existed in the preceding day of Brahmā), being born again and again, merge, in spite of themselves, O son of Pṛthā, (into the unmanifested), at the approach of night, and re-manifest at the approach of day.

Being born ... themselves: They repeatedly come forth and dissolve, being forced by the effects of their own *Karma*.

परस्तस्मात्तु भावोऽन्योऽव्यक्तोऽव्यक्तात्सनातनः।
यः स सर्वेषु भूतेषु नश्यत्सु न विनश्यति॥ २०

तस्मात् From that तु but अव्यक्तात् from the unmanifested परः that which is beyond अन्यः another, distinct अव्यक्तः Unmanifested सनातनः Eternal यः which भावः Existence सः That सर्वेषु भूतेषु all beings नश्यत्सु being destroyed न not विनश्यति dies.

20. But beyond this unmanifested, there is that other Unmanifested, Eternal Existence — that which is not destroyed at the destruction of all beings.

This unmanifested: which being the seed of the manifested, is *Avidyā* itself.

अव्यक्तोऽक्षर इत्युक्तस्तमाहुः परमां गतिम्।
यं प्राप्य न निवर्तन्ते तद्धाम परमं मम॥ २१

अव्यक्तः Unmanifested अक्षरः Imperishable इति thus उक्तः called तम् that परमां Supreme गतिम् Goal आहुः they describe यं which प्राप्य having attained न not निवर्तन्ते they return तत् that मम My परमं highest धाम state.

21. What has been called Unmanifested and Imperishable, has been described as the Goal Supreme. That is My highest state, having attained which, there is no return.

पुरुषः स परः पार्थ भक्त्या लभ्यस्त्वनन्यया ।
यस्यान्तःस्थानि भूतानि येन सर्वमिदं ततम् ।। २२

पार्थ O son of Pṛthā भूतानि beings यस्य of whom अन्तःस्थानि dwelling in येन by whom इदं this सर्वम् all ततम् pervaded तु also सः that परः Supreme पुरुषः *Puruṣa* अनन्यया whole-souled भक्त्या by devotion लभ्यः is attainable.

22. And that Supreme *Puruṣa* is attainable, O son of Pṛthā, by whole-souled devotion to Him alone, in Whom all beings dwell, and by Whom all this is pervaded.

यत्र काले त्वनावृत्तिमावृत्तिं चैव योगिनः ।
प्रयाता यान्ति तं कालं वक्ष्यामि भरतर्षभ ।। २३

भरतर्षभ O bull of the Bhāratas यत्र in which काले time (path) तु but प्रयाताः travelling योगिनः Yogis अनावृत्तिं non-return आवृत्तिं return च and एव again यान्ति go to तं that कालं time (path) वक्ष्यामि (I) shall tell.

23. Now I shall tell thee, O bull of the Bhāratas, of the time (path) travelling in which, the Yogis return, (and again of that, taking which) they do not return.

अग्निर्ज्योतिरहः शुक्लः षण्मासा उत्तरायणम् ।
तत्र प्रयाता गच्छन्ति ब्रह्म ब्रह्मविदो जनाः ॥ २४

अग्निः Fire ज्योतिः light अहः day-time शुक्लः the bright (fortnight) षण्मासाः the six months उत्तरायणम् (of) the Northern passage of the sun तत्र in that (path) प्रयाताः departed ब्रह्मविदः the knowers of Brahman जनाः people ब्रह्म Brahman गच्छन्ति go to.

24. Fire, flame, day-time, the bright fortnight, the six months of the Northern passage of the sun—taking that path, the knowers of Brahman go to Brahman.

धूमो रात्रिस्तथा कृष्णः षण्मासा दक्षिणायनम् ।
तत्र चान्द्रमसं ज्योतिर्योगी प्राप्य निवर्तते ॥ २५

धूमः Smoke रात्रिः night-time तथा also कृष्णः the dark (fortnight) षण्मासाः the six months दक्षिणायनम् (of) the Southern passage of the sun तत्र in that (path) योगी Yogī चान्द्रमसं lunar ज्योतिः light प्राप्य attaining निवर्तते returns.

25. Smoke, night-time, the dark fortnight, the six months of the Southern passage of the sun—taking that path the Yogī, attaining the lunar light, returns.

It is difficult to decide the true significance of these two verses (24 & 25). Some are inclined to think that each of the steps means a sphere; while others, a state of consciousness. Still others think, that the series beginning with fire means developing states of illumination and renunciation, and that beginning with smoke, increasing states of ignorance and attachment.

The two paths, *Devayāna* and *Pitṛyāna*, by which the souls of the dead are supposed to travel to the other world according to their deserts are mentioned in the Upaniṣads, prominently in the Chāndogya, V. x. 1,2. Bādarāyaṇa discusses these passages in the Brahma-Sūtras, IV. ii. 18-21. But an interesting light has been thrown upon the question by the late Mr. Tilak's theory of the Arctic home of the ancestors of the Aryan race. He has also dealt with this subject specially, in a paper of great value which appeared in the *Prabuddha Bhārata* (Vol. IX. p. 160). Considering the importance of the doctrine and the excellent way in which it has been elucidated by Mr. Tilak, we shall briefly note below the main heads of his argument.

The words *Pitṛyāna* and *Devayāna* are used many times in the *Ṛgveda*. But the distinction made in the Upaniṣads about the soul's path, according as a man died during the dark or the bright half of the year, was unknown to the bards of the *Ṛgveda*, who held the view that the soul of a man always travelled by the *Pitṛyāna* road, whatever the time of his death. It is therefore clear that the doctrine of the Upaniṣads was a later development, probably evolved after physical light and darkness had come to be connected with moral good and evil and the dual character of the world was established. Now, if along with this we consider that death during the Southern passage of the sun was regarded as inauspicious from the Arctic times, we can see how the distinction arose between the paths of a man's soul according as he died in the dark or the bright part of the year.

As to the series of steps in each path, since Agni was believed to be the only leader of the soul on its path, and both paths ended with the passages of the sun, the starting and halting points thus settled, it was not difficult to fill in the intermediate steps. The dual character of the world is manifested in Agni as flame and smoke. The flame was therefore the starting point of one path and smoke, of the other. Day and night, increasing and decreasing moon. Northern and Southern passages of the sun came next in natural order. The number of steps can easily be increased, and as a matter of fact has been increased in Kaushītaki and some other Upaniṣads on the same general principle.

Another point in this connection may be noted. There is nothing in the second or *Pitṛyāna* path to correspond to Agni, in the first. We must therefore either reduce the number of steps in the first path by taking the words "fire" and "flame" in appositional relation and translate the same as "fire, that is flame", or increase the steps in the second by adding "fire" as one.

शुक्लकृष्णे गती ह्येते जगतः शाश्वते मते ।
एकया यात्यनावृत्तिमन्ययावर्तते पुनः ॥ २६

हि Verily जगत: of the world शुक्लकृष्णे bright and dark एते these गती two paths शाश्वते eternal मते are considered एकया by one अनावृत्तिम् non-return याति goes to अन्यया by the other पुन: again आवर्तते returns.

26. Truly are these bright and dark paths of the world considered eternal: one leads to non-return; by the other, one returns.

The paths are eternal, because *Saṁsāra* is eternal.

नैते सृती पार्थ जानन् योगी मुह्यति कश्चन।
तस्मात्सर्वेषु कालेषु योगयुक्तो भवार्जुन॥ २७

पार्थ O son of Pṛthā एते these सृती two paths जानन् knowing कश्चन whosoever योगी Yogī न मुह्यति is not deluded तस्मात् therefore अर्जुन O Arjuna सर्वेषु in all कालेषु times योगयुक्तः steadfast in Yoga भव be (thou).

27. No Yogī, O son of Pṛthā, is deluded after knowing these paths. Therefore, O Arjuna, be thou steadfast in Yoga, at all times.

Knowing that one of the paths leads to *Saṁsāra* and the other to *Mokṣa*, the Yogī takes up the one leading to illumination and rejects the other.

वेदेषु यज्ञेषु तपःसु चैव
दानेषु यत्पुण्यफलं प्रदिष्टम्।
अत्येति तत्सर्वमिदं विदित्वा
योगी परं स्थानमुपैति चाद्यम्॥ २८

वेदेषु In the (study of the) Vedas यज्ञेषु in the (practice of) *Yajña* तपःसु in the (practice of) austerities दानेषु in (giving) gifts च and एव also यत् whatever पुण्यफलं meritorious effect प्रदिष्टम् is declared च and इदं this विदित्वा having known योगी a Yogī तत् it सर्वम् all अत्येति rises above आद्यम् primeval परं supreme स्थानम् Abode उपैति goes to.

28. Whatever meritorious effect is declared (in the Scriptures) to accrue from (the study of) the Vedas, (the performance of) *Yajñas*, (the practice of) austerities and gifts—above all this rises the Yogī, having known this, and attains to the primeval, supreme Abode.

This—the truth imparted by the Lord in answer to the question of Arjuna at the beginning of the present chapter.

इति अक्षर-ब्रह्मयोगो नामाष्टमोऽध्यायः ॥

The end of the eighth chapter, designated,
The Way to the Imperishable Brahman.

नवमोऽध्यायः
(राजविद्या-राजगुह्ययोगः)
NINTH CHAPTER
(The Way of The Kingly Knowledge & The Kingly Secret)

श्रीभगवानुवाच

इदं तु ते गुह्यतमं प्रवक्ष्याम्यनसूयवे।
ज्ञानं विज्ञानसहितं यज्ज्ञात्वा मोक्ष्यसेऽशुभात्॥ १

श्रीभगवान् The Blessed Lord उवाच said:

इदं This गुह्यतमं most profound तु indeed विज्ञानसहितं united with realisation ज्ञानं knowledge अनसूयवे to one who does not carp ते to thee प्रवक्ष्यामि shall declare यत् which ज्ञात्वा having known अशुभात् from evil (*Saṁsāra*) मोक्ष्यसे (thou) shalt be free:

The Blessed Lord said:

1. To thee, who dost not carp, verily shall I now declare this, the most profound knowledge, united with realisation, having known which, thou shalt be free from evil (*Saṁsāra*).

राजविद्या राजगुह्यं पवित्रमिदमुत्तमम्।
प्रत्यक्षावगमं धर्म्यं सुसुखं कर्तुमव्ययम्॥ २

इदम् This राजविद्या the king of sciences (i.e., the highest science) राजगुह्यं kingly secret (i.e., the deepest of all profound truths) उत्तमम् supreme पवित्रम् purifier प्रत्यक्षावगमं realisable by direct perception धर्म्यं endowed with (immense) merit कर्तुम् to perform सुसुखं very easy (च and) अव्ययम् of imperishable nature.

2. Of sciences, the highest; of profundities, the deepest; of purifiers, the supreme, is this; realisable by direct perception, endowed with (immense) merit, very easy to perform, and of an imperishable nature.

अश्रद्दधानाः पुरुषा धर्मस्यास्य परन्तप।
अप्राप्य मां निवर्तन्ते मृत्युसंसारवर्त्मनि॥ ३

परन्तप O scorcher of foes अस्य of this धर्मस्य (of) Dharma अश्रद्दधानाः without *Śraddhā* पुरुषाः persons मां Me अप्राप्य without attaining मृत्युसंसारवर्त्मनि in the path of rebirth fraught with death (मृत्युः death संसारः rebirth वर्त्मनि in the path) निवर्तन्ते return.

3. Persons without *Śraddhā* for this Dharma, return, O scorcher of foes, without attaining Me, to the path of rebirth fraught with death.

Without ... Dharma: Who have no faith in this knowledge of the Self, regarding the physical body itself as the Self.

मया ततमिदं सर्वं जगदव्यक्तमूर्तिना।
मत्स्थानि सर्वभूतानि न चाहं तेष्ववस्थितः॥४

अव्यक्तमूर्तिना By the unmanifested form मया by Me इदं this सर्वं all जगत् world ततम् pervaded सर्वभूतानि all beings मत्स्थानि exist in Me अहं I च and तेषु in them न not अवस्थितः dwelling.

4. All this world is pervaded by Me in My unmanifested form: all beings exist in Me, but I do not dwell in them.

Unmanifested: being invisible to the senses.

Exist in Me: have an individual exisience through Me, the Self, underlying them all.

Do not dwell in them: like corporeal things—in contact with them, or contained as though in a receptacle.

न च मत्स्थानि भूतानि पश्य मे योगमैश्वरम्।
भूतभृन्न च भूतस्थो ममात्मा भूतभावनः॥५

च And भूतानि beings न not मत्स्थानि dwelling in Me मे My ऐश्वरम् Divine योगम् Yoga पश्य behold मम My आत्मा Self भूतभृत् supporting the beings च and भूतभावनः bringing forth the beings न not भूतस्थः dwelling in the beings.

5. Nor do beings exist in Me (in reality), behold My Divine Yoga! Bringing forth and supporting the beings, My Self does not dwell in them.

Vide VII. 12.

Nor do, etc.: Because of the Self being unattached to or unconnected with any object. "Devoid of attachment, He is never attached."—*Bṛh. Upa.* III. ix. 26.

यथाकाशस्थितो नित्यं वायुः सर्वत्रगो महान्।
तथा सर्वाणि भूतानि मत्स्थानीत्युपधारय॥ ६

वायुः Wind नित्यं always सर्वत्रगः moving everywhere महान् mighty यथा just as आकाशस्थितः rests in the *Ākāśa* तथा so सर्वाणि all भूतानि beings मत्स्थानि dwell in Me इति thus उपधारय know.

6. As the mighty wind, moving always everywhere, rests ever in the *Ākāśa*, know thou, that even so do all beings rest in Me.

Rests ever in the Ākāśa: without being attached to it. The idea is that beings rest in the Lord without contact with, and so without producing any effect on Him.

सर्वभूतानि कौन्तेय प्रकृतिं यान्ति मामिकाम्।
कल्पक्षये पुनस्तानि कल्पादौ विसृजाम्यहम्॥ ७

कौन्तेय O son of Kuntī सर्वभूतानि all beings कल्पक्षये at the end of the *Kalpa* मामिकाम् My प्रकृतिं *Prakṛti* यान्ति go to पुनः again कल्पादौ at the beginning of the *Kalpa* तानि them अहम् I विसृजामि send forth.

7. At the end of a *Kalpa*, O son of Kuntī, all beings go back to My *Prakṛti*: at the beginning of (another) *Kalpa*, I send them forth again.

Prakṛti: The inferior one composed of the three *Guṇas*. *Kalpa*: a period of cosmic manifestation.

**प्रकृतिं स्वामवष्टभ्य विसृजामि पुनः पुनः।
भूतग्राममिमं कृत्स्नमवशं प्रकृतेर्वशात् ॥ ८**

स्वाम् My own प्रकृतिं *Prakṛti* अवष्टभ्य having animated प्रकृते: of *Prakṛti* वशात् from the sway इमं this कृत्स्नम् whole अवशं helpless भूतग्रामम् multitude of beings पुन: पुन: again and again विसृजामि (I) send forth.

8. Animating My *Prakṛti*, I project again and again this whole multitude of beings, helpless under the sway of *Prakṛti*.

Animating My Prakṛti: invigorating and fertilising the *Prakṛti* dependent on Him, which had gone to sleep at the universal dissolution, at the end of the *Kalpa*.

**न च मां तानि कर्माणि निबध्नन्ति धनञ्जय।
उदासीनवदासीनमसक्तं तेषु कर्मसु ॥ ९**

धनञ्जय O Dhanañjaya तानि those कर्माणि acts तेषु कर्मसु in those acts असक्तं unattached उदासीनवत् as one neutral or indifferent आसीनम् sitting च and मां Me न निबध्नन्ति do not bind.

9. Those acts do not bind Me, sitting as one neutral, unattached to them, O Dhanañjaya.

Those acts: which involve the unequal creation and dissolution of the universe.

As in the case of *Iśvara*, so in the case of others also, the absence of the egotistic feeling of agency and attachment for results, is the cause of freedom (from *Dharma* and *Adharma*).

मयाऽध्यक्षेण प्रकृतिः सूयते सचराचरम्।
हेतुनाऽनेन कौन्तेय जगद्विपरिवर्तते॥ १०

अध्यक्षेण By reason of proximity (lit. presiding over) मया by Me प्रकृतिः *Prakṛti* सचराचरम् the moving and the unmoving सूयते produces कौन्तेय O son of Kuntī अनेन through this हेतुना causc (इदं this) जगत् world विपरिवर्तते wheels round and round.

10. By reason of My proximity, *Prakṛti* produces all this, the moving and the unmoving; the world wheels round and round, O son of Kuntī, because of this.

In verses VII to X the Lord defines His position, following the *Arundhatī-Nyāya*. When a bride is brought to her husband's house for the first time, he shows her a very tiny star, called *Arundhatī*. To do this, he has to direct her gaze the right way, which he does by asking her to look at something near and something big, in the direction of the star, e.g., a branch of a tree. Next, he draws her attention to a large bright star observed beyond this branch, and so on, till by several steps, he succeeds in leading her eyes to the right thing. This method of leading to a subtle object through easy steps, is called *Arundhatī-Nyāya*. The Lord begins by stating that He projects all beings at the beginning of evolution: *Prakṛti* is only an instrument in His hands. Next, He says, He is not affected by that act, since He sits by, as one neutral, perfectly unattached. Lastly, He leads up to the final truth that really He does nothing, that it is *Prakṛti*, who animated by His proximity produces all that is. It is His Light that lights up *Prakṛti*, and makes her live and act. That is all the relation between Him and her.

अवजानन्ति मां मूढा मानुषीं तनुमाश्रितम्।
परं भावमजानन्तो मम भूतमहेश्वरम्॥ ११

भूतमहेश्वरम् Great Lord of beings मम My परं higher भावम् state or nature अजानन्तः unaware of मूढाः fools मानुषीं human तनुम् body or form आश्रितम् dwelling मां Me अवजानन्ति disregard.

11. Unaware of My higher state, as the great Lord of beings, fools disregard Me, dwelling in the human form.

Great Lord: Supreme Self.

मोघाशा मोघकर्माणो मोघज्ञाना विचेतसः।
राक्षसीमासुरीं चैव प्रकृतिं मोहिनीं श्रिताः॥ १२

मोघाशाः Of vain hopes मोघकर्माणः of vain works मोघज्ञानाः of vain knowledge विचेतसः senseless मोहिनीं delusive राक्षसीम् of the nature of *Rākṣasas* च and आसुरीं of the nature of *Asuras* प्रकृतिं nature श्रिताः (are) possessed of एव verily.

12. Of vain hopes, of vain works, of vain knowledge, and senseless, they verily are possessed of the delusive nature of *Rākṣasas* and *Asuras*.

Vain—because they neglect their own Self. They see no Self beyond the body.

They—refers to those described in the preceding *Śloka*.

Rākṣasas have *Rājasika* nature, *Asuras*, *Tāmasika*.

महात्मानस्तु मां पार्थ दैवीं प्रकृतिमाश्रिताः ।
भजन्त्यनन्यमनसो ज्ञात्वा भूतादिमव्ययम् ।। १३

तु But पार्थ O son of Pṛthā महात्मान: great-souled ones दैवीं divine प्रकृतिम् *Prakṛti* आश्रिता: possessed of अनन्यमनस: with a mind devoted to nothing else भूतादिम् origin of beings अव्ययम् immutable मां Me ज्ञात्वा knowing भजन्ति worship.

13. But the great-souled ones, O son of Pṛthā, possessed of the Divine *Prakṛti*, knowing Me to be the origin of beings and immutable, worship Me with a single mind.

सततं कीर्तयन्तो मां यतन्तश्च दृढव्रताः ।
नमस्यन्तश्च मां भक्त्या नित्ययुक्ता उपासते ।। १४

सततं Always कीर्तयन्त: glorifying मां Me दृढव्रता: of firm resolve यतन्त: striving च and भक्त्या with devotion नमस्यन्त: bowing down च and नित्ययुक्ता: always steadfast मां Me उपासते (they) worship.

14. Glorifying Me always and striving with firm resolve, bowing down to Me in devotion, always steadfast, they worship Me.

ज्ञानयज्ञेन चाप्यन्ये यजन्तो मामुपासते ।
एकत्वेन पृथक्त्वेन बहुधा विश्वतोमुखम् ।। १५

अन्ये Others अपि too च and ज्ञानयज्ञेन with the *Yajña* of knowledge यजन्त: sacrificing माम् Me उपासते (they) worship एकत्वेन as one पृथक्त्वेन as different विश्वतोमुखम् the All-Formed बहुधा in various ways.

15. Others, too, sacrificing by the *Yajña* of knowledge (i.e., seeing the Self in all), worship Me the All-Formed, as one, as distinct, as manifold.

All-Formed: He who has assumed all the manifold forms in the universe.

As one: identifying himself with the All-Formed—the Advaita view.

As distinct: making a distinction in essence between the Lord and himself—the Dualistic view.

As manifold: as the various divinities, Brahmā, Rudra, etc.

अहं क्रतुरहं यज्ञः स्वधाहमहमौषधम् ।
मन्त्रोऽहमहमेवाज्यमहमग्निरहं हुतम् ॥ १६

अहं I क्रतु: the Kratu अहं I यज्ञ: the *Yajña* अहम् I स्वधा the *Svadhā* अहम् I औषधम् the *Auṣadha* अहम् I मन्त्र: the *Mantra* अहम् I आज्यम् the *Ājya* एव also अहम् I अग्नि: the fire अहं I हुतम् the oblation.

16. I am the *Kratu*, I the *Yajña*, I the *Svadhā*, I the *Auṣadha*, I the *Mantra*, I the *Ājya*, I the fire, and I the oblation.

Kratu: is a particular Vedic rite.
Yajña: The worship enjoined in the *Smṛti*.
Svadhā: food offered to the manes (*Pitṛs*).
Auṣadha: all vegetable food and medicinal herbs.
Mantra: the chant with which oblation is offered.
Ājya: articles of oblation.
The fire: into which the offering is poured.

पिताहमस्य जगतो माता धाता पितामहः ।
वेद्यं पवित्रमोङ्कार ऋक् साम यजुरेव च ।। १७
गतिर्भर्ता प्रभुः साक्षी निवासः शरणं सुहृत् ।
प्रभवः प्रलयः स्थानं निधानं बीजमव्ययम् ।। १८

अहम् I अस्य of this जगत: world पिता Father माता Mother धाता the Sustainer पितामह: the Grandfather वेद्यं the (one) thing to be known पवित्रम् the purifier ओंकार: (the syllable) '*Om*' ऋक् the *Ṛk* साम *Sāman* यजु: *Yajus* एव also च and.

गति: The goal भर्ता Supporter प्रभु: Lord साक्षी the Witness निवास: Abode शरणं Refuge सुहृत् Friend प्रभव: Origin प्रलय: Dissolution स्थानं Substratum निधानं Storehouse बीजम् the Seed अव्ययम् immutable.

17. I am the Father of this world—the Mother, the Sustainer, the Grandfather, the Purifier, the (one) thing to be known, (the syllable) *Om*, and also the *Ṛk*, *Sāman*, and *Yajus*.

18. The Goal, the Supporter, the Lord, the Witness, the Abode, the Refuge, the Friend, the Origin, the Dissolution, the Substratum, the Storehouse, the Seed immutable.

Sustainer: by dispensing fruit of action
Seed: cause of the origin of all things.
Immutable: because it endures so long as the *Saṁsāra* endures.

तपाम्यहमहं वर्षं निगृह्णाम्युत्सृजामि च ।
अमृतं चैव मृत्युश्च सदसच्चाहमर्जुन ।। १९

अर्जुन O Arjuna अहम् I तपामि give heat अहं I वर्षं the rain उत्सृजामि send forth च and निगृह्णामि withhold अमृतं immortality च and एव also मृत्युः death च and अहम I सत् being च and असत् non-being.

19. (As sun) I give heat; I withhold and send forth rain; I am immortality and also death; being and non-being am I, O Arjuna!

Being: The manifested world of effects.

Non-being: means, the cause which is unmanifested only and not non-existence, otherwise we have to conceive existence coming out of non-existence, which is absurd. The *Śruti* says, "How can existence come out of non-existence?"—*Chānd. Upa.* VI. ii. 2.

त्रैविद्या मां सोमपाः पूतपापा
यज्ञैरिष्ट्वा स्वर्गतिं प्रार्थयन्ते ।
ते पुण्यमासाद्य सुरेन्द्रलोक-
मश्नन्ति दिव्यान्दिवि देवभोगान् ॥ २०

त्रैविद्याः The knowers of the three Vedas यज्ञैः by *Yajñas* मां Me इष्ट्वा worshipping सोमपाः the drinkers of *Soma* पूतपापाः purified from sin स्वर्गतिं passage to heaven प्रार्थयन्ते pray ते they पुण्यम् holy सुरेन्द्रलोकम् the world of the Lord of the *Devas* आसाद्य reaching दिवि in heaven दिव्यान् divine देवभोगान् the pleasures of the *Devas* अश्नन्ति enjoy.

20. The knowers of the three Vedas, worshipping Me by *Yajña*, drinking the *Soma*, and (thus) being purified from sin, pray for passage to heaven;

reaching the holy world of the Lord of the *Devas*, they enjoy in heaven the divine pleasures of the *Devas*.

Lord of the Devas: Indra, who is called *Śatakratu*, because he had performed a hundred sacrifices.

ते तं भुक्त्वा स्वर्गलोकं विशालं
क्षीणे पुण्ये मर्त्यलोकं विशन्ति ।
एवं त्रयीधर्ममनुप्रपन्ना
गतागतं कामकामा लभन्ते ।। २१

ते They तं that विशालं vast स्वर्गलोकं the *Svarga*—world भुक्त्वा having enjoyed पुण्ये merit क्षीणे on the exhaustion of मर्त्यलोकं the mortal world विशन्ति enter एवं thus त्रयीधर्मम् injunctions of the three (Vedas) अनुप्रपन्नाः abiding by कामकामाः desiring pleasures गतागतं the state of going and that of coming लभन्ते attain to.

21. Having enjoyed the vast *Svarga*-world, they enter the mortal world, on the exhaustion of their merit. Thus, abiding by the injunctions of the three (Vedas), desiring pleasures, they (constantly) come and go.

Injunctions: Ritualistic, the *Karma-Kāṇḍa*.

अनन्याश्चिन्तयन्तो मां ये जनाः पर्युपासते ।
तेषां नित्याभियुक्तानां योगक्षेमं वहाम्यहम् ।। २२

अनन्याः Non-separate मां Me चिन्तयन्तः meditating ये who जनाः persons पर्युपासते worship (Me) in all things

नित्याभियुक्तानां ever zealously engaged तेषां to them अहम् I योगक्षेमं the supply of what is lacking and the preservation of what is already possessed वहामि carry.

22. Persons who, meditating on Me as non-separate, worship Me in all beings, to them thus ever zealously engaged, I carry what they lack and preserve what they already have.

Ananyāḥ: as non-separate, i.e., looking upon the Supreme Being as not separate from their own self. Or *Ananyāḥ* may mean, without any other (thought). Then the translation of the *Śloka* should be—persons who worship Me in all beings, never harbouring any other thought, to them, etc.

I *carry, etc.*: Because while other devotees work for their own gain and safety, those who do not see anything as separate from themselves, do not do so; they even do not cherish a desire for life; so the Lord secures to them gain and safety.

येऽप्यन्यदेवता भक्ता यजन्ते श्रद्धयाऽन्विताः ।
तेऽपि मामेव कौन्तेय यजन्त्यविधिपूर्वकम् ।। २३

कौन्तेय O son of Kuntī श्रद्धया with Ś*raddh*ā अन्विताः endued (with) भक्ताः devotees ये who अन्यदेवताः other gods अपि even यजन्ते worship ते they अपि too अविधिपूर्वकम् by the wrong method माम् Me एव alone यजन्ति worship.

23. Even those devotees, who endued with *Śraddhā*, worship other gods, they too worship Me alone, O son of Kuntī , (but) by the wrong method.

Wrong method—ignorantly, not in the way by which they can get *Mokṣa*.

अहं हि सर्वयज्ञानां भोक्ता च प्रभुरेव च।
न तु मामभिजानन्ति तत्त्वेनातश्च्यवन्ति ते ॥ २४

हि Indeed सर्वयज्ञानां of all *Yajñas* अहं I एव alone भोक्ता enjoyer च and प्रभुः Lord च and ते they तु but माम् Me तत्त्वेन in reality न अभिजानन्ति do not know अतः hence च्यवन्ति (they) all return.

24. For I alone am the Enjoyer, and Lord of all *Yajñas*; but because they do not know Me in reality, they return (to the mortal world).

They return—by worshipping other gods they attain no doubt to the spheres of their sacrifice, but after the exhaustion of this merit, they fall from those spheres and return to the mortal world.

यान्ति देवव्रता देवान् पितॄन्यान्ति पितृव्रताः।
भूतानि यान्ति भूतेज्या यान्ति मद्याजिनोऽपि माम् ॥ २५

देवव्रताः Votaries of the *Devas* देवान् the Devas यान्ति go to पितृव्रताः the votaries of the *Pitṛs* पितॄन् the *Pitṛs* यान्ति go to भूतेज्याः the worshippers of *Bhūtas* भूतानि *Bhūtas* यान्ति go to मद्याजिनः My votaries अपि too माम् Me यान्ति go to.

25. Votaries of the *Devas* go to the *Devas*; to the *Pitṛs*, go their votaries; to the *Bhūtas*, go the *Bhūta* worshippers; My votaries too come unto Me.

Bhūtas: beings lower than the *Devas,* but higher than human beings.

Me: The Imperishable.

पत्रं पुष्पं फलं तोयं यो मे भक्त्या प्रयच्छति।
तदहं भक्त्युपहृतमश्नामि प्रयतात्मनः ॥ २६

यः Whoever मे to Me भक्त्या with devotion पत्रं a leaf पुष्पं a flower फलं a fruit तोयं water प्रयच्छति offers अहं I प्रयतात्मनः of the pure-minded भक्त्युपहृतम् the devout gift तत् that अश्नामि accept.

26. Whoever with devotion offers Me a leaf, a flower, a fruit, or water, that I accept—the devout gift of the pure-minded.

Not only does the single-minded devotion to the Supreme lead to imperishable result, but it is also so easy and simple to perform—says Kṛṣṇa in this *Śloka*.

यत्करोषि यदश्नासि यज्जुहोषि ददासि यत्।
यत्तपस्यसि कौन्तेय तत्कुरुष्व मदर्पणम् ॥ २७

कौन्तेय O son of Kuntī यत् whatever करोषि thou doest यत् whatever अश्नासि thou eatest यत् whatever जुहोषि thou offerest in sacrifice यत् whatever ददासि thou givest away यत् whatever तपस्यसि thou practisest as austerity तत् that मदर्पणम् offering unto Me कुरुष्व do.

27. Whatever thou doest, whatever thou eatest, whatever thou offerest in sacrifice, whatever thou givest away, whatever austerity thou practisest, O son of Kuntī, do that as an offering unto Me.

शुभाशुभफलैरेवं मोक्ष्यसे कर्मबन्धनैः ।
सन्न्यासयोगयुक्तात्मा विमुक्तो मामुपैष्यसि ।। २८

एवं Thus शुभाशुभफलैः from good and evil results कर्मबन्धनैः from the bondages of actions मोक्ष्यसे (thou) shalt be freed विमुक्तः liberated सन्न्यासयोगयुक्तात्मा with the heart steadfast in the Yoga of renunciation माम् unto Me उपैष्यसि (thou) shalt come.

28. Thus shalt thou be freed from the bondages of actions, bearing good and evil results, with the heart steadfast in the Yoga of renunciation, and liberated thou shalt come unto Me.

The Yoga of renunciation: This way of purification of the heart by offering everything to the Lord.

Liberated, *etc*.: thou shalt be liberated while in the body, and at its death, become Me.

समोऽहं सर्वभूतेषु न मे द्वेष्योऽस्ति न प्रियः ।
ये भजन्ति तु मां भक्त्या मयि ते तेषु चाप्यहम् ।। २९

अहं I सर्वभूतेषु to all beings समः the same मे to Me न not द्वेष्यः hateful न not प्रियः dear अस्ति is ये those तु but मां Me भक्त्या with devotion भजन्ति worship ते they मयि in Me च and अहम् I अपि too तेषु in them.

29. I am the same to all beings: to Me there is none hateful or dear. But those who worship Me with devotion, are in Me, and I too am in them.

I am like fire. As fire gives heat to those who draw near to it, and not to those who move away from it, even so do I. My grace falls upon My devotees, but not owing to any attachment on My part. As the sun's light, though pervading everywhere, is reflected in a clean mirror, so also I, the Supreme Lord, present as a matter of course everywhere, manifest Myself in these persons only, from whose minds all the dirt of ignorance has been removed by devotion.

अपि चेत् सुदुराचारो भजते मामनन्यभाक्।
साधुरेव स मन्तव्यः सम्यग्व्यवसितो हि सः ।। ३०

सुदुराचार: A very wicked person अपि even चेत् if अनन्यभाक् with devotion to none else माम् Me भजते worships स: he साधु: good एव verily मन्तव्य: should be regarded हि indeed स: he सम्यक् rightly व्यवसित: resolved.

30. If even a very wicked person worships Me, with devotion to none else, he should be regarded as good, for he has rightly resolved.

He has rightly resolved: He is one who has formed a holy resolution, to abandon the evil ways of his life.

क्षिप्रं भवति धर्मात्मा शश्वच्छान्तिं निगच्छति।
कौन्तेय प्रतिजानीहि न मे भक्तः प्रणश्यति ।। ३१

क्षिप्रं Soon धर्मात्मा righteous भवति (he) becomes शश्वत् eternal शान्तिं peace निगच्छति attains to कौन्तेय O son of Kuntī मे My भक्त: devotee न प्रणश्यति is never destroyed (इति this) प्रतिजानीहि know (do thou proclaim boldly).

31. Soon does he become righteous, and attain eternal Peace, O son of Kuntī; boldly canst thou proclaim, that My devotee is never destroyed.

मां हि पार्थ व्यपाश्रित्य येऽपि स्युः पापयोनयः ।
स्त्रियो वैश्यास्तथा शूद्रास्तेऽपि यान्ति परां गतिम् ।। ३२

पार्थ O son of Pṛthā ये who अपि also पापयोनयः of inferior birth स्युः might be स्त्रियः women वैश्याः Vaiśyas तथा as well as शूद्राः Śūdras ते they अपि even मां Me व्यपाश्रित्य taking refuge in परां the Supreme गतिम् Goal हि indeed यान्ति attain.

32. For, taking refuge in Me, they also, O son of Pṛthā, who might be of inferior birth—women, Vaiśyas, as well as Śūdras—even they attain to the Supreme Goal.

Of inferior birth . . . Śūdras: Because by birth, the Vaiśyas are engaged only in agriculture, etc., and the women and *śūdras* were debarred from the study of the Vedas.

किं पुनर्ब्राह्मणाः पुण्या भक्ता राजर्षयस्तथा ।
अनित्यमसुखं लोकमिमं प्राप्य भजस्व माम् ।। ३३

किं पुनः How much more पुण्याः holy ब्राह्मणाः Brāhmaṇas तथा also भक्ताः devoted राजर्षयः *Rājarṣis* अनित्यम् transient असुखं joyless इमं the लोकम् world प्राप्य having attained भजस्व do thou worship माम् Me.

33. What need to mention holy Brāhmaṇas, and devoted *Rājarṣis*! Having obtained this transient, joyless world, worship thou Me.

Rājarṣis: kings who have attained to sainthood (*ṛṣihood*).

What need, etc.: How much more easily then do the holy Brāhmaṇas and the devoted royal saints attain that Goal!

Having ... world: Being born in this human body which is hard to get, one should exert oneself immediately for perfection, without depending on the future, as everything in this world is transient, and without seeking for happiness, as this world is joyless.

मन्मना भव मद्भक्तो मद्याजी मां नमस्कुरु।
मामेवैष्यसि युक्त्वैवमात्मानं मत्परायणः ।। ३४

मन्मना: With mind filled with Me मद्भक्त: My devotee मद्याजी sacrificer unto Me भव be thou मां to Me नमस्कुरु bow down एवम् thus मत्परायण: taking Me as the Supreme Goal आत्मानं heart युक्त्वा having made steadfast माम् Me एव alone एष्यसि thou shalt come to.

34. Fill thy mind with Me, be My devotee, sacrifice unto Me, bow down to Me; thus having made thy heart steadfast in Me, taking Me as the Supreme Goal, thou shalt come to Me.

इति राजविद्या-राजगुह्ययोगो नाम नवमोऽध्यायः ।।

The end of the ninth chapter, designated, *The Way of the Kingly Knowledge and the Kingly Secret*.

दशमोऽध्यायः
(विभूतियोगः)

TENTH CHAPTER
(The Glimpses of Divine Glory)

श्रीभगवानुवाच

भूय एव महाबाहो शृणु मे परमं वचः ।
यत्तेऽहं प्रीयमाणाय वक्ष्यामि हितकाम्यया ॥ १

श्रीभगवान् The Blessed Lord उवाच said:

महाबाहो O mighty-armed भूयः again एव verily मे My परमं supreme वचः word शृणु hear (thou) यत् which प्रीयमाणाय who art delighted (to hear) ते to thee अहं I हितकाम्यया wishing (thy) welfare वक्ष्यामि will tell.

The Blessed Lord said:

1. Again, O mighty-armed, do thou listen to My supreme word, which I, wishing thy welfare, will tell thee who art delighted (to hear Me).

Supreme: as revealing the unsurpassed truth.

न मे विदुः सुरगणाः प्रभवं न महर्षयः ।
अहमादिर्हि देवानां महर्षीणां च सर्वशः ॥ २

न Not सुरगणा: the hosts of Devas न nor महर्षय: the great *Ṛṣis* मे My प्रभवं origin विदु: do know हि for अहम् I देवानां of the Devas महर्षीणां of the great *Ṛṣis* च and सर्वश: in every way आदि: source.

2. Neither the hosts of Devas, nor the great *Ṛṣis,* know My origin, for in every way I am the source of all the Devas and the great *Ṛṣis.*

Prabhavam: higher origin (birth)—though birthless, yet taking various manifestations of power. Or it may mean, great Lordly power.

In every way: not only as their producer, but also as their efficient cause, and the guide of their intellect, etc.

यो मामजमनादिं च वेत्ति लोकमहेश्वरम् ।
असंमूढः स मर्त्येषु सर्वपापैः प्रमुच्यते ।। ३

य: Who माम् Me अनादिं beginningless अजम् birthless च and लोकमहेश्वरम् the great Lord of worlds वेत्ति knows स: he मर्त्येषु among mortals असंमूढ: undeluded सर्वपापै: from all sins प्रमुच्यते is freed.

3. He who knows Me, birthless and beginningless, the great Lord of worlds—he, among mortals, is undeluded, he is freed from all sins.

All sins: consciously or unconsciously incurred.

बुद्धिर्ज्ञानमसंमोहः क्षमा सत्यं दमः शमः ।
सुखं दुःखं भवोऽभावो भयं चाभयमेव च ।। ४

अहिंसा समता तुष्टिस्तपो दानं यशोऽयशः ।
भवन्ति भावा भूतानां मत्त एव पृथग्विधाः ॥ ५

बुद्धिः Intellect ज्ञानम् knowledge असंमोहः non-delusion क्षमा forbearance सत्यं truth दमः restraint of the external senses शमः calmness of the heart सुखं happiness दुःखं misery भवः birth अभावः death भयं fear च and एव even अभयम् fearlessness च as well as अहिंसा non-injury समता evenness तुष्टिः contentment तपः austerity दानं benevolence यशः good name अयशः ill-fame भूतानां of beings पृथग्विधाः of different kinds भावाः qualities मत्तः from Me एव alone भवन्ति arise.

4–5. Intellect, knowledge, non-delusion, forbearance, truth, restraint of the external senses, calmness of heart, happiness, misery, birth, death, fear, as well as fearlessness, non-injury, evenness, contentment, austerity, benevolence, good name, (as well as) ill-fame—(these) different kinds of qualities of beings arise from Me alone.

Arise, etc.: according to their respective *Karma.*

महर्षयः सप्त पूर्वे चत्वारो मनवस्तथा ।
मद्भावा मानसा जाता येषां लोक इमाः प्रजाः ॥ ६

सप्त Seven महर्षयः great *Ṛṣis* पूर्वे ancient चत्वारः four तथा as well as मनवः Manus मद्भावाः possessed of powers like Me मानसाः from mind जाताः born लोके in this world इमाः these येषां from whom प्रजाः creatures.

6. The seven great *Ṛṣis* as well as the four ancient *Manus,* possessed of powers like Me (due to their thoughts being fixed on Me), were born of (My) mind; from them are these creatures in the world.

The four ancient Manus: The four *Manus* of the past ages known as *Sāvarṇas.*

एतां विभूतिं योगं च मम यो वेत्ति तत्त्वतः ।
सोऽविकम्पेन योगेन युज्यते नात्र संशयः ॥ ७

यः Who मम Mine एतां these विभूतिं manifold manifestations of (My) being योगं Yoga power च and तत्त्वतः in reality वेत्ति knows सः he अविकम्पेन unshakable योगेन in Yoga युज्यते becomes established अत्र here न संशयः no doubt.

7. He who in reality knows these manifold manifestations of My being and (this) Yoga power of Mine, becomes established in the unshakable Yoga; there is no doubt about it.

This Yoga power: i.e., the fact that the great Ṛṣis and the *Manus* possessed their power and wisdom, as partaking of a very small portion of the Lord's infinite power and wisdom.

Unshakeable Yoga: Samādhi, the state of steadiness in right realisation.

अहं सर्वस्य प्रभवो मत्तः सर्वं प्रवर्तते ।
इति मत्वा भजन्ते मां बुधा भावसमन्विताः ॥ ८

अहं I सर्वस्य of all प्रभव: the origin मत्त: from Me सर्वं everything प्रवर्तते evolves इति thus मत्वा thinking बुधा: the wise भावसमन्विता: with loving consciousness मां Me भजन्ते worship.

8. I am the origin of all, from Me everything evolves—thus thinking, the wise worship Me with loving consciousness.

Loving consciousness: of the One Self in all.

मच्चित्ता मद्‌गतप्राणा बोधयन्तः परस्परम्।
कथयन्तश्च मां नित्यं तुष्यन्ति च रमन्ति च ॥ ९

मच्चित्ता: With (their) minds wholly in Me मद्‌गतप्राणा: with (their) senses absorbed in Me परस्परम् mutually बोधयन्त: enlightening च and नित्यं always कथयन्त: speaking of मां Me च and तुष्यन्ति (they) are satisfied रमन्ति (they) are delighted च and.

9. With their minds wholly in Me, with their senses absorbed in Me, enlightening one another, and always speaking of Me, they are satisfied and delighted.

Satisfied: when there is cessation of all thirst.

Says the *Purāṇa*: All the pleasures of the senses in the world, and also all the great happiness in the divine spheres, are not worth a sixteenth part of that which comes from the cessation of all desires.

तेषां सततयुक्तानां भजतां प्रीतिपूर्वकम् ।
ददामि बुद्धियोगं तं येन मामुपयान्ति ते ॥ १०

सततयुक्तानां Ever steadfast प्रीतिपूर्वकम् with affection भजतां serving तेषां to them तं that बुद्धियोगं *Buddhi-Yoga* ददामि (I) give येन by which ते they माम् Me उपयान्ति come unto.

10. To them, ever steadfast and serving Me with affection, I give that *Buddhi-Yoga* by which they come unto Me.

Buddhi-Yoga: Devotion of right knowledge, through *Dhyāna,* of My essential nature as devoid of all limitations. See II. 39.

तेषामेवानुकम्पार्थमहमज्ञानजं तमः ।
नाशयाम्यात्मभावस्थो ज्ञानदीपेन भास्वता ॥ ११

तेषाम् For them अनुकम्पार्थम् out of compassion एव mere अहम् I आत्मभावस्थ: abiding in (their) hearts भास्वता luminous ज्ञानदीपेन by the lamp of knowledge अज्ञानजं born of ignorance तम: the darkness (of their mind) नाशयामि (I) destroy.

11. Out of mere compassion for them, I, abiding in their hearts, destroy the darkness (in them) born of ignorance, by the luminous lamp of knowledge.

Luminous lamp of knowledge: characterised by discrimination; fed by the oil of contentment due to *Bhakti*; fanned by the wind of absorbing meditation on Me; furnished with the wick of pure consciousness evolved by the constant cultivation of *Brahmacarya* and other pious virtues; held in the reservoir of the heart devoid of worldliness; placed in the wind-sheltered recess of the mind, withdrawn from the sense-objects, and untainted by attachment and aversion; shining with the light of right knowledge, engendered by incessant practice of concentration.— Śaṅkara.

अर्जुन उवाच

परं ब्रह्म परं धाम पवित्रं परमं भवान्।
पुरुषं शाश्वतं दिव्यमादिदेवमजं विभुम्॥ १२
आहुस्त्वामृषयः सर्वे देवर्षिर्नारदस्तथा।
असितो देवलो व्यासः स्वयं चैव ब्रवीषि मे॥ १३

अर्जुनः Arjuna उवाच said:

भवान् Thou परं Supreme ब्रह्म Brahman परं Supreme धाम Abode परमं Supreme पवित्रं Purifier (च and) सर्वे all ऋषयः the *Ṛṣis* देवर्षिः *Deva-Ṛṣi* नारदः Nārada तथा as well as असितः Asita देवलः Devala व्यासः Vyāsa त्वाम् Thee शाश्वतं the eternal पुरुषं *Puruṣa* दिव्यम् Self-luminous आदिदेवम् the first *Deva* अजं Birthless विभुम् the All-pervading आहुः (they) declared स्वयं Thyself च and एव also मे to me ब्रवीषि (Thou) sayest.

Arjuna said:

12–13. The Supreme Brahman, the Supreme Abode, the Supreme Purifier, art Thou. All the *Ṛṣis,* the *Deva-Ṛṣi* Nārada as well as Asita, Devala, and Vyāsa have declared Thee as the Eternal, the Self-luminous *Puruṣa,* the first *Deva,* Birthless, and All-pervading. So also Thou Thyself sayest to me.

सर्वमेतदृतं मन्ये यन्मां वदसि केशव।
न हि ते भगवन् व्यक्तिं विदुर्देवा न दानवाः ।। १४

केशव O Keśava मां to me यत् what वदसि (Thou) sayest एतत् that सर्वम् all ऋतं true मन्ये (I) regard हि verily भगवन् O Bhagavan ते Thy व्यक्तिं manifestation न neither देवाः *Devas* न nor दानवाः *Dānavas* विदुः do know.

14. I regard all this that Thou sayest to me as true, O Keśava. Verily, O Bhagavan, neither the *Devas* nor the *Dānavas* know Thy manifestation.

Bhagavān: is he in whom ever exist in their fulness, all powers, all Dharma, all glory, all success, all renunciation, and all freedom. Also he that knows the origin and dissolution and the future of all beings, as well as knowledge and ignorance, is called Bhagavān.

स्वयमेवात्मनात्मानं वेत्थ त्वं पुरुषोत्तम।
भूतभावन भूतेश देवदेव जगत्पते ।। १५

पुरुषोत्तम O Supreme *Puruṣa* भूतभावन O Source of beings भूतेश O Lord of beings देवदेव O *Deva* of *Devas* जगत्पते O Ruler of the world त्वं Thou स्वयम् Thyself एव verily आत्मना by Thyself आत्मानं Thyself वेत्थ (Thou) knowest.

15. Verily, Thou Thyself knowest Thyself by Thyself, O Supreme *Puruṣa,* O Source of beings, O Lord of beings, O *Deva* of *Devas,* O Ruler of the world.

वक्तुमर्हस्यशेषेण दिव्या ह्यात्मविभूतयः ।
याभिर्विभूतिभिर्लोकानिमांस्त्वं व्याप्य तिष्ठसि ।। १६

याभि: By which विभूतिभि: (divine) attributes त्वं Thou इमान् all these लोकान् worlds व्याप्य having filled तिष्ठसि existest दिव्या: divine आत्मविभूतय: Thy attributes हि indeed अशेषेण without reserve वक्तुम् to speak of अर्हसि (Thou) shouldst.

16. Thou shouldst indeed speak, without reserve, of Thy divine attributes by which, filling all these worlds, Thou existest.

Since none else can do so.

कथं विद्यामहं योगिंस्त्वां सदा परिचिन्तयन् ।
केषु केषु च भावेषु चिन्त्योऽसि भगवन्मया ।। १७

योगिन् O Yogī सदा ever परिचिन्तयन् meditating कथं how त्वां Thee अहं I विद्याम् shall know भगवन् O Bhagavan मया by me केषु केषु in what and what भावेषु aspects, things च and चिन्त्य: to be thought of असि (Thou) art.

17. How shall I, O Yogī, meditate ever to know Thee? In what things, O Bhagavan, art Thou to be thought of by me?

In what things, etc.: In order that the mind even thinking of external objects, may be enabled to contemplate Thee in Thy particular manifestations in them.

विस्तरेणात्मनो योगं विभूतिं च जनार्दन।
भूयः कथय तृप्तिर्हि शृण्वतो नास्ति मेऽमृतम्॥ १८

जनार्दन O Janārdana आत्मन: Thy योगं Yoga-powers विभूतिं attributes च and विस्तरेण in detail भूय: again कथय speak of हि for अमृतम् ambrosia शृण्वत: to (me) who am hearing मे to me तृप्ति: satiety न अस्ति there is not.

18. Speak to me again in detail, O Janārdana, of Thy Yoga-powers and attributes; for I am never satiated in hearing the ambrosia (of Thy speech).

Janārdana: to whom all pray for prosperity and salvation.

श्रीभगवानुवाच

हन्त ते कथयिष्यामि दिव्या ह्यात्मविभूतयः।
प्राधान्यतः कुरुश्रेष्ठ नास्त्यन्तो विस्तरस्य मे॥ १९

श्रीभगवान् The Blessed Lord उवाच said:
हन्त O कुरुश्रेष्ठ best of the Kurus दिव्या: divine आत्मविभूतय: My attributes प्राधान्यत: according to their prominence ते to thee कथयिष्यामि (I) shall speak of हि for मे My विस्तरस्य particulars अन्त: end नास्ति there is not.

The Blessed Lord said:

19. I shall speak to thee now, O best of the Kurus, of My divine attributes, according to their prominence; there is no end to the particulars of My manifestation.

According to their prominence: i.e., only where they are severally the most prominent.

अहमात्मा गुडाकेश सर्वभूताशयस्थितः ।
अहमादिश्च मध्यं च भूतानामन्त एव च ।। २०

गुडाकेश O Guḍākeśa सर्वभूताशयस्थित: existent in the heart of all beings आत्मा the Self च and अहम् I भूतानाम् of (all) beings आदि: the beginning च and मध्यं the middle अन्त: the end च and अहम् I एव also.

20. I am the Self, O Guḍākeśa, existent in the heart of all beings; I am the beginning, the middle, and also the end of all beings.

Guḍākeśa: conqueror of sleep.

Beginning, etc.: That is, the birth, the life, and the death of all beings.

आदित्यानामहं विष्णुर्ज्योतिषां रविरंशुमान् ।
मरीचिर्मरुतामस्मि नक्षत्राणामहं शशी ।। २१

अहं I आदित्यानाम् of the (twelve) *Ādityas* विष्णु: Viṣṇu ज्योतिषां of luminaries अंशुमान् the radiant रवि: the Sun मरुताम् of the winds (forty-nine wind-gods) मरीचि: Marīci अस्मि (I) am नक्षत्राणाम् of the asterisms अहं I शशी the Moon.

21. Of the *Ādityas,* I am Viṣṇu; of luminaries, the radiant Sun; of the winds I am Marīci; of the asterisms, the Moon.

वेदानां सामवेदोऽस्मि देवानामस्मि वासवः ।
इन्द्रियाणां मनश्चास्मि भूतानामस्मि चेतना ।। २२

वेदानां Of the Vedas सामवेदः *Sāma-Veda* अस्मि (I) am देवानाम् of the gods वासवः Vāsava अस्मि (I) am इन्द्रियाणां of the senses मनः Mind च and अस्मि (I) am भूतानाम् in living beings चेतना intelligence अस्मि (I) am.

22. I am the *Sāma-Veda* of the Vedas, and Vāsava (Indra) of the gods; of the senses, I am the mind; and intelligence in living beings am I.

रुद्राणां शङ्करश्चास्मि वित्तेशो यक्षरक्षसाम् ।
वसूनां पावकश्चास्मि मेरुः शिखरिणामहम् ।। २३

रुद्राणां Of the *Rudras* शङ्करः Śaṅkara च and अस्मि (I) am यक्षरक्षसाम् of the *Yakṣas* and the *Rākṣasas* वित्तेशः the Lord of wealth (Kubera) (अस्मि I am) वसूनां of the *Vasus* पावकः Pāvaka च and अस्मि (I) am शिखरिणाम् of mountains मेरुः Meru अहम् I (अस्मि am).

23. And of the *Rudras* I am Śaṅkara; of the *Yakṣas* and *Rākṣasas,* the Lord of wealth (Kubera); of the *Vasus* I am Pāvaka; and of mountains, Meru am I.

पुरोधसां च मुख्यं मां विद्धि पार्थ बृहस्पतिम् ।
सेनानीनामहं स्कन्दः सरसामस्मि सागरः ।। २४

पार्थ O son of Pṛthā मां Me पुरोधसां of the priests मुख्यं the chief बृहस्पतिम् Bṛhaspati च and विद्धि know अहं I सेनानीनाम् of generals स्कन्दः Skanda सरसाम् of bodies of water सागरः the ocean अस्मि (I) am.

24. And of priests, O son of Pṛthā, know Me the chief, Bṛhaspati; of generals, I am Skanda; of bodies of water, I am the ocean.

महर्षीणां भृगुरहं गिरामस्म्येकमक्षरम्।
यज्ञानां जपयज्ञोऽस्मि स्थावराणां हिमालयः ॥ २५

अहं I महर्षीणां of the great *Ṛṣis* भृगुः Bhṛgu गिराम् of words एकम् one अक्षरम् the syllable "Om" अस्मि (I) am यज्ञानां of *Yajñas* जपयज्ञः the *Yajña* of *Japa* (silent repetition) स्थावराणां of immovable things हिमालयः the Himālaya अस्मि (I) am.

25. Of the great *Ṛṣis* I am Bhṛgu; of words I am the one syllable "Om"; of *Yajñas* I am the *Yajña* of *Japa* (silent repetition); of immovable things the Himālaya.

Yajña of Japa: because there is no injury or loss of life involved in it, it is the best of all *Yajñas*.

अश्वत्थः सर्ववृक्षाणां देवर्षीणां च नारदः ।
गन्धर्वाणां चित्ररथः सिद्धानां कपिलो मुनिः ॥ २६

सर्ववृक्षाणां Of all trees अश्वत्थः the Aśvattha देवर्षीणां of the *Deva-Ṛṣis* च and नारदः Nārada गन्धर्वाणां of *Gandharvas*

चित्ररथः Citraratha सिद्धानां of the perfected ones कपिलः Kapila मुनिः the *Muni*.

26. Of all trees (I am) the Aśvattha, and Nārada of *Deva-Ṛṣis;* Citraratha of *Gandharvas* am I, and the *Muni* Kapila of the perfected ones.

उच्चैःश्रवसमश्वानां विद्धि माममृतोद्भवम् ।
ऐरावतं गजेन्द्राणां नराणां च नराधिपम् ॥ २७

अश्वानां Among horses अमृतोद्भवम् *Amṛta*-born उच्चैःश्रवसम् Uccaiśravas गजेन्द्राणां of lordly elephants ऐरावतं Airāvata नराणां of men नराधिपम् the king च and माम् Me विद्धि know.

27. Know Me among horses as Uccaiśravas, *Amṛta*-born; of lordly elephants Airāvata, and of men the king.

Amṛta-born: Brought forth from the ocean when it was churned for the nectar.

आयुधानामहं वज्रं धेनूनामस्मि कामधुक् ।
प्रजनश्चास्मि कन्दर्पः सर्पाणामस्मि वासुकिः ॥ २८

आयुधानाम् Of weapons अहं I वज्रं the thunderbolt धेनूनाम् of cows कामधुक् *Kāmadhuk* (Surabhi, the heavenly cow yielding all desires) अस्मि (I) am (अहं I) प्रजनः cause of offspring कन्दर्पः Kandarpa च and अस्मि (I) am सर्पाणाम् of serpents वासुकिः Vāsuki अस्मि (I) am.

28. Of weapons I am the thunderbolt, of cows I am *Kāmadhuk;* I am the Kandarpa, the cause of offspring; of serpents I am Vāsuki.

अनन्तश्चास्मि नागानां वरुणो यादसामहम्।
पितॄणामर्यमा चास्मि यमः संयमतामहम्॥ २९

नागानां Of snakes अनन्तः Ananta च and अस्मि (I) am यादसाम् of water-beings अहम् I (अस्मि am) वरुणः Varuṇa पितॄणाम् of *Pitṛs* अर्यमा Aryaman च and अस्मि (I) am संयमताम् of controllers अहम् I यमः Yama (अस्मि I am).

29. And Ananta of snakes I am, I am Varuṇa of water-beings; and Aryaman of *Pitṛs* I am, I am Yama of controllers.

प्रह्लादश्चास्मि दैत्यानां कालः कलयतामहम्।
मृगाणां च मृगेन्द्रोऽहं वैनतेयश्च पक्षिणाम्॥ ३०

दैत्यानां Of Diti's progeny च and प्रह्लादः Prahlāda अस्मि (I) am कलयताम् of measurers अहम् I कालः Time (अस्मि I am) मृगाणां of beasts अहं I च and मृगेन्द्रः the lord of beasts (lion) पक्षिणाम् of birds वैनतेयः son of Vinatā, Garuḍa च and.

30. And Prahlāda am I of Diti's progeny, of measurers I am Time; and of beasts I am the lord of beasts, and Garuḍa of birds.

पवनः पवतामस्मि रामः शस्त्रभृतामहम्।
झषाणां मकरश्चास्मि स्रोतसामस्मि जाह्नवी॥ ३१

पवताम् Of purifiers पवन: the wind अस्मि (I) am शस्त्रभृताम् of wielders of weapons (warriors) अहम् I राम: Rāma (अस्मि I am) झषाणां of fishes मकर: *Makara* (shark) च and अस्मि (I) am स्रोतसाम् of streams जाह्नवी Jāhnavī, Gangā अस्मि (I) am.

31. Of purifiers I am the wind, Rāma of warriors am I; of fishes I am the shark, of streams I am Jāhnavī (the Gaṅgā).

सर्गाणामादिरन्तश्च मध्यं चैवाहमर्जुन।
अध्यात्मविद्या विद्यानां वादः प्रवदतामहम्॥ ३२

अर्जुन O Arjuna सर्गाणाम् of manifestations आदि: the beginning च and अन्त: the end मध्यं the middle च and अहम् I एव also विद्यानां of all knowledges अध्यात्मविद्या the knowledge of the Self प्रवदताम् of disputants (च and) अहम् I वाद: *Vāda*.

32. Of manifestations I am the beginning, the middle and also the end; of all knowledges I am the knowledge of the Self, and *Vāda,* of disputants.

Vāda: Discussion is classified under three heads: 1. *Vāda*; 2. *Vitaṇḍā*; 3. *Jalpa*.

In the first, the object is to arrive at truth; in the second, idle carping at the arguments of another, without trying to establish the opposite side of the question; and in the third, the assertion of one's own opinion, and the attempt to refute that of the adversary by overbearing reply or wrangling rejoinder.

अक्षराणामकारोऽस्मि द्वन्द्वः सामासिकस्य च।
अहमेवाक्षयः कालो धाताहं विश्वतोमुखः ॥ ३३

अक्षराणाम् Of letters अकार: the letter A अस्मि (I) am सामासिकस्य of all compounds च and द्वन्द्व: (that called in Sanskrit) *Dvandva,* the copulative अहम् I एव alone अक्षय: the inexhaustible काल: Time अहं I विश्वतोमुख: the All-formed धाता the Sustainer (by distributing fruits of actions).

33. Of letters the letter A am I, and *Dvandva* of all compounds; I alone am the inexhaustible Time, I the Sustainer (by dispensing fruits of actions) All-formed.

Inexhaustible Time: i.e., Eternity. *Kāla* spoken of before is finite time.

मृत्युः सर्वहरश्चाहमुद्भवश्च भविष्यताम्।
कीर्तिः श्रीर्वाक् च नारीणां स्मृतिर्मेधा धृतिः क्षमा ॥ ३४

अहम् I सर्वहर: the all-seizing मृत्यु: Death च and भविष्यताम् of those who are to be prosperous उद्भव: the prosperity च and नारीणां of the feminine कीर्ति: Fame श्री: Prosperity (or beauty) वाक् Inspiration (lit. speech) स्मृति: Memory मेधा Intelligence धृति: Constancy क्षमा Forbearance च and (अहम् I).

34. And I am the all-seizing Death, and the prosperity of those who are to be prosperous; of the feminine qualities (I am) Fame, Prosperity

(or beauty), Inspiration, Memory, Intelligence, Constancy and Forbearance.

बृहत्साम तथा साम्नां गायत्री छन्दसामहम् ।
मासानां मार्गशीर्षोऽहमृतूनां कुसुमाकरः ॥ ३५

अहम् I तथा also साम्नां of Sāma hymns बृहत्साम *Bṛhat-Sāma* छन्दसाम् of metres अहम् I गायत्री *Gāyatrī* मासानां of months मार्गशीर्ष: *Mārgaśirṣa* ऋतूनां of seasons कुसुमाकर: the flowery season.

35. Of *Sāmas* also I am the *Bṛhat-Sāma,* of metres *Gāyatrī* am I; of months I am *Mārgaśirṣa,* of seasons the flowery season.

Mārgaśirṣa: month including parts of November and December.
Flowery season: Spring.

द्यूतं छलयतामस्मि तेजस्तेजस्विनामहम् ।
जयोऽस्मि व्यवसायोऽस्मि सत्त्वं सत्त्ववतामहम् ॥ ३६

अहम् I छलयताम् of the fraudulent द्यूतं the gambling तेजस्विनाम् of the powerful तेज: power अस्मि (I) am अहम् I जय: victory अस्मि (I) am व्यवसाय: effort अस्मि (I) am सत्त्ववताम् of the *Sāttvika* सत्त्वं the *Sattva* (अस्मि I am).

36. I am the gambling of the fraudulent, I am the power of the powerful; I am victory, I am effort, I am *Sattva* of the *Sāttvika*.

I am victory, I am effort: I am victory of the victorious, I am the effort of those who make an effort.

वृष्णीनां वासुदेवोऽस्मि पाण्डवानां धनञ्जयः ।
मुनीनामप्यहं व्यासः कवीनामुशना कविः ।। ३७

अहं I वृष्णीनां of the Vṛṣṇis वासुदेवः Vāsudeva पाण्डवानां of the Pāṇḍavas धनञ्जयः Dhanañjaya अपि also मुनीनाम् of the *Munis* व्यासः Vyāsa कवीनाम् of the sages उशना Uśanas कविः the sage अस्मि (I) am.

37. Of the Vṛṣṇis, I am Vāsudeva; of the Pāṇḍavas, Dhanañjaya; and also of the *Munis,* I am Vyāsa; of the sages, Uśanas the sage.

दण्डो दमयतामस्मि नीतिरस्मि जिगीषताम् ।
मौनं चैवास्मि गुह्यानां ज्ञानं ज्ञानवतामहम् ।। ३८

अहम् I दमयताम् of punishers दण्डः the sceptre अस्मि (I) am जिगीषताम् of those who seek to conquer नीतिः statesmanship अस्मि (I) am गुह्यानां of things secret मौनं silence च एव and also अस्मि (I) am ज्ञानवताम् of knowers ज्ञानं the knowledge.

38. Of punishers I am the sceptre; of those who seek to conquer, I am statesmanship; and also of things secret I am silence, and the knowledge of knowers am I.

यच्चापि सर्वभूतानां बीजं तदहमर्जुन ।
न तदस्ति विना यत्स्यान्मया भूतं चराचरम् ।। ३९

अर्जुन O Arjuna यत् what च and सर्वभूतानां of all beings बीजं the seed तत् that अहम् I अपि also मया विना without

Me यत् what स्यात् can exist तत् that चराचरम् moving or unmoving भूतं being न अस्ति there is not.

39. And whatsoever is the seed of all beings, that also am I, O Arjuna. There is no being, whether moving or unmoving, that can exist without Me.

नान्तोऽस्ति मम दिव्यानां विभूतीनां परन्तप।
एष तूद्देशतः प्रोक्तो विभूतेर्विस्तरो मया॥ ४०

परन्तप O scorcher of foes मम My दिव्यानां of divine विभूतीनां attributes अन्तः end न not अस्ति is एषः this तु but विभूतेः of attributes विस्तरः particulars मया by Me उद्देशतः brief statement प्रोक्तः has been stated.

40. There is no end of My divine attributes, O scorcher of foes; but this is a brief statement by Me of the particulars of My divine attributes.

यद्यद्विभूतिमत्सत्त्वं श्रीमदूर्जितमेव वा।
तत्तदेवावगच्छ त्वं मम तेजोंऽशसम्भवम्॥ ४१

विभूतिमत् Great श्रीमत् prosperous वा or एव also ऊर्जितम् powerful यत् यत् whatever सत्त्वं being तत् तत् that एव also मम My तेजोंऽशसम्भवम् a product of a part of splendour त्वं thou अवगच्छ know.

41. Whatever being there is great, prosperous, or powerful, that know thou to be a product of a part of My splendour.

अथवा बहुनैतेन किं ज्ञातेन तवार्जुन।
विष्टभ्याहमिदं कृत्स्नमेकांशेन स्थितो जगत्॥ ४२

अथवा Or अर्जुन O Arjuna एतेन by this बहुना (by) many ज्ञातेन to know तव thy किं what (avails) अहम् I इदं this कृत्स्नम् whole जगत् world एकांशेन by a portion विष्टभ्य supporting स्थित: exist.

42. Or what avails thee to know all this diversity, O Arjuna? (Know thou this that) I exist, supporting this whole world by a portion of Myself.

इति विभूतियोगो नाम दशमोऽध्याय: ॥

The end of the tenth chapter, designated,
Glimpses of the Divine Glory.

एकादशोऽध्यायः
(विश्वरूपदर्शनयोगः)
ELEVENTH CHAPTER
(The Vision of the Universal Form)

अर्जुन उवाच

मदनुग्रहाय परमं गुह्यमध्यात्मसंज्ञितम्।
यत्त्वयोक्तं वचस्तेन मोहोऽयं विगतो मम॥ १

अर्जुनः Arjuna उवाच said:

मदनुग्रहाय Out of compassion towards me परमं supremely गुह्यम् profound अध्यात्मसंज्ञितम् that which treats of the discrimination of Self and non-Self यत् that वचः words त्वया by Thee उक्तं spoken तेन by that मम my अयं this मोहः delusion विगतः is gone (has been dispelled).

Arjuna said:

1. By the supremely profound words, on the discrimination of Self, that have been spoken by Thee out of compassion towards me, this delusion of mine has been dispelled.

भवाप्ययौ हि भूतानां श्रुतौ विस्तरशो मया।
त्वत्तः कमलपत्राक्ष माहात्म्यमपि चाव्ययम्॥ २

कमलपत्राक्ष O Thou with eyes like the lotus-leaf त्वत्तः of Thee भूतानां of beings भवाप्ययौ the origin and dissolution मया by me विस्तरशः at length हि indeed श्रुतौ have been heard अव्ययम् inexhaustible माहात्म्यम् greatness अपि च and also.

2. Of Thee, O lotus-eyed, I have heard at length, of the origin and dissolution of beings, as also Thy inexhaustible greatness.

एवमेतद्यथात्थ त्वमात्मानं परमेश्वर।
द्रष्टुमिच्छामि ते रूपमैश्वरं पुरुषोत्तम॥ ३

परमेश्वर O Supreme Lord यथा as त्वम् Thou आत्मानं Thyself आत्थ hast declared एतत् it एवम् so पुरुषोत्तम O Supreme *Puruṣa* ते Thy ऐश्वरं रूपम् *Īśvara-Form* द्रष्टुम् to see इच्छामि (I) desire.

3. So it is, O Supreme Lord! as Thou hast declared Thyself. (Still) I desire to see Thy *Īśvara-Form,* O Supreme *Puruṣa.*

Thy Īśvara-Form: as possessed of omnipotence, omnipresence, infinite wisdom, strength, virtue, and splendour.

मन्यसे यदि तच्छक्यं मया द्रष्टुमिति प्रभो।
योगेश्वर ततो मे त्वं दर्शयात्मानमव्ययम्॥ ४

प्रभो O Lord यदि if तत् that मया by me द्रष्टुम् to see शक्यं capable इति as मन्यसे Thou thinkest ततः then योगेश्वर O

Lord of Yogis त्वं Thou मे me अव्ययम् immutable आत्मानम् Self दर्शय show.

4. If, O Lord, Thou thinkest me capable of seeing it, then, O Lord of Yogis, show me Thy immutable Self.

श्रीभगवानुवाच

पश्य मे पार्थ रूपाणि शतशोऽथ सहस्रशः ।
नानाविधानि दिव्यानि नानावर्णाकृतीनि च ॥ ५

श्रीभगवान् The Blessed Lord उवाच said:
पार्थ O son of Pṛthā मे My दिव्यानि celestial नानाविधानि different in kind नानावर्णाकृतीनि of various colours and shapes च and शतशः by the hundred अथ and सहस्रशः by the thousand रूपाणि forms पश्य behold.

The Blessed Lord said:
5. Behold, O son of Pṛthā, by hundreds and thousands, My different forms celestial, of various colours and shapes.

पश्यादित्यान्वसून् रुद्रानश्विनौ मरुतस्तथा ।
बहून्यदृष्टपूर्वाणि पश्याश्चर्याणि भारत ॥ ६

भारत O descendant of Bharata आदित्यान् the (twelve) *Ādityas* वसून् the (eight) *Vasus* रुद्रान् the (eleven) *Rudras* अश्विनौ the twin *Aśvins* तथा also मरुतः the *Maruts* (the forty-nine wind-gods) पश्य behold बहूनि many अदृष्टपूर्वाणि never seen before आश्चर्याणि wonders पश्य behold.

6. Behold the *Ādityas,* the *Vasus,* the *Rudras,* the twin Aś*vins,* and the *Maruts*; behold, O descendant of Bharata, many wonders never seen before.

इहैकस्थं जगत्कृत्स्नं पश्याद्य सचराचरम्।
मम देहे गुडाकेश यच्चान्यद्द्रष्टुमिच्छसि ॥ ७

गुडाकेश O Guḍākeśa (Arjuna) इह this मम My देहे (in) body एकस्थं centred in one कृत्स्नं whole सचराचरम् with the moving and the unmoving जगत् universe अन्यत् else च and यद् that द्रष्टुम् to see इच्छसि (thou) desirest अद्य now पश्य see.

7. See now, O Guḍākeśa, in this body of Mine, the whole universe centred in one—including the moving and the unmoving—and all else that thou desirest to see.

Centred in one: as part of My body.
All else: e.g., your success or defeat in the war about which you entertain a doubt (II. 6).

न तु मां शक्यसे द्रष्टुमनेनैव स्वचक्षुषा।
दिव्यं ददामि ते चक्षुः पश्य मे योगमैश्वरम् ॥ ८

अनेनैव With this स्वचक्षुषा with eye of thine तु but मां Me द्रष्टुम् to see न शक्यसे thou canst not ते (to) thee दिव्यं divine, supersensuous चक्षुः sight ददामि (I) give मे My ऐश्वरम् Supreme योगम् Yoga Power पश्य behold.

8. But thou canst not see Me with these eyes of thine; I give thee supersensuous sight; behold My supreme Yoga power.

Me: in My Universal Form.

सञ्जय उवाच

एवमुक्त्वा ततो राजन् महायोगेश्वरो हरिः ।
दर्शयामास पार्थाय परमं रूपमैश्वरम् ।। ९

सञ्जयः Sañjaya उवाच said:

राजन् O King (Dhṛtarāṣṭra) महायोगेश्वरः the Great Lord of Yoga हरिः Hari एवम् thus उक्त्वा having spoken ततः then पार्थाय unto the son of Pṛthā परमं Supreme ऐश्वरम् रूपम् *Īśvara*-Form दर्शयामास showed.

Sañjaya said:

9. Having thus spoken, O King, Hari, the Great Lord of Yoga, showed unto the son of Pṛthā, His Supreme *Īśvara*-Form:

अनेकवक्त्रनयनमनेकाद्भुतदर्शनम् ।
अनेकदिव्याभरणं दिव्यानेकोद्यतायुधम् ।। १०

अनेकवक्त्रनयनम् With numerous mouths and eyes अनेकाद्भुतदर्शनम् with numerous wondrous sight अनेकदिव्याभरणं with numerous celestial ornaments दिव्यानेकोद्यतायुधम् with numerous celestial weapons uplifted.

10. With numerous mouths and eyes, with numerous wondrous sights, with numerous celestial ornaments, with numerous celestial weapons uplifted;

दिव्यमाल्याम्बरधरं दिव्यगन्धानुलेपनम् ।
सर्वाश्चर्यमयं देवमनन्तं विश्वतोमुखम् ॥ ११

दिव्यमाल्याम्बरधरं Wearing celestial garlands and apparel दिव्यगन्धानुलेपनम् anointed with celestial-scented unguents सर्वाश्चर्यमयं the All-wonderful देवम् Resplendent अनन्तं Boundless विश्वतोमुखम् All-formed.

11. Wearing celestial garlands and apparel, anointed with celestial-scented unguents, the All-wonderful Resplendent, Boundless, and All-formed.

दिवि सूर्यसहस्रस्य भवेद्युगपदुत्थिता ।
यदि भाः सदृशी सा स्याद्भासस्तस्य महात्मनः ॥ १२

दिवि In the sky यदि if सूर्यसहस्रस्य of a thousand suns भा: splendour युगपद् at once उत्थिता भवेत् were to rise up सा that तस्य of that महात्मन: of the Mighty Being भास: splendour सदृशी like स्यात् would be.

12. If the splendour of a thousand suns were to rise up simultaneously in the sky, that would be like the splendour of that Mighty Being.

Mighty Being: The Universal Form.

The splendour of the Universal Form excels all others; it is indeed beyond compare.

तत्रैकस्थं जगत्कृत्स्नं प्रविभक्तमनेकधा।
अपश्यद्देवदेवस्य शरीरे पाण्डवस्तदा ॥ १३

तदा Then पाण्डव: the son of Pāṇḍu तत्र there देवदेवस्य of the God of gods शरीरे in the body अनेकधा in manifold ways प्रविभक्तम् divided कृत्स्नं whole जगत् universe एकस्थं resting in one अपश्यत् saw.

13. There in the body of the God of gods, the son of Pāṇḍu then saw the whole universe resting in one, with its manifold divisions.

ततः स विस्मयाविष्टो हृष्टरोमा धनञ्जयः।
प्रणम्य शिरसा देवं कृताञ्जलिरभाषत ॥ १४

ततः Then सः he धनञ्जयः Dhanañjaya विस्मयाविष्टः filled with wonder हृष्टरोमा with hairs standing on end देवं to the *Deva* शिरसा with (his) head प्रणम्य bending कृताञ्जलिः with joined palms अभाषत spoke.

14. Then Dhanañjaya, filled with wonder, with his hairs standing on end, bending down his head to the *Deva* in adoration, spoke with joined palms.

Deva: God, in His Universal Form.

अर्जुन उवाच

पश्यामि देवांस्तव देव देहे
सर्वांस्तथा भूतविशेषसङ्घान्।
ब्रह्माणमीशं कमलासनस्थ-
मृषींश्च सर्वानुरगांश्च दिव्यान्॥ १५

अर्जुन: Arjuna उवाच said:
देव O *Deva* तव Thy देहे in the body सर्वान् all देवान् the *Devas* तथा and भूतविशेषसङ्घान् hosts of all grades of beings ईशं the Lord कमलासनस्थम् seated on the lotus ब्रह्माणम् Brahmā ऋषीन् *Ṛṣis* च and सर्वान् all दिव्यान् celestial उरगान् serpents च and पश्यामि (I) see.

Arjuna said:

15. I see all the *Devas, O Deva,* in Thy body, and hosts of all grades of beings; Brahmā, the Lord, seated on the lotus, and all the *Ṛṣis* and celestial serpents.

अनेकबाहूदरवक्त्रनेत्रं
पश्यामि त्वां सर्वतोऽनन्तरूपम्।
नान्तं न मध्यं न पुनस्तवादिं
पश्यामि विश्वेश्वर विश्वरूप॥ १६

विश्वेश्वर O Lord of the universe विश्वरूप O Universal Form अनेकबाहूदरवक्त्रनेत्रं with manifold arms, stomachs, mouths, and eyes अनन्तरूपम् of boundless form त्वां Thee सर्वत: on every side पश्यामि (I) see तव of Thee पुन: also न

neither अन्तं the end न nor मध्यं the middle न nor आदिं the beginning पश्यामि do (I) see.

16. I see Thee of boundless form on every side with manifold arms, stomachs, mouths, and eyes; neither the end nor the middle, nor also the beginning of Thee do I see, O Lord of the universe, O Universal Form.

किरीटिनं गदिनं चक्रिणं च
तेजोराशिं सर्वतो दीप्तिमन्तम् ।
पश्यामि त्वां दुर्निरीक्ष्यं समन्ताद्-
दीप्तानलार्कद्युतिमप्रमेयम् ।। १७

किरीटिनं One with diadem गदिनं with club चक्रिणं with discus च and सर्वतः everywhere दीप्तिमन्तम् shining तेजोराशिं a mass of radiance दुर्निरीक्ष्यं very difficult to look at दीप्तानलार्कद्युतिम् blazing like burning fire and sun अप्रमेयम् immeasurable त्वां Thee समन्तात् all around पश्यामि (I) see.

17. I see Thee with diadem, club, and discus; a mass of radiance shining everywhere, very difficult to look at, all around blazing like burning fire and sun, and immeasurable.

त्वमक्षरं परमं वेदितव्यं
त्वमस्य विश्वस्य परं निधानम् ।
त्वमव्ययः शाश्वतधर्मगोप्ता
सनातनस्त्वं पुरुषो मतो मे ।। १८

त्वम् Thou अक्षरं the Imperishable परमं the Supreme Being वेदितव्यं the one thing to be known त्वम् Thou अस्य विश्वस्य of this universe परं the great निधानम् Refuge त्वम् Thou अव्ययः the undying शाश्वतधर्मगोप्ता Guardian of the Eternal Dharma त्वं Thou सनातनः the Ancient पुरुषः *Puruṣa* मे मतः I ween.

18. Thou art the Imperishable, the Supreme Being, the one thing to be known. Thou art the great Refuge of this universe; Thou art the undying Guardian of the Eternal Dharma, Thou art the Ancient *Puruṣa,* I ween.

अनादिमध्यान्तमनन्तवीर्य-
मनन्तबाहुं शशिसूर्यनेत्रम्।
पश्यामि त्वां दीप्तहुताशवक्त्रं
स्वतेजसा विश्वमिदं तपन्तम्॥ १९

अनादिमध्यान्तम् Without beginning, middle, or end अनन्तवीर्यम् infinite in power अनन्तबाहुं of manifold arms शशिसूर्यनेत्रम् the sun and the moon (Thy) eyes दीप्तहुताशवक्त्रं the burning fire (Thy) mouth स्वतेजसा with Thy radiance इदं this विश्वम् universe तपन्तम् heating त्वां Thee पश्यामि (I) see.

19. I see Thee without beginning, middle, or end, infinite in power, of manifold arms; the sun and the moon Thine eyes, the burning fire Thy mouth; heating the whole universe with Thy radiance.

द्यावापृथिव्योरिदमन्तरं हि
व्याप्तं त्वयैकेन दिशश्च सर्वाः।
दृष्ट्वाऽद्भुतं रूपमुग्रं तवेदं
लोकत्रयं प्रव्यथितं महात्मन्॥ २०

महात्मन् O Great-souled One द्यावापृथिव्योः (of) heaven and earth इदम् this अन्तरं space betwixt एकेन alone त्वया by Thee हि indeed व्याप्तं are filled सर्वाः all दिशः quarters च and तव Thy अद्भुतं wonderful इदं this उग्रं awful रूपम् form दृष्ट्वा having seen लोकत्रयं the three worlds प्रव्यथितं are trembling (with fear).

20. This space betwixt heaven and earth and all the quarters are filled by Thee alone; having seen this, Thy marvellous and awful Form, the three worlds are trembling with fear, O Great-souled One.

अमी हि त्वां सुरसङ्घा विशन्ति
केचिद्भीताः प्राञ्जलयो गृणन्ति।
स्वस्तीत्युक्त्वा महर्षिसिद्धसङ्घाः
स्तुवन्ति त्वां स्तुतिभिः पुष्कलाभिः॥ २१

अमी These सुरसङ्घा hosts of *Devas* हि verily त्वां Thee विशन्ति enter केचिद् some भीताः in fear प्राञ्जलयः with joined palms गृणन्ति extol महर्षिसिद्धसङ्घाः bands of great *Ṛṣis* and *Siddhas* "स्वस्ति" "May it be well" इति thus उक्त्वा saying पुष्कलाभिः splendid स्तुतिभिः with hymns त्वां Thee स्तुवन्ति praise.

21. Verily, into Thee enter these hosts of *Devas;* some extol Thee in fear with joined palms; "May it be well!" thus saying, bands of great *Ṛṣis* and *Siddhas* praise Thee with splendid hymns.

रुद्रादित्या वसवो ये च साध्या
विश्वेऽश्विनौ मरुतश्चोष्मपाश्च ।
गन्धर्वयक्षासुरसिद्धसङ्घा
वीक्षन्ते त्वां विस्मिताश्चैव सर्वे ।। २२

रुद्रादित्याः The *Rudras* and *Ādityas* वसवः *Vasus* ये those that च and साध्याः *Sādhyas* विश्वे *Viśva-Devas* अश्विनौ the two *Aśvins* मरुतः *Maruts* च and उष्मपाः *Uṣmapās* च and गन्धर्वयक्षासुरसिद्धसङ्घाः hosts of *Gandharvas, Yakṣas, Asuras* and *Siddhas* सर्वे all विस्मिताः एव quite astounded त्वां Thee च and वीक्षन्ते are looking at.

22. The *Rudras, Ādityas, Vasus, Sādhyas, Viśva-Devas,* the two *Aśvins, Maruts, Uṣmapās,* and hosts of *Gandharvas, Yakṣas, Asuras,* and *Siddhas*—all these are looking at Thee, all quite astounded.

Uṣmapās: The Pitṛs.

रूपं महत्ते बहुवक्त्रनेत्रं
महाबाहो बहुबाहूरुपादम् ।
बहूदरं बहुदंष्ट्राकरालं
दृष्ट्वा लोकाः प्रव्यथितास्तथाहम् ।। २३

महाबाहो O mighty-armed बहुवक्त्रनेत्रं with many mouths and eyes बहुबाहूरुपादम् with many arms, thighs, and feet बहूदरं with many stomachs बहुदंष्ट्राकरालं fearful with many tusks ते Thy महत् immeasurable रूपं Form दृष्ट्वा having seen लोका: worlds प्रव्यथिता: are terrified अहम् I तथा so also.

23. Having seen Thy immeasurable Form—with many mouths and eyes, O mighty-armed, with many arms, thighs, and feet, with many stomachs, and fearful with many tusks—the worlds are terrified, and so am I.

नभःस्पृशं दीप्तमनेकवर्णं
व्यात्ताननं दीप्तविशालनेत्रम्।
दृष्ट्वा हि त्वां प्रव्यथितान्तरात्मा
धृतिं न विन्दामि शमं च विष्णो॥ २४

विष्णो O Viṣṇu नभःस्पृशं touching the sky दीप्तम् shining अनेकवर्णं in many a colour व्यात्ताननं with mouths wide open दीप्तविशालनेत्रम् with large fiery eyes त्वां Thee हि indeed दृष्ट्वा on seeing प्रव्यथितान्तरात्मा terrified at heart (अहं I) धृतिं patience, courage शमं peace च and न not विन्दामि find.

24. On seeing Thee touching the sky, shining in many a colour, with mouths wide open, with large fiery eyes, I am terrified at heart, and find no courage nor peace, O Viṣṇu.

दंष्ट्राकरालानि च ते मुखानि
दृष्ट्वैव कालानलसन्निभानि।
दिशो न जाने न लभे च शर्म
प्रसीद देवेश जगन्निवास ।। २५

देवेश O Lord of *Devas* दंष्ट्राकरालानि fearful with tusks कालानलसन्निभानि (blazing) like *Pralaya*-fires च and ते Thy मुखानि mouths दृष्ट्वा एव having seen दिशः the four quarters न जाने I know not शर्म peace न च nor लभे do (I) find जगन्निवास O Abode of the universe प्रसीद have mercy.

25. Having seen Thy mouths, fearful with tusks, (blazing) like *Pralaya*-fires, I know not the four quarters, nor do I find peace; have mercy, O Lord of the *Devas,* O Abode of the universe.

Pralaya-fires: The fires which consume the worlds at the time of the final dissolution (*Pralaya*) of the universe.

I know . . . quarters: I cannot distinguish the East from the West, nor the North from the South.

अमी च त्वां धृतराष्ट्रस्य पुत्राः
सर्वे सहैवावनिपालसङ्घैः।
भीष्मो द्रोणः सूतपुत्रस्तथासौ
सहास्मदीयैरपि योधमुख्यैः ।। २६
वक्त्राणि ते त्वरमाणा विशन्ति
दंष्ट्राकरालानि भयानकानि।
केचिद्विलग्ना दशनान्तरेषु
संदृश्यन्ते चूर्णितैरुत्तमाङ्गैः ।। २७

अवनिपालसङ्घैः Hosts of kings of the earth सहैव with अमी those च and धृतराष्ट्रस्य of Dhṛtarāṣṭra सर्वे all पुत्राः sons तथा and भीष्मः Bhīṣma द्रोणः Droṇa असौ that सूतपुत्रः Sūtaputra अस्मदीयैः (with those) of ours अपि also योधमुख्यैः (with) warrior chiefs सह with त्वरमाणाः precipitately ते Thy दंष्ट्राकरालानि terrible with tusks भयानकानि fearful to behold वक्त्राणि mouths त्वां Thee विशन्ति enter केचित् some चूर्णितैः crushed to powder उत्तमाङ्गैः with (their) heads दशनान्तरेषु in the gaps betwixt the teeth विलग्नाः sticking संदृश्यन्ते are found.

26–27. All those sons of Dhṛtarāṣṭra, with hosts of monarchs, Bhīṣma, Droṇa and Sūtaputra, with the warrior chiefs of ours, enter precipitately into Thy mouth, terrible with tusks and fearful to behold. Some are found sticking in the interstices of Thy teeth, with their heads crushed to powder.

Sūtaputra: The son of a charioteer, Karṇa.

यथा नदीनां बहवोऽम्बुवेगाः
समुद्रमेवाभिमुखा द्रवन्ति ।
तथा तवामी नरलोकवीरा
विशन्ति वक्त्राण्यभिविज्वलन्ति ॥ २८

यथा As नदीनां of rivers बहवः many अम्बुवेगाः water-currents अभिमुखाः towards समुद्रम् the ocean एव verily द्रवन्ति flow तथा so अमी those नरलोकवीराः heroes in the world of men अभिविज्वलन्ति fiercely flaming तव Thy वक्त्राणि mouths विशन्ति enter.

28. Verily, as the many torrents of rivers flow towards the ocean, so do those heroes in the world of men enter Thy fiercely flaming mouths.

यथा प्रदीप्तं ज्वलनं पतङ्गा
विशन्ति नाशाय समृद्धवेगाः ।
तथैव नाशाय विशन्ति लोका-
स्तवापि वक्त्राणि समृद्धवेगाः ॥ २९

यथा As पतङ्गाः moths समृद्धवेगाः with precipitous speed नाशाय to perish प्रदीप्तं blazing ज्वलनं fire विशन्ति rush into तथा just so समृद्धवेगाः with precipitous speed लोकाः creatures अपि also नाशाय to perish एव only तव Thy वक्त्राणि mouths विशन्ति rush into.

29. As moths precipitately rush into a blazing fire only to perish, even so do these creatures also precipitately rush into Thy mouths only to perish.

28 and 29—The two similes vividly illustrate how the assembled warriors rush to destruction, out of their uncontrollable nature, with or without discrimination.

लेलिह्यसे ग्रसमानः समन्ता-
ल्लोकान्समग्रान्वदनैर्ज्वलद्भिः ।
तेजोभिरापूर्य जगत्समग्रं
भासस्तवोग्राः प्रतपन्ति विष्णो ॥ ३०

ज्वलद्भिः Flaming वदनैः with mouths समग्रान् all लोकान् the worlds ग्रसमानः swallowing समन्तात् on every side लेलिह्यसे Thou art licking Thy lips विष्णो O Viṣṇu तव Thy उग्राः fierce भासः rays तेजोभिः with radiance समग्रं the whole जगत् world आपूर्य filling प्रतपन्ति are burning.

30. Swallowing all the worlds on every side with Thy flaming mouths, Thou art licking Thy lips. Thy fierce rays, filling the whole world with radiance, are burning O Viṣṇu!

Licking Thy lips: consuming entirely, enjoying it, as it were.

आख्याहि मे को भवानुग्ररूपो
नमोऽस्तु ते देववर प्रसीद ।
विज्ञातुमिच्छामि भवन्तमाद्यं
न हि प्रजानामि तव प्रवृत्तिम् ।। ३१

उग्ररूपः Fierce in form भवान् Thou कः who (art) मे me आख्याहि tell ते to Thee नमः salutation अस्तु be देववर O Supreme *Deva* प्रसीद have mercy आद्यं the Primeval One भवन्तम् Thee विज्ञातुम् to know इच्छामि (I) desire हि indeed तव Thy प्रवृत्तिं purpose न not प्रजानामि (I) know.

31. Tell me who Thou art, fierce in form. Salutation to Thee, O Supreme *Deva,* have mercy. I desire to know Thee, O Primeval One. I know not indeed Thy purpose.

श्रीभगवानुवाच

कालोऽस्मि लोकक्षयकृत्प्रवृद्धो
लोकान्समाहर्तुमिह प्रवृत्तः ।
ऋतेऽपि त्वां न भविष्यन्ति सर्वे
येऽवस्थिताः प्रत्यनीकेषु योधाः ।। ३२

श्रीभगवान् The Blessed Lord उवाच said:

लोकक्षयकृत् World-destroying प्रवृद्धः mighty कालः Time अस्मि (I) am लोकान् world समाहर्तुम् to infold इह here प्रवृत्तः engaged त्वां thee ऋते without अपि even प्रत्यनीकेषु in hostile armies ये these योधाः warriors अवस्थिताः arrayed सर्वे न none भविष्यन्ति shall live.

The Blessed Lord said:

32. I am the mighty world-destroying Time, here made manifest for the purpose of infolding the world. Even without thee, none of the warriors arrayed in the hostile armies shall live.

Even without thee, etc.: Even without thy instrumentality, i.e., even if, thou, O Arjuna, wouldst not fight, the end of all these warriors is inevitable, because I as the all-destroying Time have already killed them; so thy instrumentality in that work is insignificant.

तस्मात्त्वमुत्तिष्ठ यशो लभस्व
जित्वा शत्रून् भुङ्क्ष्व राज्यं समृद्धम् ।
मयैवैते निहताः पूर्वमेव
निमित्तमात्रं भव सव्यसाचिन् ।। ३३

तस्मात् Therefore त्वम् thou उत्तिष्ठ do arise यशः fame लभस्व acquire शत्रून् enemies जित्वा after conquering समृद्धम् the unrivalled राज्यं dominion भुङ्क्ष्व enjoy मया by Myself एव verily एते they पूर्वम् already एव even निहताः have been slain सव्यसाचिन् O Savyasācin (त्वं thou) निमित्तमात्रं an apparent cause भव be.

33. Therefore do thou arise and acquire fame. Conquer the enemies, and enjoy the unrivalled dominion. Verily by Myself have they been already slain; be thou merely an apparent cause, O Savyasācin (Arjuna).

Be thou . . . cause: People will think thee as the vanquisher of thy enemies, whom even the Devas cannot kill, and thus thou wilt gain glory; but thou art only an instrument in My hand.

Savyasācin: one who could shoot arrows even with his left hand.

द्रोणञ्च भीष्मञ्च जयद्रथञ्च
कर्णं तथान्यानपि योधवीरान्।
मया हतांस्त्वं जहि मा व्यथिष्ठा
युध्यस्व जेतासि रणे सपत्नान्॥ ३४

द्रोणं Droṇa च and भीष्मं Bhīṣma च and जयद्रथं Jayadratha च and कर्णं Karṇa तथा as well as अन्यान् others योधवीरान् brave warriors अपि already मया by Me हतान् killed त्वं thou जहि do kill मा not व्यथिष्ठाः be distressed with fear रणे in battle सपत्नान् the enemies जेतासि shalt conquer युध्यस्व fight.

34. Droṇa, Bhīṣma, Jayadratha, Karṇa as well as other brave warriors—these already killed by Me, do thou kill. Be not distressed with fear; fight, and thou shalt conquer thy enemies in battle.

Already killed by Me: so do not be afraid of incurring sin by killing Droṇa, Bhīṣma, and others though they are venerable to you as your Guru, grandsire, etc.

Distressed with fear: as regards success because these great warriors are regarded as invincible.

सञ्जय उवाच

एतच्छ्रुत्वा वचनं केशवस्य
कृताञ्जलिर्वेपमानः किरीटी ।
नमस्कृत्वा भूय एवाह कृष्णं
सगद्गदं भीतभीतः प्रणम्य ।। ३५

सञ्जयः Sañjaya उवाच said:

केशवस्य Of Keśava एतत् this वचनं speech श्रुत्वा having heard वेपमानः trembling किरीटी the diademed one कृताञ्जलिः with joined palms नमस्कृत्वा prostrating (himself) भीतभीतः overwhelmed with fear प्रणम्य bowing down भूयः एव again सगद्गदं in a choked voice कृष्णं to Kṛṣṇa आह addressed.

Sañjaya said:

35. Having heard this speech of Keśava, the diademed one (Arjuna), with joined palms, trembling, prostrated himself, and again addressed Kṛṣṇa in a choked voice, bowing down, overwhelmed with fear.

अर्जुन उवाच

स्थाने हृषीकेश तव प्रकीर्त्या
जगत् प्रहृष्यत्यनुरज्यते च ।
रक्षांसि भीतानि दिशो द्रवन्ति
सर्वे नमस्यन्ति च सिद्धसङ्घाः ॥ ३६

अर्जुन: Arjuna उवाच said:

हृषीकेश O Hṛṣīkeśa तव Thy प्रकीर्त्या in praise जगत् the world प्रहृष्यति is delighted अनुरज्यते rejoices च and रक्षांसि *Rākṣasas* भीतानि in fear दिश: to all quarters द्रवन्ति fly सर्वे all सिद्धसङ्घा: the hosts of *Siddhas* च and नमस्यन्ति bow (to Thee) स्थाने it is meet.

Arjuna said:

36. It is meet, O Hṛṣīkeśa, that the world is delighted and rejoices in Thy praise, that *Rākṣasas* fly in fear to all quarters and all the hosts of *Siddhas* bow down to Thee in adoration.

कस्माच्च ते न नमेरन्महात्मन्
गरीयसे ब्रह्मणोऽप्यादिकर्त्रे ।
अनन्त देवेश जगन्निवास
त्वमक्षरं सदसत्तत्परं यत् ॥ ३७

महात्मन् O Great-souled One अनन्त O Infinite देवेश O Lord of the *Devas* जगन्निवास O Abode of the universe ब्रह्मण: of Brahmā अपि even गरीयसे greater आदिकर्त्रे the Primal Cause च and ते to Thee कस्मात् why न not नमेरन् they should bow सत् the Being असत् the non-Being परं

Beyond (them) यत् which अक्षरं the Imperishable तत् That च and त्वम् Thou (art).

37. And why should they not, O Great-souled One, bow to Thee, greater than, and the Primal Cause of even Brahmā, O Infinite Being, O Lord of the *Devas,* O Abode of the universe ? Thou art the Imperishable, the Being and the non-Being, (as well as) That which is Beyond (them).

Brahmā: the *Hiraṇyagarbha.*

The Being and the non-Being, etc.: The *Sat* (manifested) and the *Asat* (unmanifested), which form the *Upādhis* (adjuncts) of the *Akṣara* (Imperishable); as such He is spoken of as the *Sat* and the *Asat.* In reality, the Imperishable transcends the *Sat* and the *Asat.*

त्वमादिदेवः पुरुषः पुराण-
स्त्वमस्य विश्वस्य परं निधानम्।
वेत्ताऽसि वेद्यं च परं च धाम
त्वया ततं विश्वमनन्तरूप ॥ ३८

अनन्तरूप O boundless Form त्वम् Thou आदिदेव: the Primal *Deva* पुराण: the Ancient पुरुष: *Puruṣa* त्वम् Thou अस्य विश्वस्य of this universe परं the Supreme निधानम् Refuge वेत्ता the Knower च and वेद्यं the One Thing to be known च and परं the Supreme धाम Goal असि (Thou) art त्वया by Thee विश्वम् the universe ततं is pervaded.

38. Thou art the Primal *Deva,* the Ancient *Puruṣa*; Thou art the Supreme Refuge of this

universe, Thou art the Knower, and the One Thing to be known; Thou art the Supreme Goal. By Thee is the universe pervaded, O boundless Form.

वायुर्यमोऽग्निर्वरुणः शशाङ्कः
प्रजापतिस्त्वं प्रपितामहश्च ।
नमो नमस्तेऽस्तु सहस्रकृत्वः
पुनश्च भूयोऽपि नमो नमस्ते ।। ३९

त्वं Thou (art) वायुः Vāyu यमः Yama अग्निः Agni वरुणः Varuṇa शशाङ्कः the Moon प्रजापतिः Prajāpati प्रपितामहः the Great-grandfather च and ते to Thee नमः नमः salutation, salutation अस्तु be सहस्रकृत्वः a thousand times पुनः again च and भूयः अपि and again ते to Thee नमः नमः salutation, salutation.

39. Thou art Vāyu, Yama, Agni, Varuṇa, the Moon, Prajāpati, and the Great-grandfather. Salutation, salutation to Thee, a thousand times, and again and again salutation, salutation to Thee!

Vāyu ... Moon: The gods of wind, death, fire, waters, and the moon.

The Great-grandfather: The creator even of Brahmā who is known as the Grandfather.

नमः पुरस्तादथ पृष्ठतस्ते
नमोऽस्तु ते सर्वत एव सर्व ।
अनन्तवीर्यामितविक्रमस्त्वं
सर्वं समाप्नोषि ततोऽसि सर्वः ।। ४०

सर्व O All ते to Thee पुरस्तात् before अथ and पृष्ठत: behind नम: salutation ते to Thee सर्वत: एव on every side नम: salutation अस्तु be अनन्तवीर्या infinite in power अमितविक्रम: infinite in prowess त्वं Thou सर्वं all समाप्नोषि pervadest तत: wherefore सर्व: all असि Thou art.

40. Salutation to Thee before and behind, salutation to Thee on every side, O All! Thou, infinite in power and infinite in prowess, pervadest all; wherefore Thou art All.

On every side: As Thou art present everywhere.
Pervadest: by thy One Self.

सखेति मत्वा प्रसभं यदुक्तं
हे कृष्ण हे यादव हे सखेति।
अजानता महिमानं तवेदं
मया प्रमादात्प्रणयेन वापि॥ ४१
यच्चावहासार्थमसत्कृतोऽसि
विहारशय्यासनभोजनेषु।
एकोऽथवाप्यच्युत तत्समक्षं
तत्क्षामये त्वामहमप्रमेयम्॥ ४२

तव Thy महिमानं greatness इदं this च and अजानता unconscious of मया by me प्रमादात् from carelessness प्रणयेन due to love वा or अपि merely सखा friend इति as मत्वा regarding हे कृष्ण O Kṛṣṇa हे यादव O Yādava हे सखे O friend इति as प्रसभं presumptuously यत् whatever उक्तं said अच्युत O Acyuta विहारशय्यासनभोजनेषु while walking, reposing, sitting, or at meals एक: when alone अथवा or अपि even तत्समक्षं in company अवहासार्थम् for the sake of fun यत् in whatever way असत्कृत: disrespectfully treated असि Thou art अहम् I अप्रमेयम् Immeasurable त्वाम् Thee तत् that क्षामये implore to forgive.

41–42. Whatever I have presumptuously said from carelessness or love, addressing Thee as "O Kṛṣṇa, O Yādava, O friend" regarding Thee merely as a friend, unconscious of this Thy greatness—in whatever way I may have heen disrespectful to Thee in fun, while walking, reposing, sitting, or at meals, when alone (with Thee), O Acyuta, or in company— I implore Thee, Immeasurable One, to forgive all this.

Love: Confidence born of affection.
In company: in the presence of others.

पितासि लोकस्य चराचरस्य
त्वमस्य पूज्यश्च गुरुर्गरीयान्।
न त्वत्समोऽस्त्यभ्यधिकः कुतोऽन्यो
लोकत्रयेऽप्यप्रतिमप्रभाव ॥ ४३

अप्रतिमप्रभाव Of power incomparable त्वम् Thou चराचरस्य moving and unmoving लोकस्य of the world पिता Father असि (Thou) art पूज्य: the object of worship अस्य its च and गुरुर्गरीयान् greater than the great लोकत्रये in the three worlds अपि even त्वत्सम: equal to Thee न not अस्ति is अभ्यधिक: surpassing अन्य: any other कुत: whence.

43. Thou art the Father of the world, moving and unmoving; the object of its worship; greater than the great. There exists none who is equal to Thee in the three worlds; who then can excel Thee, O Thou of power incomparable?

None ... to Thee: There cannot be two or more *Īśvaras*; if there were, the world could not get on as it does. When one *Īśvara* desires to create, another may desire to destroy. Who knows that all the different *Īśvaras* would be of one mind, as they would all be independent of each other?

तस्मात्प्रणम्य प्रणिधाय कायं
प्रसादये त्वामहमीशमीड्यम् ।
पितेव पुत्रस्य सखेव सख्युः
प्रियः प्रियायार्हसि देव सोढुम् ॥ ४४

देव O *Deva* तस्मात् so अहम् I कायं (my) body प्रणिधाय having prostrated प्रणम्य saluting ईड्यम् adorable ईशम् Lord त्वाम् Thee प्रसादये crave forgiveness पुत्रस्य of the son पिता a father इव as सख्युः of a dear friend सखा a friend इव as प्रियायाः of one's love प्रियः a beloved one (इव as) सोढुम् to forgive अर्हसि Thou shouldest.

44. So prostrating my body in adoration, I crave Thy forgiveness, Lord adorable! As a father forgiveth his son, friend a dear friend, a beloved one his love, even so shouldst Thou forgive me, O *Deva*.

अदृष्टपूर्वं हृषितोऽस्मि दृष्ट्वा
भयेन च प्रव्यथितं मनो मे।
तदेव मे दर्शय देव रूपं
प्रसीद देवेश जगन्निवास ॥ ४५

देव O *Deva* अदृष्टपूर्वं what was never seen before दृष्ट्वा having seen हृषित: overjoyed अस्मि I am भयेन with terror च yet मे my मन: mind प्रव्यथितं is distracted तत् that रूपं Form एव only मे me दर्शय show देवेश O Lord of *Devas* जगन्निवास O Abode of the universe प्रसीद have mercy.

45. Overjoyed am I to have seen what I saw never before; yet my mind is distracted with terror. Show me, O *Deva,* only that Form of Thine. Have mercy, O Lord of *Devas,* O Abode of the universe.

किरीटिनं गदिनं चक्रहस्त-
मिच्छामि त्वां द्रष्टुमहं तथैव।
तेनैव रूपेण चतुर्भुजेन
सहस्रबाहो भव विश्वमूर्ते ॥ ४६

अहं I तथा एव as before त्वां Thee किरीटिनं diademed गदिनं bearing a mace चक्रहस्तम् with a discus in the hand द्रष्टुम् to see इच्छामि I desire सहस्रबाहो O (Thou) of thousand arms विश्वमूर्ते of universal Form तेनैव that same चतुर्भुजेन four-armed रूपेण of Form भव be.

46. Diademed, bearing a mace and a discus, Thee I desire to see as before. Assume that same four-armed Form, O Thou of thousand arms, of universal Form.

श्रीभगवानुवाच

मया प्रसन्नेन तवार्जुनेदं
रूपं परं दर्शितमात्मयोगात्।
तेजोमयं विश्वमनन्तमाद्यं
यन्मे त्वदन्येन न दृष्टपूर्वम्॥ ४७

श्रीभगवान् The Blessed Lord उवाच said.

अर्जुन O Arjuna प्रसन्नेन gracious मया by Me आत्मयोगात् by My own Yoga power तव to thee इदं this तेजोमयं resplendent अनन्तम् infinite आद्यं primeval मे of Mine परं supreme विश्वम् universal रूपं Form दर्शितम् has been shown यत् which त्वदन्येन by any other than thyself न not दृष्टपूर्वम् hath been seen before.

The Blessed Lord said:

47. Graciously have I shown to thee, O Arjuna, this Form supreme, by My own Yoga power, this resplendent, primeval, infinite universal Form of Mine, which hath not been seen before by anyone else.

न वेदयज्ञाध्ययनैर्न दानै-
र्न च क्रियाभिर्न तपोभिरुग्रैः।
एवंरूपः शक्य अहं नृलोके
द्रष्टुं त्वदन्येन कुरुप्रवीर॥ ४८

कुरुप्रवीर O great hero of the Kurus न neither वेदयज्ञाध्ययनैः by the study of the Veda and of *Yajña* न nor दानैः by gifts न च nor क्रियाभिः by rituals न nor उग्रैः severe

तपोभि: by austerities एवंरूप: in this Form अहं I त्वदन्येन by any other than thee नृलोके in the human world द्रष्टुं to be seen शक्य: possible.

48. Neither by the study of the Veda and *Yajña,* nor by gifts, nor by rituals, nor by severe austerities, am I seen in this Form, in the human world, by anyone other than thee, O great hero of the Kurus.

मा ते व्यथा मा च विमूढभावो
दृष्ट्वा रूपं घोरमीदृङ् ममेदम्।
व्यपेतभीः प्रीतमनाः पुनस्त्वं
तदेव मे रूपमिदं प्रपश्य॥ ४९

ईदृङ् So घोरम् terrible मम of Mine इदम् this रूपं Form दृष्ट्वा having seen मा not ते thine व्यथा fear विमूढभाव: bewildered state (अस्तु be) मा च nor व्यपेतभी: with (thy) fears dispelled प्रीतमना: with gladdened heart च and पुन: again त्वं thou मे of Mine तत् इदं this previous रूपम् एव Form प्रपश्य see (now).

49. Be not afraid nor bewildered, having beheld this Form of Mine, so terrific. With thy fears dispelled and with gladdened heart, now see again this previous Form of Mine.

सञ्जय उवाच

इत्यर्जुनं वासुदेवस्तथोक्त्वा
स्वकं रूपं दर्शयामास भूयः।

आश्वासयामास च भीतमेनं
भूत्वा पुनः सौम्यवपुर्महात्मा ॥ ५०

सञ्जयः Sañjaya उवाच said:

वासुदेवः Vāsudeva अर्जुनं to Arjuna इति thus उक्त्वा having spoken भूयः again तथा so स्वकं His own रूपं Form दर्शयामास showed महात्मा the Great-souled One सौम्यवपुः of gentle Form भूत्वा being पुनः again भीतम् who was terrified एनं him आश्वासयामास pacified च and.

Sañjaya said:

50. So Vāsudeva, having thus spoken to Arjuna, showed again His own Form; and the Great-souled One, assuming His gentle Form, pacified him who was terrified.

अर्जुन उवाच

दृष्ट्वेदं मानुषं रूपं तव सौम्यं जनार्दन ।
इदानीमस्मि संवृत्तः सचेताः प्रकृतिं गतः ॥ ५१

अर्जुनः Arjuna उवाच said:

जनार्दन O Janārdana तव Thy इदं this सौम्यं gentle मानुषं human रूपं Form दृष्ट्वा having seen इदानीम् now (अहं I) सचेताः with thoughts संवृत्तः composed अस्मि am प्रकृतिं (my) nature गतः restored.

Arjuna said:

51. Having seen this Thy gentle human Form, O Janārdana, my thoughts are now composed, and I am restored to my nature.

श्रीभगवानुवाच

सुदुर्दर्शमिदं रूपं दृष्टवानसि यन्मम।
देवा अप्यस्य रूपस्य नित्यं दर्शनकाङ्क्षिणः ॥ ५२

श्रीभगवान् The Blessed Lord उवाच said:

मम Mine इदं this सुदुर्दर्शम् very hard to see यत् which रूपं Form दृष्टवान् असि thou hast seen देवा: *Devas* अपि even अस्य रूपस्य of this Form नित्यं ever दर्शनकाङ्क्षिण: (are) desirous to behold.

The Blessed Lord said:

52. Very hard indeed it is to see this Form of Mine which thou hast seen. Even the *Devas* ever long to behold this Form.

नाहं वेदैर्न तपसा न दानेन न चेज्यया।
शक्य एवंविधो द्रष्टुं दृष्टवानसि मां यथा ॥ ५३

यथा As मां Me दृष्टवान् असि (thou) hast seen एवंविध: like this अहं I न neither वेदै: by the Vedas न nor तपसा by austerity न nor दानेन by gifts न nor इज्यया by sacrifice च and also द्रष्टुं to be seen शक्य: (am) possible.

53. Neither by the Vedas, nor by austerity, nor by gifts, nor by sacrifice can I be seen as thou hast seen Me.

भक्त्या त्वनन्यया शक्य अहमेवंविधोऽर्जुन।
ज्ञातुं द्रष्टुञ्च तत्त्वेन प्रवेष्टुं च परन्तप ॥ ५४

परन्तप O scorcher of foes अर्जुन Arjuna अनन्यया single-minded भक्त्या by devotion तु but एवंविध: in this Form अहम् I तत्त्वेन in reality ज्ञातुं to be known द्रष्टुं to be seen च and प्रवेष्टुं to be entered into च and also शक्य: (am) possible.

54. But by single-minded devotion I may in this form, be known, O Arjuna, and seen in reality, and also entered into, O scorcher of foes.

Single-minded devotion: That devotion which never seeks any other object but the Lord alone, and consequently cognises no other object but the Lord.

मत्कर्मकृन्मत्परमो मद्भक्तः सङ्गवर्जितः।
निर्वैरः सर्वभूतेषु यः स मामेति पाण्डव ॥ ५५

पाण्डव O Pāṇḍava य: who मत्कर्मकृत् does work for Me मत्परम: has Me for his goal मद्भक्त: is devoted to Me सङ्गवर्जित: is freed from attachment सर्वभूतेषु towards all creatures निर्वैर: bearing no enmity च and स: he माम् Me एति enters into.

55. He who does work for Me alone and has Me for his goal, is devoted to Me, is freed from attachment, and bears enmity towards no creature —he entereth into Me, O Pāṇḍava.

Does work for me alone: Serves Me alone in all forms and manner of ways, with his whole heart and soul, and thus does not become attached to them.

He alone, whose devotion takes the forms as described in this *Śloka* can know and realise Him as He is in reality, and subsequently become one with Him.

इति विश्वरूपदर्शनं नाम एकादशोऽध्यायः ॥

The end of the eleventh chapter, designated,
The Vision of the Universal Form.

द्वादशोऽध्यायः
(भक्तियोगः)
TWELFTH CHAPTER
(The Way of Devotion)

अर्जुन उवाच

एवं सततयुक्ता ये भक्तास्त्वां पर्युपासते।
ये चाप्यक्षरमव्यक्तं तेषां के योगवित्तमाः ।। १

अर्जुनः Arjuna उवाच said:

एवं Thus सततयुक्ताः ever-steadfast ये those भक्ताः devotees त्वां Thee पर्युपासते worship ये those च and अपि also अव्यक्तं the Unmanifested अक्षरम् the Imperishable तेषां of them के which योगवित्तमाः better versed in Yoga.

Arjuna said:

1. Those devotees who, ever-steadfast, thus worship Thee, and those also who worship the Imperishable, the Unmanifested—which of them are better versed in Yoga?

Thus: as declared in the last verse of the preceding chapter (XI. 55).

The Unmanifested: *Avyakta*: i.e., That which is incomprehensible to the senses, as devoid of all *Upādhis*.

श्रीभगवानुवाच

मय्यावेश्य मनो ये मां नित्ययुक्ता उपासते ।
श्रद्धया परयोपेतास्ते मे युक्ततमा मताः ॥ २

श्रीभगवान् The Blessed Lord उवाच said:

मयि On Me मनः mind आवेश्य fixing नित्ययुक्ताः ever-steadfast परया supreme श्रद्धया with *Śraddhā* उपेताः endowed ये who मां Me उपासते worship ते they युक्ततमाः the best versed in Yoga मे मताः are in My opinion.

The Blessed Lord said:

2. Those who, fixing their mind on Me, worship Me, ever-steadfast, and endowed with supreme *Śraddhā,* they in My opinion are the best versed in Yoga.

ये त्वक्षरमनिर्देश्यमव्यक्तं पर्युपासते ।
सर्वत्रगमचिन्त्यं च कूटस्थमचलं ध्रुवम् ॥ ३
संनियम्येन्द्रियग्रामं सर्वत्र समबुद्धयः ।
ते प्राप्नुवन्ति मामेव सर्वभूतहिते रताः ॥ ४

सर्वत्र Everywhere समबुद्धयः even-minded ये who तु but च also इन्द्रियग्रामं the aggregate of the senses संनियम्य having subdued अनिर्देश्यम् the Indefinable अव्यक्तं the Unmanifested सर्वत्रगम् the Omnipresent अचिन्त्यं the Unthinkable कूटस्थम् the Unchangeable अचलं the Immovable ध्रुवम् the Eternal अक्षरम् the Unchangeable पर्युपासते worship सर्वभूतहिते in the welfare of all beings रताः engaged ते they माम् Myself एव only प्राप्नुवन्ति reach.

3–4. But those also, who worship the Imperishable, the Indefinable, the Unmanifested, the Omnipresent, the Unthinkable, the Unchangeable, the Immovable, the Eternal—having subdued all the senses, even-minded everywhere, engaged in the welfare of all beings—verily, they reach only Myself.

Worship: *Upāsanā* is approaching the object of worship by way of meditating on it, in accordance with the teachings of the *Śāstras* and the Guru, and dwelling steadily in the current of that one thought, even as a thread of oil poured from one vessel to another.

Unchangeable: *Kūṭastha*: lit.. remaining like a mass. He who is seated in Māyā as its Witness.

क्लेशोऽधिकतरस्तेषामव्यक्तासक्तचेतसाम् ।
अव्यक्ता हि गतिर्दुःखं देहवद्भिरवाप्यते ॥ ५

तेषाम् Of those अव्यक्तासक्तचेतसाम् whose mind is set on the Unmanifested अधिकतरः (is) greater क्लेशः trouble हि for देहवद्भिः for the embodied अव्यक्ता the Unmanifested गतिः the goal दुःखं with hard toil अवाप्यते is reached.

5. Greater is their trouble whose minds are set on the Unmanifested; for the goal of the Unmanifested is very hard for the embodied to reach.

The embodied: Those who are attached to, or have identified themselves with, their bodies.

No comparison between the worshippers of the conditioned and unconditioned Brahman is meant here—since by the context, both reach the same goal. The path of the conditioned Brahman is described as superior only because it is easier. The path of the unconditioned Brahman is harder, because of the necessity of having to abandon all attachment to the body, from the very beginning of the practice.

ये तु सर्वाणि कर्माणि मयि सन्न्यस्य मत्पराः ।
अनन्येनैव योगेन मां ध्यायन्त उपासते ।। ६
तेषामहं समुद्धर्ता मृत्युसंसारसागरात् ।
भवामि न चिरात्पार्थ मय्यावेशितचेतसाम् ।। ७

ये Who तु but सर्वाणि all कर्माणि actions मयि in Me सन्न्यस्य resigning मत्पराः regarding Me as the Supreme Goal अनन्येन single-minded योगेन with Yoga एव verily मां Me ध्यायन्तः meditating उपासते worship पार्थ O son of Pṛthā अहं I मयि on Me आवेशितचेतसाम् of those whose mind is set तेषाम् for them मृत्युसंसारसागरात् out of the ocean of the mortal *Saṁsāra* न चिरात् ere long समुद्धर्ता the Saviour भवामि I become.

6–7. But those who worship Me, resigning all actions in Me, regarding Me as the Supreme Goal, meditating on Me with single-minded Yoga—to these whose mind is set on Me, verily, I become ere long, O son of Pṛthā, the Saviour out of the ocean of the mortal *Saṁsāra*.

Mortal Saṁsāra: The round of birth and death.

मय्येव मन आधत्स्व मयि बुद्धिं निवेशय ।
निवसिष्यसि मय्येव अत ऊर्ध्वं न संशयः ।। ८

मयि On Me एव only मन: (thy) mind आधत्स्व fix मयि in Me बुद्धिं (thy) intellect निवेशय place अत: ऊर्ध्वं hereafter मयि in Me एव alone निवसिष्यसि thou shalt live न no संशय: doubt.

8. Fix thy mind on Me only, place thy intellect in Me: (then) thou shalt no doubt live in Me hereafter.

Mind: *Manas*—purpose and thought.
Intellect: the faculty which resolves and determines.
Live in Me: as My Self.

अथ चित्तं समाधातुं न शक्नोषि मयि स्थिरम्।
अभ्यासयोगेन ततो मामिच्छाप्तुं धनञ्जय ।। ९

धनञ्जय O Dhanañjaya अथ if मयि on Me चित्तं (thy) mind स्थिरम् steadily समाधातुं to fix न शक्नोषि (thou) art unable तत: then अभ्यासयोगेन by *Abhyāsa-Yoga* माम् Me आप्तुं to reach इच्छ do (thou) seek.

9. If thou art unable to fix thy mind steadily on Me, then by *Abhyāsa-Yoga* do thou seek to reach Me, O Dhanañjaya.

Abhyāsa-Yoga: the practice of repeatedly withdrawing the mind from the objects to which it wanders, and trying to fix it on one thing.

अभ्यासेऽप्यसमर्थोऽसि मत्कर्मपरमो भव।
मदर्थमपि कर्माणि कुर्वन्सिद्धिमवाप्स्यसि ।। १०

अभ्यासे (In) *Abhyāsa* अपि also असमर्थ: unable to practise असि (if) thou art मत्कर्मपरम: intent on doing actions for My sake भव be thou मदर्थम् for My sake कर्माणि actions कुर्वन् by doing अपि even सिद्धिम् perfection अवाप्स्यसि thou shalt attain.

10. If also thou art unable to practise *Abhyāsa*, be thou intent on doing actions for My sake. Even by doing actions for My sake, thou shalt attain perfection.

अथैतदप्यशक्तोऽसि कर्तुं मद्योगमाश्रितः ।
सर्वकर्मफलत्यागं ततः कुरु यतात्मवान् ।। ११

अथ If अपि even एतत् this कर्तुं to do अशक्तः unable असि thou art ततः then मद्योगम् refuge in Me आश्रितः taking यतात्मवान् self-controlled सर्वकर्मफलत्यागं the renunciation of the fruit of all actions कुरु do.

11. If thou art unable to do even this, then taking refuge in Me, abandon the fruit of all action, being self-controlled.

In the preceding *Ślokas*—first, the concentration of the mind on the Lord is enjoined; in case of an inability to do that, *Abhyāsa-Yoga* is advised; if one finds that to be too hard, the performance of actions for the sake of the Lord alone, has been taught. Those who cannot do this even, who want to do things impelled by personal or other desires, are directed to give up the fruits of those actions to the Lord—i.e., not to anticipate, dwell, or build on, or care for, the results, knowing them to be dependent upon the Lord. Those who cannot control their desire for work are taught to practise indifference to the effects thereof.

श्रेयो हि ज्ञानमभ्यासाज्ज्ञानाद्ध्यानं विशिष्यते।
ध्यानात्कर्मफलत्यागस्त्यागाच्छान्तिरनन्तरम्॥ १२

अभ्यासात् Than (blind) *Abhyāsa* ज्ञानम् knowledge हि indeed श्रेय: better ज्ञानाद् than (mere) knowledge ध्यानं meditation (with knowledge) विशिष्यते is more esteemed ध्यानात् than meditation कर्मफलत्याग: the renunciation of the fruit of action त्यागात् from renunciation अनन्तरम् immediately शान्ति: peace (भवति follows).

12. Better indeed is knowledge than (blind) *Abhyāsa;* meditation (with knowledge) is more esteemed than (mere) knowledge; than meditation the renunciation of the fruit of action; peace immediately follows renunciation.

Renunciation of the fruit of all actions, as a means to the attainment of Bliss, is merely extolled here by the declaration of the superiority of one over another. Wherefore? Because it constitutes a common factor which immediately precedes Peace, both in the case of the man of wisdom who is steadily engaged in devout contemplation, and also of the ignorant one who, unable to tread the paths taught before, takes it up as the easiest means of Bliss.

अद्वेष्टा सर्वभूतानां मैत्रः करुण एव च।
निर्ममो निरहङ्कारः समदुःखसुखः क्षमी॥ १३
सन्तुष्टः सततं योगी यतात्मा दृढनिश्चयः।
मय्यर्पितमनोबुद्धिर्यो मद्भक्तः स मे प्रियः॥ १४

सर्वभूतानां Of (to) all creatures अद्वेष्टा free from hatred or malevolence मैत्रः friendly करुणः compassionate च and एव even निर्ममः who is free from the idea of "mineness" निरहङ्कारः free from egoism, from the notion of "I" समदुःखसुखः even-minded in pain and pleasure क्षमी forbearing सततं ever सन्तुष्टः content योगी steady in contemplation यतात्मा self-controlled दृढनिश्चयः possessed of firm conviction मयि in Me अर्पितमनोबुद्धिः with mind and intellect fixed यः who मद्भक्तः devoted to Me सः he मे to Me प्रियः (is) dear.

13–14. He who hates no creature, and is friendly and compassionate towards all, who is free from the feelings of "I and mine", even-minded in pain and pleasure, forbearing, ever content, steady in meditation, self-controlled, and possessed of firm conviction, with mind and intellect fixed on Me—he who is thus devoted to Me, is dear to Me.

यस्मान्नोद्विजते लोको लोकान्नोद्विजते च यः ।
हर्षामर्षभयोद्वेगैर्मुक्तो यः स च मे प्रियः ॥ १५

यस्मात् From whom लोकः the world न not उद्विजते is agitated, afflicted, यः who च and लोकात् from the world न not उद्विजते is agitated यः who च and हर्षामर्षभयोद्वेगैः by (from) joy, envy, fear, and anxiety मुक्तः freed सः he मे to Me प्रियः (is) dear.

15. He by whom the world is not agitated and who cannot be agitated by the world, who is freed from joy, envy, fear, and anxiety—he is dear to Me.

अनपेक्षः शुचिर्दक्ष उदासीनो गतव्यथः ।
सर्वारम्भपरित्यागी यो मद्भक्तः स मे प्रियः ।। १६

अनपेक्षः (who is), free from dependence शुचिः who is pure दक्षः prompt उदासीनः unconcerned गतव्यथः untroubled सर्वारम्भपरित्यागी renouncing every undertaking यः who मद्भक्तः devoted to Me सः he मे to Me प्रियः (is) dear.

16. He who is free from dependence, who is pure, prompt, unconcerned, untroubled, renouncing every undertaking—he who is thus devoted to Me, is dear to Me.

Free from dependence: on the body, the senses, the sense-objects, and their mutual connections.

Prompt: able to decide rightly and immediately in matters demanding prompt action.

Every undertaking: calculated to secure objects of desire, whether of this world or of the next.

यो न हृष्यति न द्वेष्टि न शोचति न काङ्क्षति ।
शुभाशुभपरित्यागी भक्तिमान् यः स मे प्रियः ।। १७

यः Who न neither हृष्यति rejoices न nor द्वेष्टि hates न nor शोचति grieves न nor काङ्क्षति desires शुभाशुभपरित्यागी renouncing good and evil यः who भक्तिमान् full of devotion सः he मे to Me प्रियः (is) dear.

17. He who neither rejoices, nor hates, nor grieves, nor desires, renouncing good and evil, full of devotion, he is dear to Me.

Hates: Frets at receiving anything undesirable.
Grieves: at parting with a beloved object.
Desires: the unattained.

समः शत्रौ च मित्रे च तथा मानापमानयोः ।
शीतोष्णसुखदुःखेषु समः सङ्गविवर्जितः ॥ १८
तुल्यनिन्दास्तुतिर्मौनी सन्तुष्टो येन केनचित् ।
अनिकेतः स्थिरमतिर्भक्तिमान्मे प्रियो नरः ॥ १९

शत्रौ To foe मित्रे to friend च and तथा also च and मानापमानयोः in honour and dishonour समः (who is) the same शीतोष्णसुखदुःखेषु in cold and heat, in pleasure and pain समः the same सङ्गविवर्जितः free from attachment तुल्यनिन्दास्तुतिः to whom censure and praise are equal मौनी who is silent येन केनचित् with anything सन्तुष्टः content अनिकेतः homeless स्थिरमतिः steady-minded भक्तिमान् full of devotion नरः (that) man मे to Me प्रियः (is) dear.

18–19. He who is the same to friend and foe, and also in honour and dishonour; who is the same in heat and cold, and in pleasure and pain; who is free from attachment; to whom censure and praise are equal; who is silent, content with anything, homeless, steady-minded, full of devotion — that man is dear to Me.

Content with anything, homeless: content with the bare means of bodily sustenance. Says the *Mahābhārata*:

येन केनचिदाच्छन्नो येन केनचिदाशितः ।

यत्र क्वचनशायी स्यात्तन्देवा ब्राह्मणं विदुः ॥

"Who is clad with anything, who is fed on any food, who lies down anywhere, him the gods call a *Brāhmaṇa.*"—Śānti-Parva.

ये तु धर्म्यामृतमिदं यथोक्तं पर्युपासते ।
श्रद्दधाना मत्परमा भक्तास्तेऽतीव मे प्रियाः ॥ २०

ये Who तु indeed यथोक्तं as declared (above) इदं this धर्म्यामृतम् Immortal Dharma पर्युपासते follow श्रद्दधानाः endued with *Śraddhā* मत्परमाः regarding Me as the Supreme Goal भक्ताः devoted ते they अतीव exceedingly मे to Me प्रियाः (are) dear.

20. And they who follow this Immortal Dharma, as described above, endued with *Śraddhā* regarding Me as the Supreme Goal, and devoted—they are exceedingly dear to Me.

इति भक्तियोगो नाम द्वादशोऽध्यायः ॥

The end of the twelfth chapter, designated,
The Way of Devotion.

त्रयोदशोऽध्यायः
(क्षेत्रक्षेत्रज्ञविभागयोगः)

THIRTEENTH CHAPTER
(The Discrimination of The Kṣetra and The Kṣetrajña)

अर्जुन उवाच

प्रकृतिं पुरुषं चैव क्षेत्रं क्षेत्रज्ञमेव च।
एतद्वेदितुमिच्छामि ज्ञानं ज्ञेयं च केशव ।।

अर्जुनः Arjuna उवाच said:

केशव O Keśava प्रकृतिं the *Prakṛti* पुरुषं *Puruṣa* च and एव also क्षेत्रं *Kṣetra* क्षेत्रज्ञम् the knower of the *Kṣetra* च and एव also ज्ञानं knowledge ज्ञेयं what ought to be known च and एतत् this वेदितुम् to know इच्छामि (I) desire.

Arjuna said:

Prakṛti and *Puruṣa*, also the *Kṣetra* and the knower of the *Kṣetra*, knowledge, and that which ought to be known—these, O Keśava, I desire to learn.

This verse is omitted in many editions.

श्रीभगवानुवाच

इदं शरीरं कौन्तेय क्षेत्रमित्यभिधीयते।
एतद्यो वेत्ति तं प्राहुः क्षेत्रज्ञ इति तद्विदः ॥ १

श्रीभगवान् The Blessed Lord उवाच said:

कौन्तेय O son of Kuntī इदं this शरीरं body क्षेत्रम् *Kṣetra* इति thus अभिधीयते is called यः who एतत् this वेत्ति knows तद्विदः who know of them तं him क्षेत्रज्ञः the knower of the *Kṣetra* इति as प्राहुः they call.

The Blessed Lord said:

1. This body, O son of Kuntī, is called, *Kṣetra*, and he who knows it is called *Kṣetrajña* by those who know of them (*Kṣetra* and *Kṣetrajña*).

Kṣetra: Literally, field; the body is so called because the fruits of action are reaped in it as in a field.

क्षेत्रज्ञं चापि मां विद्धि सर्वक्षेत्रेषु भारत।
क्षेत्रक्षेत्रज्ञयोर्ज्ञानं यत्तज्ज्ञानं मतं मम ॥ २

भारत O descendant of Bharata सर्वक्षेत्रेषु in all *Kṣetras* अपि also मां Me च and क्षेत्रज्ञं the *Kṣetrajña* विद्धि do thou know क्षेत्रक्षेत्रज्ञयोः of *Kṣetra* and *Kṣetrajña* यत् which ज्ञानं knowledge तत् that ज्ञानं knowledge मम by Me मतं is considered to be.

2. Me do thou also know, O descendant of Bharata, to be *Kṣetrajña* in all *Kṣetras*. The knowledge of *Kṣetra* and *Kṣetrajña* is considered by Me to be *the* knowledge.

तत्क्षेत्रं यच्च यादृक् च यद्विकारि यतश्च यत्।
स च यो यत्प्रभावश्च तत्समासेन मे शृणु ॥ ३

तत् The क्षेत्रं *Kṣetra* यत् what (is) च and यादृक् what its properties च and यद्विकारि what its modifications यतः from what (causes) च and यत् what (effects arise) सः he (is) च and यः who यत्प्रभावः what its powers च and तत् that समासेन in brief मे from Me शृणु hear.

3. What the *Kṣetra* is, what its properties are, what its modifications are, what effects arise from what causes, and also who He is and what His powers are, hear that from Me in brief.

That: the true nature of *Kṣetra* and *Kṣetrajña* in all these specific aspects.

ऋषिभिर्बहुधा गीतं छन्दोभिर्विविधैः पृथक्।
ब्रह्मसूत्रपदैश्चैव हेतुमद्भिर्विनिश्चितैः ॥ ४

ऋषिभिः By *Ṛṣis* विविधैः various छन्दोभिः in chants पृथक् distinctive बहुधा in many ways गीतं has been sung विनिश्चितैः convincing हेतुमद्भिः full of reasoning ब्रह्मसूत्रपदैः in phrases indicative of Brahman च and एव also.

4. (This truth) has been sung by *Ṛṣis* in many ways, in various distinctive chants, in passages indicative of Brahman, full of reasoning, and convincing.

महाभूतान्यहङ्कारो बुद्धिरव्यक्तमेव च।
इन्द्रियाणि दशैकं च पञ्च चेन्द्रियगोचराः ॥ ५
इच्छा द्वेषः सुखं दुःख सङ्घातश्चेतना धृतिः ।
एतत्क्षेत्रं समासेन सविकारमुदाहृतम् ॥ ६

महाभूतानि The great Elements अहङ्कारः Egoism बुद्धिः Intellect अव्यक्तम् the Unmanifested (*Mūlā Prakṛti*) च and एवं also दश ten इन्द्रियाणि the senses एकं the one (mind) च and पञ्च five इन्द्रियगोचराः objects of the senses च and इच्छा desire द्वेषः hatred सुखं pleasure दुःखं pain सङ्घातः the aggregate, the body चेतना intelligence धृतिः fortitude एतत् this सविकारम् with its modifications क्षेत्रं *Kṣetra* समासेन briefly उदाहृतम् has been described.

5-6. The great Elements, Egoism, Intellect, as also the Unmanifested (*Mūlā Prakṛti*), the ten senses and the one (mind), and the five objects of the senses; desire, hatred, pleasure, pain, the aggregate, intelligence, fortitude—the *Kṣetra* has been thus briefly described with its modifications.

The *Sāṅkhyas* speak of those mentioned in the fifth *Śloka* as the twenty-four *Tattvas* or Principles.

The great Elements: *Mahābhūtas*—pervade all *Vikāras*, modifications of matter.

Aggregate: *Saṁghāta*—combination of the body and the senses.

Desire and other qualities which the *Vaiśeṣikas* speak of as inherent attributes of the Ātman, are spoken of in the sixth *Śloka* as merely the attributes of *Kṣetra*, and not the attributes of *Kṣetrajña*. Desire and other qualities mentioned here, stand for all the qualities of the *Antaḥ-karaṇa* or inner sense—as mere mental states. Each of them, being knowable, is *Kṣetra*.

The *Kṣetra*, of which the various modifications in their totality are spoken of as "this body" in the first *Śloka*, has been here dwelt upon in all its different forms, from "The great Elements" to "fortitude".

अमानित्वमदम्भित्वमहिंसा क्षान्तिरार्जवम् ।
आचार्योपासनं शौचं स्थैर्यमात्मविनिग्रहः ।। ७

अमानित्वम् Humility अदम्भित्वम् unpretentiousness अहिंसा non-injury क्षान्तिः forbearance आर्जवम् uprightness आचार्योपासनं service to the teacher शौचं purity स्थैर्यम् steadiness आत्मविनिग्रहः self-control.

7. Humility, unpretentiousness, non-injury, forbearance, uprightness, service to the teacher, purity, steadiness, self-control;

Ācārya: one who teaches the means of attaining *Mokṣa*.

Purity: external and internal. The former consists in washing away the dirt from the body by means of water, etc., and the latter—the purity of mind—consists in the removal from it of the dirt of attachment and other passions, by the recognition of evil in all objects of the senses.

इन्द्रियार्थेषु वैराग्यमनहङ्कार एव च ।
जन्ममृत्युजराव्याधिदुःखदोषानुदर्शनम् ।। ८

इन्द्रियार्थेषु Of sense-objects वैराग्यम् renunciation अनहङ्कारः absence of egoism एव also च and जन्ममृत्युजराव्याधि-

दुःखदोषानुदर्शनम् reflection on the evils of birth, death, old age, sickness, and pain.

8. The renunciation of sense-objects, and also absence of egoism; reflection on the evils of birth, death, old age, sickness, and pain;

Sense-objects: such as sound, touch, etc., of pleasures seen or unseen.

Pain: whether *Ādhyātmika,* i.e., arising in one's own person caused by diseases etc.; or *Ādhibhautika*, i.e., produced by external agents, or *Ādhidaivika*, i.e., produced by supernatural beings.

Reflection.... pain: or the passage may be interpreted as— reflection on the evils and miseries of birth, death, old age, and sickness. Birth, etc., are all miseries, not that they are miseries in themselves, but because they produce misery. From such reflection arises indifference to sense-pleasures, and the senses turn towards the Innermost Self for knowledge.

असक्तिरनभिष्वङ्गः पुत्रदारगृहादिषु ।
नित्यं च समचित्तत्वमिष्टानिष्टोपपत्तिषु ।। ९

असक्तिः Non-attachment पुत्रदारगृहादिषु with son, wife, home, and the rest अनभिष्वङ्गः non-identification of self इष्टानिष्टोपपत्तिषु in the occurrence of the desirable and the undesirable नित्यं constant समचित्तत्वम् even-mindedness च and.

9. Non-attachment, non-identification of self with son, wife, home, and the rest, and constant even-mindedness in the occurrence of the desirable and the undesirable;

Identification of self: as in the case of a person who feels happy or miserable when another to whom he is attached, is happy or miserable, and who feels himself alive or dead when his beloved one is alive or dead.

मयि चानन्ययोगेन भक्तिरव्यभिचारिणी।
विविक्तदेशसेवित्वमरतिर्जनसंसदि ।। १०

मयि To Me अनन्ययोगेन by the Yoga of non-separation अव्यभिचारिणी unswerving भक्ति: devotion च and विविक्तदेश-सेवित्वम् resort to sequestered places जनसंसदि for the society of men अरति: distaste;

10. Unswerving devotion to Me by the Yoga of non-separation, resort to sequestered places, distaste for the society of men;

Resort... places: favourable to 'equanimity of mind, so that uninterrupted meditation on the Self, and the like, may be possible.

Society of men: of the unenlightened and undisciplined people, not of the pure and holy, because association with the latter leads to *Jñāna*.

अध्यात्मज्ञाननित्यत्वं तत्त्वज्ञानार्थदर्शनम्।
एतज्ज्ञानमिति प्रोक्तमज्ञानं यदतोऽन्यथा ।। ११

अध्यात्मज्ञाननित्यत्वम् Constant application to spiritual knowledge तत्त्वज्ञानार्थदर्शनम् understanding of the end of true knowledge एतत् this ज्ञानम् knowledge इति thus प्रोक्तम् is declared यद् what अत: to it अन्यथा opposed अज्ञानं ignorance.

11. Constant application to spiritual knowledge, understanding of the end of true knowledge — this is declared to be knowledge, and what is opposed to it is ignorance.

These attributes—from "Humility" to "Understanding of the end of true knowledge"—are declared to be knowledge, because they are the means conducive to knowledge.

ज्ञेयं यत्तत्प्रवक्ष्यामि यज्ज्ञात्वाऽमृतमश्नुते।
अनादिमत्परं ब्रह्म न सत्तन्नासदुच्यते॥ १२

यत् Which ज्ञेयं has to be known तत् that प्रवक्ष्यामि I shall describe यत् which ज्ञात्वा knowing अमृतम् Immortality अश्नुते (one) attains to तत् it अनादिमत् the beginningless परं Supreme ब्रह्म Brahman न neither सत् being न nor असद् non-being उच्यते is called.

12. I shall describe that which has to be known, knowing which one attains to immortality, the beginningless Supreme Brahman. It is called neither being nor non-being.

सर्वतः पाणिपादं तत्सर्वतोऽक्षिशिरोमुखम्।
सर्वतः श्रुतिमल्लोके सर्वमावृत्य तिष्ठति॥ १३

सर्वत: Everywhere पाणिपादं with hands and feet सर्वत: everywhere अक्षिशिरोमुखम् with eyes, heads, and mouths सर्वत: everywhere श्रुतिमत् with ears तत् That लोके in the universe सर्वम् all आवृत्य pervading तिष्ठति exists.

13. With hands and feet everywhere, with eyes, heads, and mouths everywhere, with ears everywhere in the universe — That exists pervading all.

सर्वेन्द्रियगुणाभासं सर्वेन्द्रियविवर्जितम्।
असक्तं सर्वभृच्चैव निर्गुणं गुणभोक्तृ च॥ १४

सर्वेन्द्रियगुणाभासं Shining by the functions of all the senses सर्वेन्द्रियविवर्जितम् (yet) without the senses असक्तं devoid of all attachment or relativity, Absolute सर्वभृत् sustaining all चैव yet निर्गुणं devoid of *Guṇas* गुणभोक्तृ experiencer of the *Guṇas* च and.

14. Shining by the functions of all the senses, yet without the senses; Absolute, yet sustaining all; devoid of *Guṇas*, yet their experiencer.

बहिरन्तश्च भूतानामचरं चरमेव च।
सूक्ष्मत्वात्तदविज्ञेयं दूरस्थं चान्तिके च तत्॥ १५

भूतानाम् (Of all) beings बहिः without च and अन्तः within अचरं the unmoving चरम् the moving एव also च and सूक्ष्मत्वात् because of its subtlety तत् It अविज्ञेयं (is) incomprehensible दूरस्थं is far च and अन्तिके near च and तत् It.

15. Without and within (all) beings, the unmoving and also the moving; incomprehensible because of Its subtlety; It is far and near.

Incomprehensible: to the unillumined, though knowable in Itself.

Far: when unknown.

Near: to the illumined, because It is their own Self.

अविभक्तं च भूतेषु विभक्तमिव च स्थितम्।
भूतभर्तृ च तज्ज्ञेयं ग्रसिष्णु प्रभविष्णु च ।। १६

भूतेषु In beings च and अविभक्तं impartible विभक्तम् divided च yet इव as if स्थितम् existing भूतभर्तृ as sustaining beings च and ग्रसिष्णु devouring प्रभविष्णु as generating च as well तत् It ज्ञेयं is to be known.

16. Impartible, yet It exists as if divided in beings; It is to be known as sustaining beings, and devouring, as well as generating (them).

Devouring: at the time of *Pralaya*.

Generating: at the time of *Utpatti* or origin of the universe.

ज्योतिषामपि तज्ज्योतिस्तमसः परमुच्यते।
ज्ञानं ज्ञेयं ज्ञानगम्यं हृदि सर्वस्य धिष्ठितम्।। १७

. ज्योतिषाम् Of lights अपि even ज्योति: Light तमस: darkness परम् beyond तत् It उच्यते is said (to bc) ज्ञानं Knowledge ज्ञेयं the One Thing to be known ज्ञानगम्यं the Goal of knowledge सर्वस्य of all हृदि in the heart धिष्ठितम् dwelling.

17. The Light even of lights, It is said to be beyond darkness; Knowledge, and the One Thing to be known, the Goal of knowledge, dwelling in the hearts of all.

The Light even of lights: The illuminator of all illuminating things, such as the sun, etc., and *Buddhi*, etc. Indeed, these latter shine only when illuminated by the Light of the consciousness of the Self.

इति क्षेत्रं तथा ज्ञानं ज्ञेयं चोक्तं समासतः ।
मद्भक्त एतद्विज्ञाय मद्भावायोपपद्यते ।। १८

इति Thus क्षेत्रं *Kṣetra* तथा and ज्ञानं knowledge ज्ञेयं that which has to be known च and समासत: briefly उक्तं have been stated मद्भक्त: My devotee एतत् this विज्ञाय knowing मद्भावाय for My state उपपद्यते is fitted.

18. Thus *Kṣetra*, knowledge, and that which has to be known, have been briefly stated. Knowing this, My devotee is fitted for My state.

प्रकृतिं पुरुषं चैव विद्ध्यनादी उभावपि ।
विकारांश्च गुणांश्चैव विद्धि प्रकृतिसम्भवान् ।। १९

प्रकृतिं *Prakṛti* पुरुषं *Puruṣa* च and एव indeed उभौ both अपि also अनादी beginningless विद्धि know (thou) विकारान् (all) modifications च and गुणान् *Guṇas* च and एव also प्रकृतिसम्भवान् born of *Prakṛti* विद्धि know (thou).

19. Know thou that *Prakṛti* and *Puruṣa* are both beginningless; and also know that all modifications and *Guṇas* are born of *Prakṛti*.

Modifications: *Vikāras*—From *Buddhi* down to the physical body.

कार्यकरणकर्तृत्वे हेतुः प्रकृतिरुच्यते।
पुरुषः सुखदुःखानां भोक्तृत्वे हेतुरुच्यते।। २०

कार्यकरणकर्तृत्वे In the production of the body and the senses प्रकृतिः *Prakṛti* हेतुः the cause उच्यते is said (to be) पुरुषः *Puruṣa* सुखदुःखानां of pleasure and pain भोक्तृत्वे in the experience हेतुः the cause उच्यते is said (to be).

20. In the production of the body and the senses, *Prakṛti* is said to be the cause; in the experience of pleasure and pain, *Puruṣa* is said to be the cause.

Senses: five organs of perception, five of action, mind, intellect, and egoism.

Puruṣa: the *Jīva* is meant here.

Kārya: The effect, the physical body. *Karaṇa*: Senses. Some read *Kāraṇa*, and explain "*Kārya* and *Kāraṇa*" as "effect and cause".

पुरुषः प्रकृतिस्थो हि भुङ्क्ते प्रकृतिजान्गुणान्।
कारणं गुणसङ्गोऽस्य सदसद्योनिजन्मसु।। २१

हि Indeed पुरुषः *Puruṣa* प्रकृतिस्थः seated in *Prakṛti* प्रकृतिजान् born of *Prakṛti* गुणान् the *Guṇas* भुङ्क्ते experiences अस्य its सदसद्योनिजन्मसु of birth in good and evil wombs गुणसङ्गः attachment to the *Guṇas* कारणं the reason.

21. *Puruṣa* seated in *Prakṛti*, experiences the *Guṇas* born of *Prakṛti*; the reason of his birth in good and evil wombs is his attachment to the *Guṇas*.

Seated in: identifying himself with.

Guṇas: manifesting themselves as pleasure, pain, and delusion.

उपद्रष्टानुमन्ता च भर्ता भोक्ता महेश्वरः ।
परमात्मेति चाप्युक्तो देहेऽस्मिन्पुरुषः परः ।। २२

अस्मिन् देहे In this body पुरुषः *Puruṣa* परः Supreme उपद्रष्टा the Looker-on अनुमन्ता the Permitter च and भर्ता Supporter भोक्ता the Experiencer महेश्वरः the Great Lord परमात्मा the Highest Self च and इति thus अपि also उक्तः is called.

22. And the Supreme *Puruṣa* in this body is also called the Looker-on, the Permitter, the Supporter, the Experiencer, the Great Lord, and the Highest Self.

Looker-on, the Permitter: He himself does not participate in the activities of the bodily organs, the mind and the *Buddhi*, being quite apart from them, yet appears to be so engaged. And being a looker-on, He never stands in the way of the activities of *Prakṛti* as manifested in the body. Indeed, all the consciousness or intelligence that manifests itself in the activities of life is but the reflection of the All-pervading, Absolute, and Perfect Intelligence—the Supreme Spirit.

य एवं वेत्ति पुरुषं प्रकृतिं च गुणैः सह ।
सर्वथा वर्तमानोऽपि न स भूयोऽभिजायते ।। २३

यः Who एवं thus पुरुषं the *Puruṣa* गुणैः सह with *Guṇas* प्रकृतिं *Prakṛti* च and वेत्ति knows सः he सर्वथा in whatever way वर्तमानः living अपि even भूयः again न not अभिजायते is born.

23. He who knows thus the *Puruṣa* and the *Prakṛti* together with the *Guṇas*, whatever his life, is not born again.

Whatever his life, *etc*.: Whether he be engaged in prescribed or forbidden acts, he is not born again. For, the acts, the seeds of rebirth, of a knower of Truth are burnt by the fire of knowledge, and thus cannot be effective causes to bring about births. In his case they are mere semblances of *Karma*; a burnt cloth, for instance, cannot serve the purposes of a cloth.

ध्यानेनात्मनि पश्यन्ति केचिदात्मानमात्मना।
अन्ये सांख्येन योगेन कर्मयोगेन चापरे ॥ २४

केचिद् Some ध्यानेन by meditation आत्मनि in their own intelligence आत्मना by the purified heart आत्मानम् the Self पश्यन्ति behold अन्ये others सांख्येन योगेन by the path of knowledge अपरे others च again कर्मयोगेन by Karma-Yoga.

24. Some by meditation behold the Self in their own intelligence by the purified heart, others by the path of knowledge, others again by Karma-Yoga.

अन्ये त्वेवमजानन्तः श्रुत्वान्येभ्य उपासते।
तेऽपि चातितरन्त्येव मृत्युं श्रुतिपरायणाः ॥ २५

अन्ये Others तु again एवम् thus अजानन्तः not knowing अन्येभ्यः from others श्रुत्वा as (they have) heard उपासते worship ते they अपि च and also श्रुतिपरायणाः regarding what they have heard as the Supreme Refuge मृत्युं death अतितरन्ति go beyond एव even.

25. Others again, not knowing thus, worship as they have heard from others. Even they go beyond death, regarding what they have heard as the Supreme Refuge.

Not knowing thus: not able to know the Self described above, by one of the several methods as pointed out.

From others: *Ācāryas* or spiritual teachers.

Regarding: following with *Śraddhā*.

What they have heard: i.e., they solely depend upon the authority of others' instructions.

यावत्सञ्जायते किञ्चित्सत्त्वं स्थावरजङ्गमम्।
क्षेत्रक्षेत्रज्ञसंयोगात्तद्विद्धि भरतर्षभ।। २६

भरतर्षभ O bull of the Bhāratas यावत् किञ्चित् whatever स्थावरजङ्गमम् the moving and the unmoving सत्त्वं being सञ्जायते is born तत् it क्षेत्रक्षेत्रज्ञसंयोगात् from the union of *Kṣetra* and *Kṣetrajña* विद्धि know (to be).

26. Whatever being is born, the moving or the unmoving, O bull of the Bhāratas, know it to be from the union of *Kṣetra* and *Kṣetrajña*.

Union ... Kṣetrajña: The union of *Kṣetra* and *Kṣetrajña*, of the object and the subject, is of the nature of mutual *Adhyāsa* which consists in confounding them as well as their attributes with each other, owing to the absence of discrimination of their real nature. This false knowledge vanishes when one is able to separate *Kṣetra* from *Kṣetrajña*.

समं सर्वेषु भूतेषु तिष्ठन्तं परमेश्वरम्।
विनश्यत्स्वविनश्यन्तं यः पश्यति स पश्यति।। २७

सर्वेषु All भूतेषु in beings समं equally तिष्ठन्तं existing विनश्यत्सु in the dying अविनश्यन्तं deathless परमेश्वरम् the Supreme Lord य: who पश्यति sees स: he पश्यति sees.

27. He sees, who sees the Supreme Lord existing equally in all beings, the deathless in the dying.

समं पश्यन् हि सर्वत्र समवस्थितमीश्वरम्।
न हिनस्त्यात्मनात्मानं ततो याति परां गतिम्॥ २८

हि Since सर्वत्र everywhere समं equally समवस्थितम् existent ईश्वरम् the Lord पश्यन् seeing आत्मना by self आत्मानं Self न not हिनस्ति injures तत: so परां highest गतिम् the Goal याति (he) goes to.

28. Since seeing the Lord equally existent everywhere, he injures not Self by self, and so goes to the highest Goal.

He injures . . . by self: like the ignorant man either by ignoring the Self in others (*Avidyā* or nescience), or regarding the non-Self (physical body, etc.) as the Self (*Mithyā-jñāna* or false knowledge)—the two veils that hide the true nature of the Self.

प्रकृत्यैव च कर्माणि क्रियमाणानि सर्वशः।
यः पश्यति तथात्मानमकर्तारं स पश्यति॥ २९

य: Who च and कर्माणि actions प्रकृत्या by *Prakṛti* एव alone सर्वश: all क्रियमाणानि being done तथा and आत्मानम् the Self अकर्तारं actionless पश्यति sees स: he पश्यति sees.

29. He sees, who sees that all actions are done by *Prakṛti* alone and that the Self is actionless.

यदा भूतपृथग्भावमेकस्थमनुपश्यति ।
तत एव च विस्तारं ब्रह्म सम्पद्यते तदा ।। ३०

यदा When भूतपृथग्भावम् the separate existence of all beings एकस्थम् inherent in the One अनुपश्यति sees ततः from That एव alone विस्तारं (their) expansion च and तदा then ब्रह्म Brahman सम्पद्यते (he) becomes.

30. When he sees the separate existence of all beings inherent in the One, and their expansion from That (One) alone, he then becomes Brahman.

अनादित्वान्निर्गुणत्वात्परमात्मायमव्ययः ।
शरीरस्थोऽपि कौन्तेय न करोति न लिप्यते ।। ३१

कौन्तेय O son of Kuntī अनादित्वात् being without beginning निर्गुणत्वात् being devoid of *Guṇas* अयम् this अव्ययः immutable परमात्मा Supreme Self शरीरस्थः existing in the body अपि though न neither करोति acts न nor लिप्यते is affected.

31. Being without beginning and devoid of *Guṇas*, this Supreme Self, immutable, O son of Kuntī, though existing in the body neither acts nor is affected.

Being without beginning: having no cause.

Neither . . . affected: Because the Self is not the doer, therefore He, is not touched by the fruit of action.

यथा सर्वगतं सौक्ष्म्यादाकाशं नोपलिप्यते।
सर्वत्रावस्थितो देहे तथात्मा नोपलिप्यते॥ ३२

यथा As सर्वगतं the all-pervading आकाशं *Ākāśa* सौक्ष्म्यात् because of its subtlety न not उपलिप्यते is tainted तथा so सर्वत्र everywhere देहे in the body अवस्थित: existent आत्मा the Self न not उपलिप्यते is tainted.

32. As the all-pervading *Ākāśa*, because of its subtlety, is not tainted, so the Self existent everywhere in the body, is not tainted.

यथा प्रकाशयत्येकः कृत्स्नं लोकमिमं रविः।
क्षेत्रं क्षेत्री तथा कृत्स्नं प्रकाशयति भारत॥ ३३

भारत O descendant of Bharata यथा as एक: the one रवि: sun इमं this कृत्स्नं all लोकम् world प्रकाशयति illumines तथा so क्षेत्री He who abides in the *Kṣetra* कृत्स्नं the whole क्षेत्रं *Kṣetra* प्रकाशयति illumines.

33. As the one sun illumines all this world, so does He who abides in the *Kṣetra*, O descendant of Bharata, illumine the whole *Kṣetra*.

क्षेत्रक्षेत्रज्ञयोरेवमन्तरं ज्ञानचक्षुषा।
भूतप्रकृतिमोक्षं च ये विदुर्यान्ति ते परम्॥ ३४

एवम् Thus क्षेत्रक्षेत्रज्ञयो: between the *Kṣetra* and the *Kṣetrajña* अन्तरं the distinction भूतप्रकृतिमोक्षं the emancipation from the *Prakṛti* of beings च and (also)

ज्ञानचक्षुषा with the eye of knowledge ये who विदुः perceive ते they परम् the Supreme यान्ति go to.

34. They who thus with the eye of knowledge perceive the distinction between the *Kṣetra* and the *Kṣetrajña*, and also the emancipation from the *Prakṛti* of beings, they go to the Supreme.

Prakṛti of beings: the material nature or delusion of beings due to *Avidyā*.

इति क्षेत्रक्षेत्रज्ञविभागयोगो नाम त्रयोदशोऽध्यायः ॥

The end of the thirteenth chapter, designated, *The Discrimination of the Kṣetra and the Kṣetrajña.*

चतुर्दशोऽध्याय:
(गुणत्रयविभागयोग:)

FOURTEENTH CHAPTER
(The Discrimination of The Three Guṇas)

श्रीभगवानुवाच

परं भूय: प्रवक्ष्यामि ज्ञानानां ज्ञानमुत्तमम्।
यज्ज्ञात्वा मुनय: सर्वे परां सिद्धिमितो गता: ।। १

श्रीभगवान् The Blessed Lord उवाच said:

ज्ञानानां Of all knowledge उत्तमम् the best परं supreme ज्ञानम् knowledge भूय: again प्रवक्ष्यामि I shall tell यत् which ज्ञात्वा having known सर्वे all मुनय: the *Munis* इत: after this life परां high सिद्धिम् perfection गता: have attained to.

The Blessed Lord said:

1. Again I shall tell thee that supreme knowledge which is above all knowledge, having known which all the *Munis* have attained to high perfection after this life.

After this life: after being freed from this bondage of the body.

इदं ज्ञानमुपाश्रित्य मम साधर्म्यमागताः ।
सर्गेऽपि नोपजायन्ते प्रलये न व्यथन्ति च ।। २

इदं This ज्ञानम् knowledge उपाश्रित्य having devoted to मम साधर्म्यम् My Being आगताः have attained to सर्गे at the time of creation अपि न neither उपजायन्ते are born प्रलये at the time of dissolution न च nor व्यथन्ति are (they) troubled.

2. They who, having devoted themselves to this knowledge, have attained to My Being, are neither born at the time of creation, nor are they troubled at the time of dissolution.

मम योनिर्महद्ब्रह्म तस्मिन् गर्भं दधाम्यहम् ।
सम्भवः सर्वभूतानां ततो भवति भारत ।। ३

भारत O descendant of Bharata महत् the great ब्रह्म *Prakṛti* मम My योनिः womb तस्मिन् in that अहम् I गर्भं the germ दधामि place ततः thence सर्वभूतानां of all beings सम्भवः the birth भवति is.

3. My womb is the great *Prakṛti*; in that I place the germ; from thence, O descendant of Bharata, is the birth of all beings.

Brahma: This word is derived from *Bṛmh*, "to expand", and means here the vast seed or womb (the *Prakṛti*) out of which the cosmos is evolved or expanded.

I place the germ: I infuse the reflection of My Intelligence, and this act of impregnation is the cause of the evolution of the cosmos.

सर्वयोनिषु कौन्तेय मूर्तयः सम्भवन्ति याः ।
तासां ब्रह्म महद्योनिरहं बीजप्रदः पिता ॥ ४

कौन्तेय O son of Kuntī सर्वयोनिषु in all the wombs याः whatever मूर्तयः forms सम्भवन्ति are produced तासां their महत् the great ब्रह्म *Prakṛti* योनिः womb अहं I बीजप्रदः seed-giving पिता Father.

4. Whatever forms are produced, O son of Kuntī, in all the wombs, the great *Prakṛti* is their womb, and I the seed-giving Father.

सत्त्वं रजस्तम इति गुणाः प्रकृतिसम्भवाः ।
निबध्नन्ति महाबाहो देहे देहिनमव्ययम् ॥ ५

महाबाहो O mighty-armed सत्त्वं *Sattva* रजः *Rajas* तमः *Tamas* इति these प्रकृतिसम्भवाः born of *Prakṛti* गुणाः *Guṇas* देहे in the body अव्ययम् the indestructible देहिनम् the embodied one निबध्नन्ति bind fast.

5. *Sattva*, *Rajas*, and *Tamas*—these *Guṇas*, O mighty-armed, born of *Prakṛti*, bind fast in the body the indestructible embodied one.

These Guṇas: are the primary constituents of the *Prakṛti* and are the bases of all substances; they cannot therefore be said to be attributes or qualities inhering in the substances as opposed to the substances.

Embodied one: he who abides in the body as if identified therewith.

तत्र सत्त्वं निर्मलत्वात्प्रकाशकमनामयम्।
सुखसङ्गेन बध्नाति ज्ञानसङ्गेन चानघ॥ ६

अनघ O sinless one तत्र of these निर्मलत्वात् from its stainlessness प्रकाशकम् luminous अनामयम् free from evil सत्त्वं *Sattva* सुखसङ्गेन by attachment to happiness ज्ञानसङ्गेन by attachment to knowledge च and बध्नाति binds.

6. Of these *Sattva*, because of its stainlessness, luminous and free from evil, binds, O sinless one, by attachment to happiness, and by attachment to knowledge.

Binds by attachment to happiness, etc.: Binds the Self by the consciousness of happiness and knowledge in the shape of "I am happy", "I am wise", which belongs properly to the *Kṣetra*, but which is associated with the Self, the Absolute Intelligence and Bliss, through *Avidyā*.

रजो रागात्मकं विद्धि तृष्णासङ्गसमुद्भवम्।
तन्निबध्नाति कौन्तेय कर्मसङ्गेन देहिनम्॥ ७

कौन्तेय O son of Kuntī रागात्मकं of the nature of passion रजः *Rajas* तृष्णासङ्गसमुद्भवम् giving rise to thirst and attachment विद्धि know तत् it कर्मसङ्गेन by attachment to action देहिनम् the embodied one निबध्नाति binds fast.

7. Know *Rajas* to be of the nature of passion, giving rise to thirst and attachment; it binds fast, O son of Kuntī, the embodied one, by attachment to action.

It binds, etc.: Though the Self is not the agent, *Rajas* makes him act with the idea, "*I* am the doer".

तमस्त्वज्ञानजं विद्धि मोहनं सर्वदेहिनाम् ।
प्रमादालस्यनिद्राभिस्तन्निबध्नाति भारत ॥ ८

भारत O descendant of Bharata तमः *Tamas* तु and अज्ञानजं born of ignorance सर्वदेहिनाम् all embodied beings मोहनं stupefying विद्धि know तत् it प्रमादालस्यनिद्राभिः by miscomprehension, indolence, and sleep निबध्नाति binds fast.

8. And know *Tamas* to be born of ignorance, stupefying all embodied beings; it binds fast, O descendant of Bharata, by miscomprehension, indolence, and sleep.

Stupefying: causing delusion or non-discrimination.

सत्त्वं सुखे सञ्जयति रजः कर्मणि भारत ।
ज्ञानमावृत्य तु तमः प्रमादे सञ्जयत्युत ॥ ९

भारत O descendant of Bharata सत्त्वं *Sattva* सुखे to happiness सञ्जयति attaches रजः *Rajas* कर्मणि to action उत while तमः *Tamas* तु indeed ज्ञानम् discrimination आवृत्य shrouding प्रमादे to miscomprehension सञ्जयति attaches.

9. *Sattva* attaches to happiness, and *Rajas* to action, O descendant of Bharata; while *Tamas*, verily, shrouding discrimination, attaches to miscomprehension.

रजस्तमश्चाभिभूय सत्त्वं भवति भारत।
रजः सत्त्वं तमश्चैव तमः सत्त्वं रजस्तथा॥ १०

भारत O descendant of Bharata सत्त्वं *Sattva* रज: *Rajas* तम: *Tamas* च and अभिभूय predominating over भवति arises रज: *Rajas* सत्त्वं *Sattva* तम: च and *Tamas* एव likewise तथा so तम: *Tamas* सत्त्वं *Sattva* रज: *Rajas* च and.

10. *Sattva* arises, O descendant of Bharata, predominating over *Rajas* and *Tamas*; likewise *Rajas* over *Sattva* and *Tamas*; so *Tamas* over *Sattva* and *Rajas*.

When one or the other of the *Guṇas* asserts itself, predominating over the other two, it produces its own effect—*Sattva* produces knowledge and happiness; *Rajas*, action; *Tamas*, veiling of discrimination, etc.

सर्वद्वारेषु देहेऽस्मिन्प्रकाश उपजायते।
ज्ञानं यदा तदा विद्याद्विवृद्धं सत्त्वमित्युत॥ ११

यदा When अस्मिन् in this देहे body सर्वद्वारेषु through every sense ज्ञानं (of) intelligence प्रकाश: light उपजायते shines तदा then उत indeed सत्त्वम् *Sattva* विवृद्धं (is) predominant इति that विद्यात् (it) should be known.

11. When through every sense in this body, the light of intelligence shines, then it should be known that *Sattva* is predominant.

Every sense: lit., all the gates. All the senses are for the Self the gateways of perception.

लोभः प्रवृत्तिरारम्भः कर्मणामशमः स्पृहा।
रजस्येतानि जायन्ते विवृद्धे भरतर्षभ ।। १२

भरतर्षभ O bull of the Bhāratas लोभ: greed प्रवृत्ति: activity कर्मणाम् of actions आरम्भ: the undertaking अशम: unrest स्पृहा longing एतानि these रजसि *Rajas* विवृद्धे having become predominant जायन्ते arise.

12. Greed, activity, the undertaking of actions, unrest, longing — these arise when *Rajas* is predominant, O bull of the Bhāratas.

Unrest: being agitated with joy, attachment, etc.

अप्रकाशोऽप्रवृत्तिश्च प्रमादो मोह एव च।
तमस्येतानि जायन्ते विवृद्धे कुरुनन्दन ।। १३

कुरुनन्दन O descendant of Kuru अप्रकाश: darkness अप्रवृत्ति: inertness च and प्रमाद: miscomprehension मोह: delusion एव also च and एतानि these तमसि *Tamas* विवृद्धे having become predominant जायन्ते arise.

13. Darkness, inertness, miscomprehension, and delusion — these arise when *Tamas* is predominant, O descendant of Kuru.

Darkness, *inertness*: Absence of discrimination, and its results, e.g., inertness, etc.

यदा सत्त्वे प्रवृद्धे तु प्रलयं याति देहभृत्।
तदोत्तमविदां लोकानमलान्प्रतिपद्यते ।। १४

यदा तु When सत्त्वे *Sattva* प्रवृद्धे having become predominant देहभृत् the embodied one प्रलयं death याति meets तदा then उत्तमविदां of the knowers of the Highest अमलान् the spotless लोकान् worlds प्रतिपद्यते (he) attains.

14. If the embodied one meets death when *Sattva* is predominant, then he attains to the spotless regions of the worshippers of the Highest.

Spotless regions: The *Brahma-loka* and the like.
The Highest: Deities such as *Hiraṇyagarbha*.

रजसि प्रलयं गत्वा कर्मसङ्गिषु जायते।
तथा प्रलीनस्तमसि मूढयोनिषु जायते।। १५

रजसि In *Rajas* प्रलयं death गत्वा meeting कर्मसङ्गिषु among those attached to action जायते (he) is born तथा so तमसि in *Tamas* प्रलीन: dying मूढयोनिषु in the wombs of the irrational जायते (he) is born.

15. Meeting death in *Rajas,* he is born among those attached to action; so dying in *Tamas*, he is born in the wombs of the irrational.

Meeting . . . Rajas: If he dies when *Rajas* is predominant in him.

कर्मणः सुकृतस्याहुः सात्त्विकं निर्मलं फलम्।
रजसस्तु फलं दुःखमज्ञानं तमसः फलम्।। १६

सुकृतस्य Good कर्मणः of action निर्मलं pure सात्त्विकं *Sāttvika*
फलम् the fruit आहुः they say रजसः of *Rajas* तु verily दुःखम्
pain फलं the fruit तमसः of *Tamas* अज्ञानं ignorance फलम्
the fruit.

16. The fruit of good action, they say, is *Sāttvika*
and pure; verily, the fruit of *Rajas* is pain, and
ignorance is the fruit of *Tamas*.

Rajas: means *Rājasika* action, and *Tamas*, *Tāmasika*
action, as this section treats of actions.

सत्त्वात्सञ्जायते ज्ञानं रजसो लोभ एव च।
प्रमादमोहौ तमसो भवतोऽज्ञानमेव च॥ १७

सत्त्वात् From *Sattva* ज्ञानं wisdom सञ्जायते arises रजसः
from *Rajas* लोभः greed एव indeed च and तमसः from
Tamas अज्ञानम् ignorance प्रमादमोहौ miscomprehension
and delusion एव even च and भवतः arise.

17. From *Sattva* arises wisdom, and from *Rajas*
greed; miscomprehension, delusion and ignorance
arise from *Tamas*.

ऊर्ध्वं गच्छन्ति सत्त्वस्था मध्ये तिष्ठन्ति राजसाः।
जघन्यगुणवृत्तिस्था अधो गच्छन्ति तामसाः॥ १८

सत्त्वस्थाः The *Sattva*-abiding ऊर्ध्वं upwards गच्छन्ति
go राजसाः the *Rājasika* मध्ये in the middle तिष्ठन्ति dwell
जघन्यगुणवृत्तिस्था: abiding in the function of the lowest
Guṇa तामसाः the *Tāmasika* अधः downwards गच्छन्ति go.

18. The *Sattva*-abiding go upwards; the *Rājasika* dwell in the middle; and the *Tāmasika*, abiding in the function of the lowest *Guṇa*, go downwards.

नान्यं गुणेभ्यः कर्तारं यदा द्रष्टानुपश्यति।
गुणेभ्यश्च परं वेत्ति मद्भावं सोऽधिगच्छति॥ १९

यदा When द्रष्टा the seer गुणेभ्य: than the *Guṇas* अन्यं other कर्तारं agent न no अनुपश्यति beholds गुणेभ्य: than the *Guṇas* च and परं higher वेत्ति knows तथा then स: he मद्भावं My being अधिगच्छति attains to.

19. When the seer beholds no agent other than the *Guṇas* and knows That which is higher than the *Guṇas*, he attains to My being.

The Guṇas: which transform themselves into the bodies, senses, and sense-objects, and which in all their modifications constitute the agent in all actions.

Knows . . . the Guṇas: Sees Him who is distinct from the *Guṇas*, who is the Witness of the *Guṇas* and of their functions.

गुणानेतानतीत्य त्रीन्देही देहसमुद्भवान्।
जन्ममृत्युजरादुःखैर्विमुक्तोऽमृतमश्नुते॥ २०

देहसमुद्भवान् Out of which the body is evolved एतान् these त्रीन् three गुणान् *Guṇas* अतीत्य having gone beyond जन्ममृत्युजरादु:खै: from birth, death, decay, and pain विमुक्त: freed देही the embodied one अमृतम् immortality अश्नुते attains to.

20. The embodied one having gone beyond these three *Guṇas*, out of which the body is evolved, is freed from birth, death, decay, and pain, and attains to immortality.

अर्जुन उवाच

कैर्लिङ्गैस्त्रीन्गुणानेतानतीतो भवति प्रभो।
किमाचारः कथं चैतांस्त्रीन्गुणानतिवर्तते ॥ २१।

अर्जुनः Arjuna उवाच said:

प्रभो O Lord कैः by what लिङ्गैः marks एतान् these त्रीन् three गुणान् *Guṇas* अतीतः भवति has gone beyond किमाचारः what (is his) conduct कथं how च and एतान् these त्रीन् three गुणान् *Guṇas* अतिवर्तते does (he) pass beyond.

Arjuna said:

21. By what marks, O Lord, is he (known) who has gone beyond these three *Guṇas* ? What is his conduct, and how does he pass beyond these three *Guṇas* ?

श्रीभगवानुवाच

प्रकाशं च प्रवृत्तिं च मोहमेव च पाण्डव।
न द्वेष्टि सम्प्रवृत्तानि न निवृत्तानि काङ्क्षति ॥ २२

श्रीभगवान् The Blessed Lord उवाच said:

पाण्डव O Pāṇḍava प्रकाशं light (the effect of *Sattva*) प्रवृत्तिं activity (the effect of *Rajas*) मोहम् delusion (the effect of *Tamas*) एव च and also सम्प्रवृत्तानि (when) come forth

न not द्वेष्टि (he) hates निवृत्तानि when absent न nor काङ्क्षति longs for;

The Blessed Lord said:

22. He who hates not the appearance of light (the effect of *Sattva*), activity (the effect of *Rajas*), and delusion (the effect of *Tamas*), (in his own mind), O Pāṇḍava nor longs for them when absent;

This answers Arjuna's first question. The man of right knowledge does not hate the effects of the three *Guṇas* when they clearly present themselves as objects of consciousness; nor does he long after things which have disappeared.

उदासीनवदासीनो गुणैर्यो न विचाल्यते।
गुणा वर्तन्त इत्येव योऽवतिष्ठति नेङ्गते॥ २३

यः Who उदासीनवद् like one unconcerned आसीनः sitting गुणैः by the *Guṇas* न not विचाल्यते is moved गुणाः the *Guṇas* वर्तन्ते operate इत्येव (knowing) that अवतिष्ठति is Self-centred न not इङ्गते swerves;

23. He who, sitting like one unconcerned, is moved not by the *Guṇas*, who knowing that the *Guṇas* operate, is Self-centred and swerves not;

समदुःखसुखः स्वस्थः समलोष्टाश्मकाञ्चनः।
तुल्यप्रियाप्रियो धीरस्तुल्यनिन्दात्मसंस्तुतिः॥ २४

यः Who समदुःखसुखः alike in pleasure and pain स्वस्थः Self-abiding समलोष्टाश्मकाञ्चनः regarding a clod of earth, a stone, and gold alike तुल्यप्रियाप्रिय: the same to agreeable and disagreeable धीर: firm तुल्यनिन्दात्मसंस्तुति: the same in censure and praise;

24. Alike in pleasure and pain, Self-abiding, regarding a clod of earth, a stone and gold alike; the same to agreeable and disagreeable, firm, the same in censure and praise;

Self-abiding: He remains in his own true nature.

मानापमानयोस्तुल्यस्तुल्यो मित्रारिपक्षयोः ।
सर्वारम्भपरित्यागी गुणातीतः स उच्यते ।। २५

य: Who मानापमानयो: in honour and disgrace तुल्य: the same मित्रारिपक्षयो: to friend and foe तुल्य: the same सर्वारम्भपरित्यागी relinquishing all undertakings स: he गुणातीत: gone beyond the *Guṇas* उच्यते is said.

25. The same in honour and disgrace, the same to friend and foe, relinquishing all undertakings—he is said to have gone beyond the *Guṇas*.

Inclining to neither of the dual throng, he firmly treads the path of Self-knowledge, and rises above the *Guṇas*.

These three *ślokas* are in answer to Arjuna's second question.

मां च योऽव्यभिचारेण भक्तियोगेन सेवते ।
स गुणान्समतीत्यैतान् ब्रह्मभूयाय कल्पते ।। २६

यः Who च and मां Me अव्यभिचारेण unswerving भक्तियोगेन with devotion सेवते serves सः he एतान् these गुणान् *Guṇas* समतीत्य going beyond ब्रह्मभूयाय for becoming Brahman कल्पते is fitted.

26. And he who serves Me with unswerving devotion, he, going beyond the *Guṇas*, is fitted for becoming Brahman.

This answers Arjuna's third question.

ब्रह्मणो हि प्रतिष्ठाहममृतस्याव्ययस्य च।
शाश्वतस्य च धर्मस्य सुखस्यैकान्तिकस्य च॥ २७

हि For अहम् I ब्रह्मणः of Brahman प्रतिष्ठा the abode अव्ययस्य the Immutable अमृतस्य the Immortal च and शाश्वतस्य everlasting धर्मस्य of Dharma ऐकान्तिकस्य Absolute सुखस्य of Bliss च and.

27. For I am the abode of Brahman, the Immortal and Immutable, of everlasting Dharma and of Absolute Bliss.

I: the *Pratyagātman*, the true Inner-Self.

इति गुणत्रयविभागयोगो नाम चतुर्दशोऽध्यायः॥

The end of the fourteenth chapter, designated, *The Discrimination of the Three Guṇas*.

पञ्चदशोऽध्यायः
(पुरुषोत्तमयोगः)

FIFTEENTH CHAPTER
(The Way to The Supreme Spirit)

श्रीभगवानुवाच

ऊर्ध्वमूलमधःशाखमश्वत्थं प्राहुरव्ययम्।
छन्दांसि यस्य पर्णानि यस्तं वेद स वेदवित्॥ १

श्रीभगवान् The Blessed Lord उवाच said:

ऊर्ध्वमूलम् Rooted above अधःशाखम् branching below अव्ययम् eternal अश्वत्थं *Aśvattha* प्राहुः they speak of छन्दांसि the Vedas यस्य whose पर्णानि leaves तं it यः who वेद knows सः he वेदवित् (is) Veda-knower.

The Blessed Lord said:

1. They speak of an eternal *Aśvattha* rooted above and branching below whose leaves are the Vedas; he who knows it, is a Veda-knower.

Aśvattha: literally, that which does not endure till tomorrow: the *Saṁsāra*, the ever-changing, phenomenal world.

Brahman with Its unmanifested energy, Māyā, is spoken as the One *"above"*, for It is supreme over all things. The One above is the root of this Tree of *Saṁsāra*, as such it is said to have its root above. *Mahat, Ahaṁkāra, Tanmātras,* etc., are its branches evolving to grosser and grosser states—hence it is said to be branching *"below"*. As leaves protect a tree, so do the Vedas protect the Tree of *Saṁsāra*, by treating of *Dharma* and *Adharma*, with their causes and fruits.

Eternal: because this Tree of *Saṁsāra* rests on a continuous series of births without beginning and end, and it cannot be cut down except by the knowledge, "I am Brahman."

अधश्चोर्ध्वं प्रसृतास्तस्य शाखा
गुणप्रवृद्धा विषयप्रवालाः ।
अधश्च मूलान्यनुसन्ततानि
कर्मानुबन्धीनि मनुष्यलोके ॥ २

तस्य Its गुणप्रवृद्धाः nourished by the *Guṇas* विषयप्रवालाः sense-objects (are) its buds शाखाः branches अधः below ऊर्ध्वं above च and प्रसृताः spread मनुष्यलोके in the human world कर्मानुबन्धीनि originating action मूलानि the roots अधः below च and अनुसन्ततानि are stretched forth.

2. Below and above spread its branches, nourished by the *Guṇas*; sense-objects are its buds; and below in the human world stretch forth the roots, originating action.

Below: from man downwards.

Above: up to *Brahmā*.

Roots: The tap-root is the Lord "above"; the secondary roots are the *Saṁskāras*, attachment, aversion, etc. It is these that, being in perpetual succession the cause and consequence of good and evil deeds, bind one fast to actions—*Dharma* and *Adharma*.

न रूपमस्येह तथोपलभ्यते
नान्तो न चादिर्न च सम्प्रतिष्ठा।
अश्वत्थमेनं सुविरूढमूल-
मसङ्गशस्त्रेण दृढेन छित्त्वा।। ३
ततः पदं तत्परिमार्गितव्यं
यस्मिन्गता न निवर्तन्ति भूयः।
तमेव चाद्यं पुरुषं प्रपद्ये
यतः प्रवृत्तिः प्रसृता पुराणी।। ४

इह Here अस्य its रूपम् form न not उपलभ्यते is perceived तथा as such न neither अन्त: (its) end न nor आदि: (its) origin न च nor सम्प्रतिष्ठा (its) existence एनं this सुविरूढमूलम् firm-rooted अश्वत्थम् *Aśvattha* दृढेन strong असङ्गशस्त्रेण with the axe of non-attachment छित्वा having cut asunder तत: then तत् that पदं goal परिमार्गितव्यं is to be sought for यस्मिन् whither गता: going भूय: again न not निवर्तन्ति (they) return यत: whence (एषा the) पुराणी Eternal प्रवृत्ति: Activity प्रसृता streamed forth तम् in that एव च indeed आद्यं Primeval पुरुषं *Puruṣa* प्रपद्ये I seek refuge.

3–4. Its form is not here perceived as such, neither its end, nor its origin, nor its existence. Having cut asunder this firm-rooted *Aśvattha* with the strong axe of non-attachment—then that Goal is to be sought for, going whither they (the wise) do not return again. I seek refuge in that Primeval *Puruṣa* whence streamed forth the Eternal Activity.

As such: it cannot be said to exist, because it appears and vanishes every other moment. See commentary on II. 16.

Tat: *That*—Śaṅkara and Ānandagiri read "*Tataḥ*", and explain it as beyond or above the *Aśvattha*, the Tree of *Saṁsāra*.

The Eternal Activity: this ever-passing work of projection, this ever-flowing current of evolution, the world of phenomena.

निर्मानमोहा जितसङ्गदोषा
अध्यात्मनित्या विनिवृत्तकामाः ।
द्वन्द्वैर्विमुक्ताः सुखदुःखसंज्ञै-
र्गच्छन्त्यमूढाः पदमव्ययं तत् ॥ ५

निर्मानमोहाः Free from pride and delusion जितसङ्गदोषाः with the evil of attachment conquered अध्यात्मनित्याः ever dwelling in the Self विनिवृत्तकामाः with desires completely receded सुखदुःखसंज्ञैः known as pleasure and pain द्वन्द्वैः from the pairs of opposites विमुक्ताः liberated अमूढाः the undeluded तत् that अव्ययं Eternal पदम् Goal गच्छन्ति reach.

5. Free from pride and delusion, with the evil of attachment conquered, ever dwelling in the Self, with desires completely receded, liberated from the pairs of opposites known as pleasure and pain, the undeluded reach that Goal Eternal.

न तद्भासयते सूर्यो न शशाङ्को न पावकः ।
यद्गत्वा न निवर्तन्ते तद्धाम परमं मम ।। ६

यत् Whither गत्वा going न not निवर्तन्ते (they) return तत् that सूर्य: the sun न not भासयते illumines न nor शशाङ्क: the moon न nor पावक: fire तत् that मम My परमं Supreme धाम Abode.

6. That the sun illumines not, nor the moon, nor fire; that is My Supreme Abode, going whither they return not.

ममैवांशो जीवलोके जीवभूतः सनातनः ।
मनःषष्ठानीन्द्रियाणि प्रकृतिस्थानि कर्षति ।। ७

मम एव Of Myself सनातन: eternal अंश: portion जीवभूत: having become a living soul प्रकृतिस्थानि abiding in the *Prakṛti* मन:षष्ठानि with mind as the sixth इन्द्रियाणि the (five) senses जीवलोके in the world of life कर्षति draws (to itself).

7. An eternal portion of Myself having become a living soul in the world of life, draws (to itself) the (five) senses with mind for the sixth, abiding in *Prakṛti*.

The Jīva or the individual soul is that aspect of the Supreme Self which manifests itself in every one as the doer and enjoyer, being limited by the *Upādhis* set up by *Avidyā*; but in reality, both are the same. It is like the *Ākāśa* (space) in the jar, which is a portion of the infinite *Ākāśa*, and becomes one with the latter on the destruction of the jar, the cause of limitation.

शरीरं यदवाप्नोति यच्चाप्युत्क्रामतीश्वरः ।
गृहीत्वैतानि संयाति वायुर्गन्धानिवाशयात् ।। ८

ईश्वरः The Lord यत् when शरीरं a body अवाप्नोति obtains यत् when च and अपि also उत्क्रामति leaves वायुः the wind आशयात् from (their) seats गन्धान् the scents इव as एतानि these गृहीत्वा taking संयाति goes.

8. When the Lord obtains a body and when He leaves it, He takes these and goes, as the wind takes the scents from their seats (the flowers).

Lord: Jīva spoken of in the preceding *Śloka*.

When the Jīva leaves the body, then he draws round himself the senses and the *Manas*. When he enters another, he takes these again with him, i.e. he is born with these again.

श्रोत्रं चक्षुः स्पर्शनं च रसनं घ्राणमेव च ।
अधिष्ठाय मनश्चायं विषयानुपसेवते ।। ९

अयं He श्रोत्रं the ear चक्षुः the eye स्पर्शनं the (organ of) touch रसनं the (organ of) taste च and घ्राणम् the (organ of) smell एव च as also मनः the mind अधिष्ठाय presiding over विषयान् objects उपसेवते experiences.

9. Presiding over the ear, the eye, the touch, the taste, and the smell, as also the mind, He experiences objects.

उत्क्रामन्तं स्थितं वापि भुञ्जानं वा गुणान्वितम् ।
विमूढा नानुपश्यन्ति पश्यन्ति ज्ञानचक्षुषः ।। १०

उत्क्रामन्तं Transmigrating (from one body to another) स्थितं residing (in the same) वापि or भुञ्जानं experiencing गुणान्वितम् united with the *Guṇas* विमूढा: the deluded न not अनुपश्यन्ति do see (Him) ज्ञानचक्षुष: those who have the eye of wisdom पश्यन्ति do see (Him).

10. While transmigrating (from one body to another), or residing (in the same) or experiencing, or when united with the *Guṇas*—the deluded do not see Him; but those who have the eye of wisdom behold Him.

Though Ātman is nearest and comes most easily within the range of their consciousness in a variety of functions, still all do not see Him, because of their complete subservience to sense-objects.

यतन्तो योगिनश्चैनं पश्यन्त्यात्मन्यवस्थितम् ।
यतन्तोऽप्यकृतात्मानो नैनं पश्यन्त्यचेतसः ॥ ११

यतन्त: Striving (for perfection) योगिन: the *Yogis* एनं Him आत्मनि in themselves अवस्थितम् dwelling पश्यन्ति behold यतन्त: striving अपि even though अकृतात्मान: the men of unrefined self अचेतस: unintelligent एनं Him न not पश्यन्ति see.

11. The *Yogis* striving (for perfection) behold Him dwelling in themselves; but the unrefined and unintelligent, even though striving, see Him not.

The unrefined: Whose mind has not been regenerated by *Tapas* and subjugation of the senses, whose mind is not purified.

यदादित्यगतं तेजो जगद्भासयतेऽखिलम् ।
यच्चन्द्रमसि यच्चाग्नौ तत्तेजो विद्धि मामकम् ।। १२

आदित्यगतं Residing in the sun यत् which तेजः light अखिलम् the whole जगत् world भासयते illumines चन्द्रमसि in the moon च and यत् which अग्नौ in the fire च and यत् which तत् that तेजः light मामकम् Mine विद्धि know.

12. The light which residing in the sun illumines the whole world, that which is in the moon and in the fire—know that light to be Mine.

Light: may also be understood to mean the light of consciousness.

गामाविश्य च भूतानि धारयाम्यहमोजसा ।
पुष्णामि चौषधीः सर्वाः सोमो भूत्वा रसात्मकः ।। १३

अहम् I ओजसा with my energy गाम् the earth आविश्य entering भूतानि all beings धारयामि (I) support रसात्मकः watery सोमः moon च and भूत्वा becoming सर्वाः all ओषधीः the herbs पुष्णामि I nourish.

13. Entering the earth with My energy I support all beings, and I nourish all the herbs, becoming the watery moon.

Energy: *Ojas*—The energy of *Īśvara*, whereby the vast heaven and the earth are firmly held.

Nourish: by infusing sap into them.

The watery moon: The *Soma*, moon, is considered as the repository or the embodiment of all fluids (*Rasas*).

अहं वैश्वानरो भूत्वा प्राणिनां देहमाश्रितः।
प्राणापानसमायुक्तः पचाम्यन्नं चतुर्विधम्॥ १४

अहं I वैश्वानरः (the fire) *Vaiśvānara* भूत्वा becoming प्राणिनां of living beings देहम् in the body आश्रितः abiding प्राणापानसमायुक्तः associated with *Prāṇa* and *Apāna* चतुर्विधम् fourfold अन्नं the food पचामि I digest.

14. Abiding in the body of living beings as (the fire) *Vaiśvānara*, I, associated with *Prāṇa* and *Apāna*, digest the fourfold food.

See IV. 29.

Vaiśvānara: The fire abiding in the stomach.

Fourfold food: Food which has to be eaten by (1) mastication, (2) sucking, (3) licking, and (4) swallowing.

सर्वस्य चाहं हृदि सन्निविष्टो
मत्तः स्मृतिर्ज्ञानमपोहनं च।
वेदैश्च सर्वैरहमेव वेद्यो
वेदान्तकृद्वेदविदेव चाहम्॥ १५

अहं I सर्वस्य of all हृदि in the heart सन्निविष्टः centred च and मत्तः from Me स्मृतिः memory ज्ञानम् perception अपोहनं (their) loss च as well as सर्वैः all वेदैः by the Vedas च and अहम् I एव verily वेद्यः that which has to be known वेदान्तकृद् the Author of the Vedānta वेदविद् the Knower of the Veda च and अहम् I एव indeed.

15. I am centred in the hearts of all; memory and perception as well as their loss come from Me.

I am verily that which has to be known by all the Vedas, I indeed am the Author of the Vedānta, and the Knower of the Veda am I.

Memory: of what is experienced in the past births; and *knowledge*—of things transcending the ordinary limits of space, time, and visible nature—Ānandagiri.

Come from Me: as the result of their good or evil deeds.

I indeed . . . Vedānta: It is I who am the Teacher of the wisdom of the Vedānta, and cause it to be handed down in regular succession.

द्वाविमौ पुरुषौ लोके क्षरश्चाक्षर एव च ।
क्षरः सर्वाणि भूतानि कूटस्थोऽक्षर उच्यते ॥ १६

क्षर: The Perishable अक्षर: the Imperishable च and द्वौ two एव indeed इमौ these पुरुषौ (two) *Puruṣas* (beings) लोके in the world सर्वाणि all भूतानि beings क्षर: (are) the Perishable कूटस्थ: the *Kūṭastha* अक्षर: the Imperishable उच्यते is called.

16. There are two *Puruṣas* in the world—the Perishable and the Imperishable. All beings are the Perishable, and the *Kūṭastha* is called the Imperishable.

Two Puruṣas: Two categories—arranged in two separate groups of beings—spoken of as "*Puruṣas*", as they are the *Upādhis* of the *Puruṣa*.

Imperishable: *Māyā-Śakti* of the Lord, the germ from which the perishable being is born.

Kūṭastha: That which manifests Itself in various forms of illusion and deception. It is said to be imperishable, as the seed of *Saṁsāra* is endless—in the sense that it does not perish in the absence of *Brahma-Jñāna*.

उत्तमः पुरुषस्त्वन्यः परमात्मेत्युदाहृतः ।
यो लोकत्रयमाविश्य बिभर्त्यव्यय ईश्वरः ।। १७

अन्यः Another तु but उत्तमः the Supreme पुरुषः *Puruṣa* परमात्मा the Highest Self इति thus उदाहृतः called यः who ईश्वरः Lord अव्ययः the Immutable लोकत्रयम् the three worlds आविश्य pervading बिभर्ति sustains (them).

17. But (there is) another, the Supreme *Puruṣa*, called the Highest Self, the Immutable Lord, who pervading the three worlds, sustains them.

Another: quite distinct from the two.
The three worlds: *Bhūḥ* (the Earth), *Bhuvaḥ* (the Mid-Region), and *Svaḥ* (the Heaven).

यस्मात्क्षरमतीतोऽहमक्षरादपि चोत्तमः ।
अतोऽस्मि लोके वेदे च प्रथितः पुरुषोत्तमः ।। १८

यस्मात् As अहम् I क्षरम् the Perishable अतीतः transcend अक्षराद् than (to) the Imperishable अपि even उत्तमः superior च and अतः therefore लोके in the world वेदे in the Veda च and पुरुषोत्तमः Puruṣottama (the Highest *Puruṣa*) इति as प्रथितः celebrated अस्मि am I.

18. As I transcend the Perishable and am above even the Imperishable, therefore am I in the world and in the Veda celebrated as Puruṣottama (the Highest *Puruṣa*).

The Perishable: The Tree of *Saṁsāra* called *Aśvattha*.
The Imperishable: Which constitutes the seed of the Tree of *Saṁsāra*.

यो मामेवमसम्मूढो जानाति पुरुषोत्तमम्।
स सर्वविद्भजति मां सर्वभावेन भारत।। १९

भारत O descendant of Bharata यः who एवम् thus असम्मूढः free from delusion पुरुषोत्तमम् the Supreme *Puruṣa* माम् Me जानाति knows सः he सर्वविद् knowing all सर्वभावेन with all his heart मां Me भजति worships.

19. He who, free from delusion, thus knows Me, the Highest Spirit, he knowing all, worships Me with all his heart, O descendant of Bharata.

इति गुह्यतमं शास्त्रमिदमुक्तं मयाऽनघ।
एतद्बुद्ध्वा बुद्धिमान्स्यात्कृतकृत्यश्च भारत।। २०

अनघ O sinless one भारत O descendant of Bharata इति thus गुह्यतमं most profound इदम् this शास्त्रम् teaching मया by Me उक्तं has been imparted एतद् this बुद्ध्वा knowing बुद्धिमान् possessed of (the highest) intelligence कृतकृत्यः (who has) accomplished all the duties च and स्यात् becomes.

20. Thus, O sinless one, has this most profound teaching been imparted by Me. Knowing this one attains the highest intelligence and will have accomplished all one's duties, O descendant of Bharata.

Highest intelligence: which realises the Brahman.

Will have accomplished . . . duties: Whatever duty one has to do in life, all that duty has been done, when the Brahman is realised.

इति पुरुषोत्तमयोगो नाम पञ्चदशोऽध्यायः ।।

The end of the fifteenth chapter, designated,
The Way to the Supreme Spirit.

षोडशोऽध्यायः
(दैवासुर-सम्पद्विभागयोगः)

SIXTEENTH CHAPTER
(The Classification of the Divine and Non-divine Attributes)

श्रीभगवानुवाच

अभयं सत्त्वसंशुद्धिर्ज्ञानयोगव्यवस्थितिः ।
दानं दमश्च यज्ञश्च स्वाध्यायस्तप आर्जवम् ।। १

श्रीभगवान् The Blessed Lord उवाच said:

अभयं Fearlessness सत्त्वसंशुद्धिः purity of heart ज्ञानयोगव्यवस्थितिः steadfastness in knowledge and Yoga दानं almsgiving दमः control of the senses यज्ञः *Yajña* स्वाध्यायः reading of the *Śastras* तपः austerity आर्जवम् uprightness;

The Blessed Lord said:

1. Fearlessness, purity of heart, steadfastness in knowledge and Yoga; almsgiving, control of the senses, *Yajña*, reading of the *Śāstras*, austerity, uprightness;

Yoga: consists in making what has been learnt from the *Śastras* and the *Ācārya* an object of one's own direct perception, by concentration and self-control.

अहिंसा सत्यमक्रोधस्त्यागः शान्तिरपैशुनम्।
दया भूतेष्वलोलुप्त्वं मार्दवं ह्रीरचापलम्॥ २

अहिंसा Non-injury सत्यम् truth अक्रोधः absence of anger त्यागः renunciation शान्तिः tranquillity अपैशुनम् absence of calumny भूतेषु to beings दया compassion अलोलुप्त्वं uncovetousness मार्दवं gentleness ह्रीः modesty अचापलम् absence of fickleness;

2. Non-injury, truth, absence of anger, renunciation, tranquillity, absence of calumny, compassion to beings, uncovetousness, gentleness, modesty, absence of fickleness;

Uncovetousness: Unaffectedness of the senses when in contact with their objects.

Absence of fickleness: Avoidance of useless actions—*Ś*ridhara.

तेजः क्षमा धृतिः शौचमद्रोहो नातिमानिता।
भवन्ति सम्पदं दैवीमभिजातस्य भारत॥ ३

तेजः Boldness क्षमा forgiveness धृतिः fortitude शौचम् purity अद्रोहः absence of hatred नातिमानिता absence of pride दैवीम् divine सम्पदं state अभिजातस्य to one born for भवन्ति (these) belong भारत O descendant of Bharata.

3. Boldness, forgiveness, fortitude, purity, absence of hatred, absence of pride; these belong to one born for a divine state, O descendant of Bharata.

दम्भो दर्पोऽभिमानश्च क्रोधः पारुष्यमेव च।
अज्ञानं चाभिजातस्य पार्थ सम्पदमासुरीम्॥ ४

पार्थ O Pārtha दम्भः ostentation दर्पः arrogance च and अभिमानः self-conceit क्रोधः anger पारुष्यम् harshness च and अज्ञानं ignorance च एव as well as आसुरीम् an *Āsurika* सम्पदम् state अभिजातस्य to one who is born for.

4. Ostentation, arrogance, and self-conceit, anger as also harshness and ignorance, belong to one who is born, O Pārtha, for an *Āsurika* state.

Āsurika: Demoniac.

दैवी सम्पद्विमोक्षाय निबन्धायासुरी मता।
मा शुचः सम्पदं दैवीमभिजातोऽसि पाण्डव॥ ५

दैवी The divine सम्पद् state विमोक्षाय for liberation आसुरी *Āsurika* निबन्धाय for bondage मता is deemed (as mature) पाण्डव O Pāṇḍava मा not शुचः grieve दैवीम् the divine सम्पदं state अभिजातः born for असि (thou) art.

5. The divine state is deemed to make for liberation, the *Āsurika* for bondage; grieve not O Pāṇḍava, thou art born for a divine state.

द्वौ भूतसर्गौ लोकेऽस्मिन् दैव आसुर एव च।
दैवो विस्तरशः प्रोक्त आसुरं पार्थ मे शृणु॥ ६

पार्थ O Pārtha अस्मिन् लोके in this world दैवः the divine आसुरः the *Āsurika* च and द्वौ two भूतसर्गौ types of beings दैवः

the divine विस्तरशः at length प्रोक्तः has been described आसुरं of the *Āsurika* मे from Me शृणु hear.

6. There are two types of beings in this world, the divine and the *Āsurika*. The divine have been described at length; hear from Me, O Pārtha, of the *Āsurika*.

प्रवृत्तिं च निवृत्तिं च जना न विदुरासुराः ।
न शौचं नापि चाचारो न सत्यं तेषु विद्यते ।। ७

आसुराः The *Āsurika* जनाः persons प्रवृत्तिं what to do च and निवृत्तिं what to refrain from न not विदुः know तेषु in them न neither शौचं purity न nor आचारः good conduct न च nor सत्यं truth विद्यते is.

7. The persons of *Āsurika* nature know not what to do and what to refrain from; neither is purity found in them nor good conduct, nor truth.

What to do ... from: What acts they should perform to achieve the end of man, nor what acts they should abstain from to avert evil.

असत्यमप्रतिष्ठं ते जगदाहुरनीश्वरम् ।
अपरस्परसम्भूतं किमन्यत्कामहैतुकम् ।। ८

जगद् The universe असत्यम् (is) without truth अप्रतिष्ठं without (moral) basis अनीश्वरम् without a God अपरस्परसम्भूतं brought about by mutual union किमन्यत् what else कामहैतुकम् with lust for its cause ते आहुः they say.

8. They say, "The universe is without truth, without a (moral) basis, without a God, brought about by mutual union, with lust for its cause; what else ?"

Without truth: As we are unreal so this universe is unreal, and the sacred scriptures that declare the truth are unreal.

What else: but lust can be the cause of the universe?—This is the view of the *Lokāyatikas*, the materialists.

एतां दृष्टिमवष्टभ्य नष्टात्मानोऽल्पबुद्धयः ।
प्रभवन्त्युग्रकर्माणः क्षयाय जगतोऽहिताः ॥ ९

अल्पबुद्धयः Of small intellect एतां this दृष्टिम् view अवष्टभ्य holding नष्टात्मानः ruined souls उग्रकर्माणः of fierce deeds अहिताः the enemies जगतः of the world क्षयाय for (its) destruction प्रभवन्ति rise.

9. Holding this view, these ruined souls of small intellect and fierce deeds, rise as the enemies of the world for its destruction.

Small intellect: as it concerns itself only with sense-objects and cannot soar higher.

काममाश्रित्य दुष्पूरं दम्भमानमदान्विताः ।
मोहाद्गृहीत्वाऽसद्ग्राहान्प्रवर्तन्तेऽशुचिव्रताः ॥ १०

दुष्पूरं Insatiable कामम् desire आश्रित्य abiding in दम्भमानमदान्विताः full of hypocrisy, pride, and arrogance मोहाद् through delusion असद्ग्राहान् evil ideas गृहीत्वा holding अशुचिव्रताः with impure resolve प्रवर्तन्ते they work.

10. Filled with insatiable desires, full of hypocrisy, pride, and arrogance, holding evil ideas through delusion, they work with impure resolve.

चिन्तामपरिमेयां च प्रलयान्तामुपाश्रिताः ।
कामोपभोगपरमा एतावदिति निश्चिताः ॥ ११

प्रलयान्ताम् Ending only with death अपरिमेयां immense चिन्ताम् cares उपाश्रिताः beset with कामोपभोगपरमाः regarding gratification of lust as the highest एतावद् that is all इति that निश्चिताः feeling sure;

11. Beset with immense cares ending only with death, regarding gratification of lust as the highest, and feeling sure that that is all;

Cares: as to the means of acquiring and preserving the innumerable objects of desire.

आशापाशशतैर्बद्धाः कामक्रोधपरायणाः ।
ईहन्ते कामभोगार्थमन्यायेनार्थसञ्चयान् ॥ १२

आशापाशशतैः By a hundred ties of hope बद्धाः bound कामक्रोधपरायणाः given over to lust and wrath कामभोगार्थम् for sensual enjoyment अन्यायेन by unjust means अर्थसञ्चयान् hoards of wealth ईहन्ते (they) strive (to secure).

12. Bound by a hundred ties of hope, given over to lust and wrath, they strive to secure by unjust means hoards of wealth for sensual enjoyment.

इदमद्य मया लब्धमिदं प्राप्स्ये मनोरथम्।
इदमस्तीदमपि मे भविष्यति पुनर्धनम्॥ १३

अद्य Today मया by me इदम् this लब्धम् has been gained इदं this मनोरथम् desire प्राप्स्ये I shall obtain इदम् this अस्ति is पुन: again (in future) मे mine इदम् this अपि also धनम् wealth भविष्यति shall be.

13. "This has been gained by me today; this desire I shall obtain; this is mine, and this wealth also shall be mine in future.

असौ मया हतः शत्रुर्हनिष्ये चापरानपि।
ईश्वरोऽहमहं भोगी सिद्धोऽहं बलवान्सुखी॥ १४

असौ That शत्रु: enemy मया by me हत: has been slain अपरान् others च and अपि also हनिष्ये shall I slay अहम् I ईश्वर: Lord अहं I भोगी enjoyer अहं I सिद्ध: (am) successful बलवान् powerful सुखी happy.

14. "That enemy has been slain by me, and others also shall I slay. I am the Lord, I enjoy, I am successful, powerful, and happy.

आढ्योऽभिजनवानस्मि कोऽन्योऽस्ति सदृशो मया।
यक्ष्ये दास्यामि मोदिष्य इत्यज्ञानविमोहिताः॥ १५

आढ्य: Rich अभिजनवान् well-born अस्मि I am मया to me सदृश: equal अन्य: else क: who अस्ति is यक्ष्ये I will sacrifice दास्यामि I will give मोदिष्ये I will rejoice इति thus अज्ञानविमोहिता: deluded by ignorance.

15. "I am rich and well-born. Who else is equal to me ? I will sacrifice, I will give, I will rejoice." Thus deluded by ignorance,

अनेकचित्तविभ्रान्ता मोहजालसमावृताः ।
प्रसक्ताः कामभोगेषु पतन्ति नरकेऽशुचौ ॥ १६

अनेकचित्तविभ्रान्ताः Bewildered by many a fancy मोहजालसमावृताः covered by the meshes of delusion कामभोगेषु to the gratification of lust प्रसक्ताः addicted अशुचौ foul नरके into a hell पतन्ति they fall.

16. Bewildered by many a fancy, covered by the meshes of delusion, addicted to the gratification of lust, they fall down into a foul hell.

आत्मसम्भाविताः स्तब्धा धनमानमदान्विताः ।
यजन्ते नामयज्ञैस्ते दम्भेनाविधिपूर्वकम् ॥ १७

आत्मसम्भाविताः Self-conceited स्तब्धाः haughty धनमानमदान्विताः filled with the pride and intoxication of wealth ते they दम्भेन out of ostentation नामयज्ञैः sacrifices in name अविधिपूर्वकम् disregarding ordinance यजन्ते they perform;

17. Self-conceited, haughty, filled with the pride and intoxication of wealth, they perform sacrifices in name, out of ostentation, disregarding ordinance;

अहङ्कारं बलं दर्पं कामं क्रोधं च संश्रिताः ।
मामात्मपरदेहेषु प्रद्विषन्तोऽभ्यसूयकाः ॥ १८

अहङ्कारं Egoism बलं power दर्पं insolence कामं lust क्रोधं wrath च and संश्रिताः possessed of आत्मपरदेहेषु in their own bodies and in those of others माम् Me (the Self within) प्रद्विषन्तः hating अभ्यसूयकाः (these) malignant people.

18. Possessed of egoism, power, insolence, lust, and wrath, these malignant people hate Me (the Self within) in their own bodies and those of others.

तानहं द्विषतः क्रूरान्संसारेषु नराधमान् ।
क्षिपाम्यजस्रमशुभानासुरीष्वेव योनिषु ॥ १९

अहं I द्विषतः malicious क्रूरान् cruel नराधमान् most degraded of men अशुभान् evil-doers संसारेषु in these worlds आसुरीषु of *Asuras* योनिषु into the wombs एव only अजस्रम् perpetually क्षिपामि (I) hurl.

19. These malicious and cruel evil-doers, most degraded of men, I hurl perpetually into the wombs of *Asuras* only, in these worlds.

Wombs of Asuras: Wombs of the most cruel beings, as tigers, snakes, etc.
Worlds: Paths of *Saṁsāra* passing through many a hell.

आसुरीं योनिमापन्ना मूढा जन्मनि जन्मनि ।
मामप्राप्यैव कौन्तेय ततो यान्त्यधमां गतिम् ॥ २०

कौन्तेय O son of Kuntī मूढा: deluded जन्मनि जन्मनि birth after birth आसुरीं *Āsurika* योनिम् wombs आपन्ना: obtaining माम् Me अप्राप्य not attaining एव still ततः than that अधमां lower गतिम् condition यान्ति (they) fall into.

20. Obtaining the *Āsurika* wombs, and deluded birth after birth, not attaining to Me, they thus fall, O son of Kuntī, into a still lower condition.

त्रिविधं नरकस्येदं द्वारं नाशनमात्मनः ।
कामः क्रोधस्तथा लोभस्तस्मादेतत्त्रयं त्यजेत् ॥ २१

कामः Lust क्रोधः anger तथा and लोभः greed इदं this त्रिविधं triple नरकस्य of hell द्वारं the gate आत्मनः of the self नाशनम् destructive एतत् these त्रयं three त्यजेत् (one) should forsake.

21. Triple is this gate of hell, destructive of the self—lust, anger and greed; therefore one should forsake these three.

Destructive of the self: making the self fit for no human end whatever.

एतैर्विमुक्तः कौन्तेय तमोद्वारैस्त्रिभिर्नरः ।
आचरत्यात्मनः श्रेयस्ततो याति परां गतिम् ॥ २२

कौन्तेय O son of Kuntī एतैः from these त्रिभिः three तमोद्वारैः gates of darkness (hell) विमुक्तः free नरः the man आत्मनः for himself श्रेयः what is good आचरति practises ततः and then परां Supreme गतिम् Goal याति goes to.

22. The man who has got beyond these three gates of darkness, O son of Kuntī, practises what is good for himself, and thus goes to the Goal Supreme.

Gates of darkness: leading to hell (*Naraka*) which is full of pain and delusion.

यः शास्त्रविधिमुत्सृज्य वर्तते कामकारतः ।
न स सिद्धिमवाप्नोति न सुखं न परां गतिम् ।। २३

यः Who शास्त्रविधिम् the ordinance of the *Śāstra* उत्सृज्य setting aside कामकारतः under the impulse of desire वर्तते acts सः he सिद्धिम् perfection न not अवाप्नोति attains to न nor सुखं happiness न nor परां Supreme गतिम् Goal.

23. He who, setting aside the ordinance of the *Śāstra*, acts under the impulse of desire, attains not to perfection, nor happiness, nor the Goal Supreme.

Perfection: fitness for attaining the end of man.

तस्माच्छास्त्रं प्रमाणं ते कार्याकार्यव्यवस्थितौ ।
ज्ञात्वा शास्त्रविधानोक्तं कर्म कर्तुमिहार्हसि ।। २४

तस्मात् So कार्याकार्यव्यवस्थितौ in ascertaining what ought to be done and what ought not to be done शास्त्रं the *Śāstra* ते thy प्रमाणं (be) authority इह here शास्त्रविधानोक्तं what is said in the ordinance of the *Śāstra* ज्ञात्वा having known कर्म action कर्तुम् to do अर्हसि thou shouldst.

24. So let the *Śāstra* be thy authority in ascertaining what ought to be done and what ought not to be done. Having known what is said in the ordinance of the *Śāstra*, thou shouldst act here.

Here: in this world.

इति दैवासुर-सम्पद्विभागयोगो नाम षोडशोऽध्यायः ॥

The end of the sixteenth chapter, designated, *The Classification of the Divine and the Non-divine Attributes.*

सप्तदशोऽध्यायः
(श्रद्धात्रय-विभागयोगः)

SEVENTEENTH CHAPTER
(The enquiry into The Threefold Śraddhā)

अर्जुन उवाच

ये शास्त्रविधिमुत्सृज्य यजन्ते श्रद्धयान्विताः ।
तेषां निष्ठा तु का कृष्ण सत्त्वमाहो रजस्तमः ॥ १

अर्जुनः Arjuna उवाच said:

कृष्ण O Kṛṣṇa ये who शास्त्रविधिम् the ordinance of the *Śāstra* उत्सृज्य setting aside श्रद्धया with *Śraddhā* तु but अन्विताः endued यजन्ते perform sacrifice तेषां their निष्ठा condition का what सत्त्वम् *Sattva* रजः *Rajas* आहो or तमः *Tamas*.

Arjuna said:

1. Those who, setting aside the ordinance of the *Śāstra*, perform sacrifice with *Śraddhā*, what is their condition, O Kṛṣṇa ? (Is it) *Sattva*, *Rajas* or *Tamas* ?

Setting . . . Śraddhā: not that they believe the ordinance of the *Śāstra* to be false, but out of laziness or because of the difficulty in adhering to them strictly, they let them alone and worship the gods, endued with *Śraddhā*.

श्रीभगवानुवाच

त्रिविधा भवति श्रद्धा देहिनां सा स्वभावजा।
सात्त्विकी राजसी चैव तामसी चेति तां शृणु ॥ २

श्रीभगवान् The Blessed Lord उवाच said:

देहिनां Of the embodied सात्त्विकी the *Sāttvika* राजसी the *Rājasika* तामसी the *Tāmasika* च and इति thus त्रिविधा threefold एव indeed श्रद्धा the *Śraddhā* भवति is सा which स्वभावजा (is) inherent in (their) nature तां of it शृणु hear (thou).

The Blessed Lord said:

2. Threefold is the *Śraddhā* of the embodied, which is inherent in their nature—the *Sāttvika*, the *Rājasika* and the *Tāmasika*. Do thou hear of it.

Inherent. . . nature: born of their past *Saṁskāras*.
It: the threefold *Śraddhā*.

सत्त्वानुरूपा सर्वस्य श्रद्धा भवति भारत।
श्रद्धामयोऽयं पुरुषो यो यच्छ्रद्धः स एव सः ॥ ३

भारत O descendant of Bharata सर्वस्य of each श्रद्धा *Śraddhā* सत्त्वानुरूपा according to his natural disposition भवति is अयं the पुरुषः man श्रद्धामयः consists of (his) *Śraddhā* यः he यच्छ्रद्धः what (his) *Śraddhā* is सः he एव verily सः that (is).

3. The *Śraddhā* of each is according to his natural disposition, O descendant of Bharata. The

man consists of his *Śraddhā*; he verily is what his *Śraddhā* is.

Natural disposition: the specific tendencies or *Saṁskāras*.

यजन्ते सात्त्विका देवान्यक्षरक्षांसि राजसाः ।
प्रेतान्भूतगणांश्चान्ये यजन्ते तामसा जनाः ॥ ४

सात्त्विका: *Sāttvika* men देवान् the *Devas* यजन्ते worship राजसा: the *Rājasika* यक्षरक्षांसि the *Yakṣas* and the *Rākṣasas* अन्ये the others तामसा: the *Tāmasika* जना: men प्रेतान् the *Pretas* भूतगणान् the hosts of *Bhūtas* च and यजन्ते worship.

4. *Sāttvika* men worship the *Devas*; *Rājasika*, the *Yakṣas* and the *Rākṣasas*; the others—the *Tāmasika* men—worship the *Pretas* and the hosts of *Bhūtas*.

अशास्त्रविहितं घोरं तप्यन्ते ये तपो जनाः ।
दम्भाहङ्कारसंयुक्ताः कामरागबलान्विताः ॥ ५
कर्शयन्तः शरीरस्थं भूतग्राममचेतसः ।
मां चैवान्तःशरीरस्थं तान्विद्ध्यासुरनिश्चयान् ॥ ६

दम्भाहङ्कारसंयुक्ता: Given to ostentation and egoism कामरागबलान्विता: endowed with the power of lust and attachment ये who अचेतस: senseless जना: men शरीरस्थं in the body भूतग्रामम् all the organs अन्त:शरीरस्थं that dwell in the body within मां Me च and कर्शयन्त: torturing अशास्त्रविहितं not enjoined by the *Śāstras* घोरं severe तप: austerity तप्यन्ते practise तान् them आसुरनिश्चयान् to be of *Āsurika* resolve विद्धि know.

5–6. Those men who practise severe austerities not enjoined by the *Śāstras,* given to ostentation and egoism, endowed with the power of lust and attachment, torture, senseless as they are, all the organs in the body, and Me dwelling in the body within; know them to be of *Āsurika* resolve.

Austerities: which cause pain to himself and to other living beings.

Endowed . . . attachment: may also be interpreted as, "possessed of lust, attachment and power".

All the organs of the body: the aggregate of all the elements composing the body.

आहारस्त्वपि सर्वस्य त्रिविधो भवति प्रियः ।
यज्ञस्तपस्तथा दानं तेषां भेदमिमं शृणु ।। ७

सर्वस्य By each of them अपि also आहार: food तु indeed त्रिविध: threefold प्रिय: liked भवति is तथा as also यज्ञ: *Yajña* तप: austerity दानं almsgiving च and तेषां their इमं this भेदम् distinction शृणु do thou hear.

7. The food also which is liked by each of them is threefold, as also is *Yajña*, austerity, and almsgiving. Do thou hear this distinction of them.

आयुःसत्त्वबलारोग्यसुखप्रीतिविवर्धनाः ।
रस्याः स्निग्धाः स्थिरा हृद्या आहाराः सात्त्विकप्रियाः ।। ८

आयु:सत्त्वबलारोग्यसुखप्रीतिविवर्धना: Those which augment आयु: vitality सत्त्वम् energy बलम् strength आरोग्यम् health सुखम् cheerfulness and प्रीति: appetite रस्या: which are savoury स्निग्धाः oleaginous स्थिराः substantial हृद्याः agreeable आहाराः the foods सात्त्विकप्रियाः (are) liked by the *Sāttvika*.

8. The foods which augment vitality, energy, strength, health, cheerfulness, and appetite, which are savoury and oleaginous, substantial and agreeable, are liked by the *Sāttvika*.

कट्वम्ललवणात्युष्णतीक्ष्णरूक्षविदाहिनः ।
आहारा राजसस्येष्टा दुःखशोकामयप्रदाः ॥ ९

कट्वम्ललवणात्युष्णतीक्ष्णरूक्षविदाहिनः Those that are कटुः bitter अम्लः sour लवणः saline अत्युष्णः excessively hot तीक्ष्णः pungent रूक्षः dry and विदाहिनः burning दुःखशोकामयप्रदाः are productive of pain, grief, and disease आहाराः the foods राजसस्य by the *Rājasika* इष्टाः are liked.

9. The foods that are bitter, sour, saline, excessively hot, pungent, dry, and burning, are liked by the *Rājasika*, and are productive of pain, grief, and disease.

Excessively: this word should be construed with each of the seven; thus, excessively bitter, excessively sour, and so on.

यातयामं गतरसं पूति पर्युषितं च यत् ।
उच्छिष्टमपि चामेध्यं भोजनं तामसप्रियम् ॥ १०

यत् Which यातयामं (is) stale गतरसं is tasteless पूति stinking पर्युषितं cooked overnight उच्छिष्टम् refuse अमेध्यं impure च and भोजनं the food तामसप्रियम् liked by the *Tāmasika*.

10. That which is stale, tasteless, stinking, cooked overnight, refuse, and impure, is the food liked by the *Tāmasika*.

Stale: *Yātayāmam*—lit., cooked three hours ago.
Refuse: left on the plate after a meal.

अफलाकाङ्क्षिभिर्यज्ञो विधिदृष्टो य इज्यते।
यष्टव्यमेवेति मनः समाधाय स सात्त्विकः॥ ११

अफलाकाङ्क्षिभि: By men desiring no fruit यष्टव्यम् to be performed for its own sake एव only इति as मन: (their) mind समाधाय fixing विधिदृष्ट: as enjoined by ordinance य: which यज्ञ: *Yajña* इज्यते is performed स: that सात्त्विक: is *Sāttvika*.

11. That *Yajña* is *Sāttvika* which is performed by men desiring no fruit, as enjoined by ordinance, with their mind fixed on the *Yajña* only, for its own sake.

अभिसन्धाय तु फलं दम्भार्थमपि चैव यत्।
इज्यते भरतश्रेष्ठ तं यज्ञं विद्धि राजसम्॥ १२

फलं Fruit अभिसन्धाय seeking for तु but दम्भार्थम् for ostentation अपि also एव indeed च and यत् which इज्यते is performed भरतश्रेष्ठ O best of the Bhāratas तं that यज्ञं *Yajña* राजसम् *Rājasika* विद्धि know (it to be).

12. That which is performed, O best of the Bhāratas, seeking for fruit and for ostentation, know it to be a *Rājasika Yajña*.

विधिहीनमसृष्टान्नं मन्त्रहीनमदक्षिणम् ।
श्रद्धाविरहितं यज्ञं तामसं परिचक्षते ।। १३

विधिहीनम् Without keeping to ordinance असृष्टान्नं in which no food is distributed मन्त्रहीनम् which is devoid of *Mantras* अदक्षिणम् which is devoid of gifts श्रद्धाविरहितं devoid of *Śraddhā* यज्ञं *Yajña* तामसं *Tāmasika* परिचक्षते is said to be.

13. The *Yajña* performed without heed to ordinance, in which no food is distributed, which is devoid of *Mantras*, gifts, and *Śraddhā*, is said to be *Tāmasika*.

देवद्विजगुरुप्राज्ञपूजनं शौचमार्जवम् ।
ब्रह्मचर्यमहिंसा च शारीरं तप उच्यते ।। १४

देवद्विजगुरुप्राज्ञपूजनं Worship of the *Devas*, the twice-born, the *Gurus*, and the wise शौचम् purity आर्जवम् straightforwardness ब्रह्मचर्यम् continence अहिंसा non-injury च and शारीरं of the body तपः the austerity उच्यते is called.

14. Worship of the *Devas*, the twice-born, the *Gurus*, and the wise, as well as purity, straightforwardness, continence, and non-injury are called the austerity of the body.

अनुद्वेगकरं वाक्यं सत्यं प्रियहितं च यत् ।
स्वाध्यायाभ्यसनं चैव वाङ्मयं तप उच्यते ।। १५

अनुद्वेगकरं Causing no vexation सत्यं true प्रियहितं agreeable and beneficial च as also यत् which वाक्यं speech स्वाध्यायाभ्यसनं regular study of Vedas च एव and also वाङ्मयं of speech तप: the austerity उच्यते is said (to form)

15. Speech which causes no vexation, and is truthful, as also agreeable and beneficial, and regular study of the Vedas—these are said to form the austerity of speech.

Speech, to be an austerity, must form an invariable combination of all the four attributes mentioned in the *Śloka*; if it lacks in one or other of them, it will no longer be an austerity of speech.

मनःप्रसादः सौम्यत्वं मौनमात्मविनिग्रहः ।
भावसंशुद्धिरित्येतत्तपो मानसमुच्यते ।। १६

मन:प्रसाद: Serenity of mind सौम्यत्वं kindliness मौनम् silence आत्मविनिग्रह: self-control भावसंशुद्धि: honesty of motive इति एतत् this मानसम् mental तप: the austerity उच्यते is called.

16. Serenity of mind, kindliness, silence, self-control, honesty of motive—this is called the mental austerity.

Silence: *Maunam*—is the result of the control of thought so far as it concerns speech. Or it may mean, the condition of the *Muni*, i.e., practice of meditation.

श्रद्धया परया तप्तं तपस्तत्त्रिविधं नरैः ।
अफलाकाङ्क्षिभिर्युक्तैः सात्त्विकं परिचक्षते ॥ १७

अफलाकाङ्क्षिभिः Desiring no fruit युक्तैः steadfast नरैः by men परया great श्रद्धया with *Śraddhā* तप्तं practised तत् that त्रिविधं threefold तपः austerity सात्त्विकं *Sāttvika* परिचक्षते (sages) call.

17. This threefold austerity practised by steadfast men with great *Śraddhā*, desiring no fruit, is said to be *Sāttvika*.

Steadfast: unaffected in success and failure.

सत्कारमानपूजार्थं तपो दम्भेन चैव यत् ।
क्रियते तदिह प्रोक्तं राजसं चलमध्रुवम् ॥ १८

सत्कारमानपूजार्थं With the object of gaining praise, honour, and worship दम्भेन with ostentation च एव and यत् which तपः austerity क्रियते is practised इह here चलम् unstable अध्रुवम् transitory तद् that राजसं *Rājasika* प्रोक्तं is said (to be).

18. That austerity which is practised with the object of gaining praise, honour, and worship, and with ostentation, is here said to be *Rājasika* — unstable and transitory.

With ostentation: for mere show, hypocritically, with no sincere belief.

Here: is explained also in the sense of "of this world", i.e. yielding fruit only in this world.

मूढग्राहेणात्मनो यत्पीडया क्रियते तपः ।
परस्योत्सादनार्थं वा तत्तामसमुदाहृतम् ॥ १९

मूढग्राहेण Out of a foolish notion आत्मनः of self पीडया with torture परस्य of another उत्सादनार्थं for the purpose of ruining वा or यत् which तपः austerity क्रियते is practised तत् that तामसम् *Tāmasika* उदाहृतम् is declared (to be).

19. That austerity which is practised out of a foolish notion, with self-torture or for the purpose of ruining another, is declared to be *Tāmasika*.

दातव्यमिति यद्दानं दीयतेऽनुपकारिणे ।
देशे काले च पात्रे च तद्दानं सात्त्विकं स्मृतम् ॥ २०

देशे In a fit place काले in a fit time च and पात्रे to a worthy person च and दातव्यम् to give is right इति with this idea अनुपकारिणे to one who does no service (in return) यद् which दानं gift दीयते is given तद् that दानं gift सात्त्विकं *Sāttvika* स्मृतम् is held to be.

20. "To give is right"—gift given with this idea, to one who does no service in return, in a fit place and to a worthy person, that gift is held to be *Sāttvika*.

Who ... return: one who cannot, or who though able is not expected to return the good.

यत्तु प्रत्युपकारार्थं फलमुद्दिश्य वा पुनः ।
दीयते च परिक्लिष्टं तद्दानं राजसं स्मृतम् ॥ २१

यत् What तु and प्रत्युपकारार्थं with a view to receiving in return फलम् च and the fruit उद्दिश्य looking for वा or पुन: again परिक्लिष्टं reluctantly दीयते is given तद् that दानं gift राजसं *Rājasika* स्मृतम् is held to be.

21. And what is given with a view to receiving in return, or looking for the fruit, or again reluctantly, that gift is held to be *Rājasika*.

अदेशकाले यद्दानमपात्रेभ्यश्च दीयते ।
असत्कृतमवज्ञातं तत्तामसमुदाहृतम् ।। २२

अदेशकाले At the wrong place or time अपात्रेभ्य: च and to unworthy persons असत्कृतम् without regard अवज्ञातं with disdain यद् that दानम् gift दीयते is given तत् that तामसम् *Tāmasika* उदाहृतम् is declared to be.

22. The gift that is given at the wrong place or time, to unworthy persons, without regard or with disdain, that is declared to be *Tāmasika*.

ॐ तत्सदिति निर्देशो ब्रह्मणस्त्रिविधः स्मृतः ।
ब्राह्मणास्तेन वेदाश्च यज्ञाश्च विहिताः पुरा ।। २३

ॐ *Om* तत् *Tat* सद् *Sat* इति this ब्रह्मण: of Brahman त्रिविध: triple निर्देश: designation स्मृत: has been declared तेन by that ब्राह्मणा: the *Brāhmaṇas* च and वेदा: the Vedas च and यज्ञा: the *Yajñas* पुरा of old विहिता: were made.

23. "*Om-Tat-Sat*" — this has been declared to be the triple designation of Brahman. By that were

made of old the *Brāhmaṇas*, the Vedas, and the *Yajñas*.

Om-Tat-Sat : *Om* is the principal name of the Lord, because it means all that is manifest and the beyond. It also means "Yes". *Tat* means "That"; the Indefinable, that which can only be described indirectly as "That which". *Sat* means Reality, which is ever permanent in one mode of being.

तस्मादोमित्युदाहृत्य यज्ञदानतपःक्रियाः ।
प्रवर्तन्ते विधानोक्ताः सततं ब्रह्मवादिनाम् ।। २४

तस्माद् Therefore ओम् *Om* इति उदाहृत्य uttering ब्रह्मवादिनाम् of the followers of the Vedas विधानोक्ता: as enjoined in the ordinances यज्ञदानतप:क्रिया: the acts of sacrifice, gift, and austerity सततं always प्रवर्तन्ते begun.

24. Therefore, uttering "Om", are the acts of sacrifice, gift, and austerity as enjoined in the ordinances, always begun by the followers of the Vedas.

तदित्यनभिसन्धाय फलं यज्ञतपःक्रियाः ।
दानक्रियाश्च विविधाः क्रियन्ते मोक्षकाङ्क्षिभिः ।। २५

तद् *Tat* इति thus (uttering) फलं the fruit अनभिसन्धाय without aiming at मोक्षकाङ्क्षिभि: by seekers of *Mokṣa* विविधा: various यज्ञतप:क्रिया: acts of *Yajña* and austerity दानक्रिया: acts of gift च and क्रियन्ते are performed.

25. Uttering "*Tat*", without aiming at fruits, are the various acts of *Yajña*, austerity, and gift performed by the seekers of *Mokṣa*.

सद्भावे साधुभावे च सदित्येतत्प्रयुज्यते ।
प्रशस्ते कर्मणि तथा सच्छब्दः पार्थ युज्यते ।। २६

पार्थ O Pārtha सद्भावे in the sense of reality साधुभावे in the sense of goodness च and सद् *Sat* इति as एतत् this प्रयुज्यते is used तथा so long प्रशस्ते auspicious कर्मणि in (the sense of) an act च and सत् *Sat* शब्दः the word युज्यते is used.

26. The word "*Sat*" is used in the sense of reality and of goodness; and so also, O Pārtha, the word "*Sat*" is used in the sense of an auspicious act.

यज्ञे तपसि दाने च स्थितिः सदिति चोच्यते ।
कर्म चैव तदर्थीयं सदित्येवाभिधीयते ।। २७

यज्ञे In *Yajña* तपसि in austerity दाने in gift च and स्थितिः steadiness सद् *Sat* इति so उच्यते is called च also तदर्थीयं in connection with these, or, for the sake of the Lord कर्म action च एव as also सद् *Sat* इति एव so अभिधीयते is called.

27. Steadiness in *Yajña*, austerity, and gift is also called "*Sat*", as also action in connection with these (or, action for the sake of the Lord) is called "*Sat*".

अश्रद्धया हुतं दत्तं तपस्तप्तं कृतं च यत् ।
असदित्युच्यते पार्थ न च तत्प्रेत्य नो इह ।। २८

अश्रद्धया Without *Śraddhā* हुतं is sacrificed दत्तं given तप्तं is practised तपः austerity च and यत् whatever कृतं performed असद् *Asat* इति so उच्यते is called पार्थ O Pārtha तत् it न च neither प्रेत्य hereafter (after death) नो nor इह here.

28. Whatever is sacrificed, given, or performed and whatever austerity is practised without *Śraddhā*, it is called *Asat*, O Pārtha; it is naught here or hereafter.

It is naught here or hereafter: Though costing much trouble it is of no use here as it is not acceptable to the wise ones, nor can it produce any effect conducive to good hereafter.

इति श्रद्धात्रय-विभागयोगो नाम सप्तदशोऽध्यायः ॥

The end of the seventeenth chapter, designated,
The Enquiry into the Threefold Śraddhā.

अष्टादशोऽध्यायः
(मोक्ष-सन्न्यासयोगः)

EIGHTEENTH CHAPTER
(The Way of Liberation in Renunciation)

अर्जुन उवाच

सन्न्यासस्य महाबाहो तत्त्वमिच्छामि वेदितुम्।
त्यागस्य च हृषीकेश पृथक्केशिनिषूदन॥ १

अर्जुनः Arjuna उवाच said:

हृषीकेश O Hṛṣīkeśa महाबाहो O mighty-armed केशिनिषूदन O Slayer of Keśi सन्न्यासस्य of *Sannyāsa* त्यागस्य of *Tyāga* च as also पृथक् severally तत्त्वम् truth वेदितुम् to know इच्छामि I desire.

Arjuna said:

1. I desire to know severally, O mighty-armed, the truth of *Sannyāsa*, O *Hṛṣīkeśa*, as also of *Tyāga*, O slayer of Keśi.

Sannyāsa and *Tyāga* both mean renunciation.
Keśi: was an Asura.

श्रीभगवानुवाच

काम्यानां कर्मणां न्यासं सन्न्यासं कवयो विदुः ।
सर्वकर्मफलत्यागं प्राहुस्त्यागं विचक्षणाः ।। २

श्रीभगवान् The Blessed Lord उवाच said:
कवय: The sages काम्यानां *Kāmya* कर्मणां of actions न्यासं the renunciation सन्न्यासं (as) *Sannyāsa* विदु: understand विचक्षणा: the wise सर्वकर्मफलत्यागं the abandonment of the fruit of all works त्यागं (as) *Tyāga* प्राहु: delare.

The Blessed Lord said:
2. The renunciation of *Kāmya* actions, the sages understand as *Sannyāsa*; the wise declare the abandonment of the fruit of all works as *Tyāga*.

Kāmya: which are accompanied with a desire for fruits.

त्याज्यं दोषवदित्येके कर्म प्राहुर्मनीषिणः ।
यज्ञदानतपःकर्म न त्याज्यमिति चापरे ।। ३

एके Some मनीषिण: philosophers कर्म (all) actions दोषवद् as an evil इति that त्याज्यं should be relinquished प्राहु: declare अपरे others च whilst यज्ञदानतप:कर्म the work of *Yajña*, gift, and austerity न not त्याज्यम् should be relinquished इति that.

3. Some philosophers declare that all actions should be relinquished as an evil, whilst others (say) that the work of *Yajña*, gift, and austerity should not be relinquished.

निश्चयं शृणु मे तत्र त्यागे भरतसत्तम।
त्यागो हि पुरुषव्याघ्र त्रिविधः सम्प्रकीर्तितः ॥ ४

भरतसत्तम O best of the Bhāratas पुरुषव्याघ्र O tiger among men तत्र about that त्यागे in relinquishment मे from Me निश्चयं the final truth शृणु hear त्यागः relinquishment हि for त्रिविधः of three kinds सम्प्रकीर्तितः has been declared (to be).

4. Hear from Me the final truth about relinquishment, O best of the Bhāratas. For relinquishment has been declared to be of three kinds, O tiger among men.

यज्ञदानतपःकर्म न त्याज्यं कार्यमेव तत्।
यज्ञो दानं तपश्चैव पावनानि मनीषिणाम् ॥ ५

यज्ञदानतपःकर्म The work of *Yajña*, gift, and austerity न not त्याज्यं should be relinquished तत् it कार्यम् should be performed एव indeed यज्ञः *Yajña* दानं gift तपः austerity च and एव indeed मनीषिणाम् to the wise पावनानि are purifying.

5. The work of *Yajña*, gift, and austerity should not be relinquished, but it should indeed be performed; (for) *Yajña*, gift, and austerity are purifying to the wise.

एतान्यपि तु कर्माणि सङ्गं त्यक्त्वा फलानि च।
कर्तव्यानीति मे पार्थ निश्चितं मतमुत्तमम् ॥ ६

पार्थ O Pārtha एतानि these कर्माणि works अपि even तु but सङ्गं attachment फलानि the fruits च and त्यक्त्वा leaving कर्तव्यानि should be performed इति such मे My निश्चितं certain उत्तमम् best मतम् conviction.

6. But even these works, O Pārtha should be performed, leaving attachment and the fruits; such is My best and certain conviction.

नियतस्य तु सन्न्यासः कर्मणो नोपपद्यते।
मोहात्तस्य परित्यागस्तामसः परिकीर्तितः ॥ ७

नियतस्य Obligatory कर्मणः of action तु but सन्न्यासः the renunciation न not उपपद्यते is proper मोहात् from delusion तस्य of the same परित्यागः abandonment तामसः *Tāmasika* परिकीर्तितः is declared.

7. But the renunciation of obligatory action is not proper. Abandonment of the same from delusion is declared to be *Tāmasika*.

Since it is purifying in the case of the ignorant.

दुःखमित्येव यत्कर्म कायक्लेशभयात्त्यजेत्।
स कृत्वा राजसं त्यागं नैव त्यागफलं लभेत् ॥ ८

दुःखम् (It is) painful इति because एव only कायक्लेशभयात् from fear of bodily trouble यत् which कर्म action त्यजेत् relinquishes स he राजसं *Rājasika* त्यागं relinquishment कृत्वा performing त्यागफलं the fruit of relinquishment न not एव लभेत् obtains.

8. He who from fear of bodily trouble relinquishes action, because it is painful, thus performing a *Rājasika* relinquishment, he obtains not the fruit thereof.

Fruit: i.e. *Mokṣa*, which comes out of the renunciation of all actions accompanied with wisdom.

कार्यमित्येव यत्कर्म नियतं क्रियतेऽर्जुन।
सङ्गं त्यक्त्वा फलं चैव स त्यागः सात्त्विको मतः ॥ ९

अर्जुन O Arjuna सङ्गं attachment फलं fruit च एव and त्यक्त्वा leaving कार्यम् it ought to be done इति because एव only यत् which नियतं obligatory कर्म action क्रियते is performed सः such त्यागः relinquishment सात्त्विकः *Sāttvika* मतः is regarded.

9. When obligatory work is performed, O Arjuna, only because it ought to be done, leaving attachment and fruit, such relinquishment is regarded as *Sāttvika*.

न द्वेष्ट्यकुशलं कर्म कुशले नानुषज्जते।
त्यागी सत्त्वसमाविष्टो मेधावी छिन्नसंशयः ॥ १०

सत्त्वसमाविष्टः Endued with *Sattva* मेधावी with a steady understanding छिन्नसंशयः with his doubts dispelled त्यागी the relinquisher अकुशलं disagreeable कर्म action न not द्वेष्टि hates कुशले to an agreeable one न nor अनुषज्जते is attached.

10. The relinquisher endued with *Sattva* and a steady understanding, and with his doubts dispelled, hates not a disagreeable work nor is attached to an agreeable one.

न हि देहभृता शक्यं त्यक्तुं कर्माण्यशेषतः।
यस्तु कर्मफलत्यागी स त्यागीत्यभिधीयते॥ ११

देहभृता by an embodied being अशेषत: entirely कर्माणि actions त्यक्तुं to relinquish न not हि indeed शक्यं can be य: who तु but कर्मफलत्यागी relinquisher of the fruits of action स: he त्यागी relinquisher इति thus अभिधीयते is called.

11. Actions cannot be entirely relinquished by an embodied being, but he who relinquishes the fruits of action is called a relinquisher.

अनिष्टमिष्टं मिश्रं च त्रिविधं कर्मणः फलम्।
भवत्यत्यागिनां प्रेत्य न तु सन्न्यासिनां क्वचित्॥ १२

अत्यागिनां To non-relinquishers प्रेत्य after death अनिष्टम् disagreeable इष्टं agreeable मिश्रं mixed च and त्रिविधं threefold कर्मण: of action फलम् fruit भवति accrues तु but सन्न्यासिनां to relinquishers क्वचित् ever न not.

12. The threefold fruit of action—disagreeable, agreeable, and mixed—accrues to non-relinquishers after death, but never to relinquishers.

पञ्चैतानि महाबाहो कारणानि निबोध मे।
सांख्ये कृतान्ते प्रोक्तानि सिद्धये सर्वकर्मणाम्॥ १३

महाबाहो O mighty-armed सांख्ये in the wisdom कृतान्ते which is the end of all action सर्वकर्मणाम् of all works सिद्धये for the accomplishment प्रोक्तानि as declared एतानि these पञ्च five कारणानि causes मे from Me निबोध learn.

13. Learn from Me, O mighty-armed, these five causes for the accomplishment of all works as declared in the wisdom which is the end of all action.

Wisdom: *Sāṅkhya*—literally, in which all the things that are to be known are expounded, therefore, the highest wisdom.

अधिष्ठानं तथा कर्ता करणं च पृथग्विधम्।
विविधाश्च पृथक् चेष्टा दैवं चैवात्र पञ्चमम्॥ १४

अधिष्ठानं The body तथा also कर्ता the agent पृथग्विधम् various करणं the senses विविधा: of a manifold kind पृथक् different चेष्टा: functions अत्र of these पञ्चमम् the fifth दैवं the presiding divinity च एव and also.

14. (They are) the body, the agent, the various senses, the different functions of a manifold kind, and also the presiding divinity, the fifth of these.

Presiding divinity: Each of the senses has its god who presides over it, and by whose aid it discharges its own functions; e.g., *Āditya* (the Sun) is the presiding divinity of the eye, by whose aid it sees and acts; and so on with the other senses.

शरीरवाङ्मनोभिर्यत्कर्म प्रारभते नरः ।
न्याय्यं वा विपरीतं वा पञ्चैते तस्य हेतवः ।। १५

नरः A man शरीरवाङ्मनोभिः by (this) body, speech, and mind यत् whatever न्याय्यं right वा or विपरीतं the reverse कर्म action प्रारभते performs एते these पञ्च five तस्य its हेतवः causes.

15. Whatever action a man performs by his body, speech, and mind—whether right or the reverse—these five are its causes.

तत्रैवं सति कर्तारमात्मानं केवलं तु यः ।
पश्यत्यकृतबुद्धित्वान्न स पश्यति दुर्मतिः ।। १६

एवं Thus सति being तत्र there (the case) केवलं the Absolute आत्मानं the Self तु verily अकृतबुद्धित्वात् through a non-purified understanding यः who कर्तारम् as the agent पश्यति looks upon सः he दुर्मतिः of perverted mind न not पश्यति sees.

16. Such being the case, he who through a non-purified understanding looks upon his Self, the Absolute, as the agent—he of perverted mind sees not.

यस्य नाहंकृतो भावो बुद्धिर्यस्य न लिप्यते ।
हत्वापि स इमाँल्लोकान्न हन्ति न निबध्यते ।। १७

यस्य Whose अहंकृत: of egoism भाव: the notion न not यस्य whose बुद्धि: intelligence न not लिप्यते is affected स: he इमान् these लोकान् people हत्वा killing अपि though न not हन्ति kills न nor निबध्यते is bound.

17. He who is free from the notion of egoism, whose intelligence is not affected (by good or evil), though he kills these people, he kills not, nor is bound (by the action).

He whose self-consciousness, by the force of long, strenuous, and properly-trained self-concentration, is ever identified with Brahman, and not with the five causes of action as mentioned in *Śloka* 14—he whose self-consciousness never mistakes itself for the body, mind, and the like, even when performing physical acts—he is ever free from the taint of action.

ज्ञानं ज्ञेयं परिज्ञाता त्रिविधा कर्मचोदना।
करणं कर्म कर्तेति त्रिविधः कर्मसंग्रहः॥ १८

ज्ञानं Knowledge ज्ञेयं the known परिज्ञाता the knower त्रिविधा threefold कर्मचोदना the cause of action करणं the instrument कर्म the object कर्ता the agent इति the त्रिविध: threefold कर्मसंग्रह: the basis of action.

18. Knowledge, the known and the knower form the threefold cause of action. The instrument, the object, and the agent are the threefold basis of action.

Basis: because the threefold action inheres in these three.

ज्ञानं कर्म च कर्ता च त्रिधैव गुणभेदतः ।
प्रोच्यते गुणसंख्याने यथावच्छृणु तान्यपि ।। १९

गुणसंख्याने In the (science of) enumeration of the *Guṇas* (Sāṅkhya philosophy) ज्ञानं knowledge कर्म action च and कर्ता agent च and गुणभेदतः from the distinction of *Guṇas* त्रिधा of three kinds एव only प्रोच्यते are declared (to be) तानि them अपि also यथावत् duly शृणु hear.

19. Knowledge, action and agent are declared in the Sāṅkhya philosophy to be of three kinds only, from the distinction of *Guṇas*: hear them also duly.

Sāṅkhya: the Science of the *Guṇas* by Kapila. Though the Sāṅkhya view is in conflict with the supreme Truth of Vedānta—the oneness or non-duality of Brahman—yet the former view is given here, because it is an authority on the science of *Guṇas*.

Duly: described according to the science, according to reason.

सर्वभूतेषु येनैकं भावमव्ययमीक्षते ।
अविभक्तं विभक्तेषु तज्ज्ञानं विद्धि सात्त्विकम् ।। २०

येन By which विभक्तेषु in the separate सर्वभूतेषु (in) all beings अविभक्तं inseparate एकं the one अव्ययम् indestructible भावम् Substance ईक्षते (one) sees तत् that ज्ञानं knowledge सात्त्विकम् to be *Sāttvika* विद्धि know (thou).

20. That by which the one indestructible Substance is seen in all beings, inseparate in the separated, know that knowledge to be *Sāttvika*.

Inseparate: undifferentiated; permeating all.

पृथक्त्वेन तु यज्ज्ञानं नानाभावान्पृथग्विधान्।
वेत्ति सर्वेषु भूतेषु तज्ज्ञानं विद्धि राजसम्॥ २१।

पृथक्त्वेन As different from one another तु but यत् which ज्ञानं knowledge सर्वेषु all भूतेषु in beings पृथग्विधान् of distinct kinds नानाभावान् various entities वेत्ति knows तत् that ज्ञानं knowledge राजसम् as *Rājasika* विद्धि know (thou).

21. But the knowledge which sees in all beings various entities of distinct kinds as different from one another, know thou that knowledge as *Rājasika*.

Entities: Souls.
Different from one another: Different in different bodies.

यत्तु कृत्स्नवदेकस्मिन् कार्ये सक्तमहैतुकम्।
अतत्त्वार्थवदल्पं च तत्तामसमुदाहृतम्॥ २२

यत् Which तु but एकस्मिन् one single कार्ये to effect कृत्स्नवद् as if it were the whole सक्तम् confined अहैतुकम् without reason अतत्त्वार्थवद् without foundation in truth अल्पं trivial च and तत् that तामसम् *Tāmasika* उदाहृतम् is declared.

22. Whilst that which is confined to one single effect as if it were the whole, without reason, without foundation in truth, and trivial—that is declared to be *Tāmasika*.

One single effect: such as the body—thinking it to be the Self.

नियतं सङ्गरहितमरागद्वेषतः कृतम् ।
अफलप्रेप्सुना कर्म यत्तत्सात्त्विकमुच्यते ।। २३

अफलप्रेप्सुना By one not desirous of the fruit नियतं ordained सङ्गरहितम् free from attachment अरागद्वेषतः without love or hatred कृतम् done यत् which कर्म action तत् that सात्त्विकम् *Sāttvika* उच्यते is declared.

23. An ordained action done without love or hatred by one not desirous of the fruit and free from attachment, is declared to be *Sāttvika*.

यत्तु कामेप्सुना कर्म साहंकारेण वा पुनः ।
क्रियते बहुलायासं तद्राजसमुदाहृतम् ।। २४

कामेप्सुना By one desiring results साहंकारेण with self-conceit वा or बहुलायासं with much effort यत् which तु but पुनः again कर्म the action क्रियते is performed तद् that राजसम् *Rājasika* उदाहृतम् is declared.

24. But the action which is performed desiring results, or with self-conceit and with much effort, is declared to be *Rājasika*.

अनुबन्धं क्षयं हिंसामनपेक्ष्य च पौरुषम् ।
मोहादारभ्यते कर्म यत्तत्तामसमुच्यते ।। २५

अनुबन्धं The consequence क्षयं loss (of power and wealth) हिंसाम् injury (to others) पौरुषम् (one's own) ability च and अनपेक्ष्य without heeding मोहाद् through delusion यत् which कर्म action आरभ्यते is undertaken तत् that तामसम् *Tāmasika* उच्यते is declared.

25. That action is declared to be *Tāmasika* which is undertaken through delusion, without heed to the consequence, loss (of power and wealth), injury (to others), and (one's own) ability.

मुक्तसङ्गोऽनहंवादी धृत्युत्साहसमन्वितः।
सिद्ध्यसिद्ध्योर्निर्विकारः कर्ता सात्त्विक उच्यते॥ २६

मुक्तसङ्गः: Who is free from attachment अनहंवादी non-egotistic धृत्युत्साहसमन्वितः endued with fortitude and enthusiasm सिद्ध्यसिद्ध्योः in success or failure निर्विकारः unaffected कर्ता an agent सात्त्विकः *Sāttvika* उच्यते is called.

26. An agent who is free from attachment, non-egotistic, endued with fortitude and enthusiasm, and unaffected in success or failure, is called *Sāttvika*.

रागी कर्मफलप्रेप्सुर्लुब्धो हिंसात्मकोऽशुचिः।
हर्षशोकान्वितः कर्ता राजसः परिकीर्तितः॥ २७

रागी Passionate कर्मफलप्रेप्सुः desirous of the fruits of action लुब्धः greedy हिंसात्मकः malignant अशुचिः impure हर्षशोकान्वितः (easily) affected by elation or dejection कर्ता (such) an agent राजसः *Rājasika* परिकीर्तितः is called.

27. He who is passionate, desirous of the fruits of action, greedy, malignant, impure, easily elated or dejected, such an agent is called *Rājasika*.

Elated or dejected: at the success or failure of the action in which he is engaged.

अयुक्तः प्राकृतः स्तब्धः शठो नैष्कृतिकोऽलसः।
विषादी दीर्घसूत्री च कर्ता तामस उच्यते॥ २८

अयुक्तः Unsteady प्राकृतः vulgar स्तब्धः arrogant शठः dishonest नैष्कृतिकः malicious अलसः indolent विषादी desponding दीर्घसूत्री procrastinating च and कर्ता (such) an agent तामसः *Tāmasika* उच्यते is called.

28. Unsteady, vulgar, arrogant, dishonest, malicious, indolent, desponding, and procrastinating, such an agent is called *Tāmasika*.

बुद्धेर्भेदं धृतेश्चैव गुणतस्त्रिविधं शृणु।
प्रोच्यमानमशेषेण पृथक्त्वेन धनञ्जय॥ २९

धनञ्जय O Dhanañjaya बुद्धेः of intellect धृतेः of fortitude च एव and also गुणतः according to the *Guṇas* त्रिविधं triple पृथक्त्वेन severally अशेषेण exhaustively प्रोच्यमानम् as I declare भेदं the distinction शृणु hear (thou).

29. Hear thou the triple distinction of intellect and fortitude, according to the *Guṇas*, as I declare them exhaustively and severally, O Dhanañjaya.

Dhanañjaya: the conqueror of wealth—human and divine, earthly and celestial; an epithet of Arjuna.

प्रवृत्तिं च निवृत्तिं च कार्याकार्ये भयाभये।
बन्धं मोक्षं च या वेत्ति बुद्धिः सा पार्थ सात्त्विकी॥ ३०

पार्थ O Pārtha या which प्रवृत्तिं the path of work निवृत्तिं the path of renunciation च and कार्याकार्ये right and wrong action भयाभये fear and fearlessness बन्धं bondage मोक्षं liberation च and वेत्ति knows सा that सात्त्विकी *Sāttvika* बुद्धिः intellect.

30. That which knows the paths of work and renunciation, right and wrong action, fear and fearlessness, bondage and liberation, that intellect, O Pārtha, is *Sāttvika*.

Fear . . . liberation: the cause of fear and the cause of fearlessness; similarly, the cause of bondage and the cause of liberation.

यया धर्ममधर्मं च कार्यं चाकार्यमेव च।
अयथावत्प्रजानाति बुद्धिः सा पार्थ राजसी।। ३१

पार्थ O Pārtha यया by which धर्मम् Dharma अधर्मं *Adharma* कार्यं right action अकार्यम् wrong action च and अयथावत् in a distorted way प्रजानाति apprehends सा that राजसी *Rājasika* बुद्धिः intellect.

31. That which has a distorted apprehension of Dharma and its opposite and also of right action and its opposite, that intellect, O Pārtha, is *Rājasika*.

अधर्मं धर्ममिति या मन्यते तमसावृता।
सर्वार्थान्विपरीतांश्च बुद्धिः सा पार्थ तामसी।। ३२

पार्थ O Pārtha या which अधर्मं *Adharma* धर्मम् Dharma इति as मन्यते regards सर्वार्थान् all things विपरीतान् perverted च and तमसा in darkness आवृता enveloped सा that बुद्धिः intellect तामसी *Tāmasika*.

32. That which, enveloped in darkness, regards *Adharma* as Dharma and views all things in a perverted light, that intellect, O Pārtha, is *Tāmasika*.

धृत्या यया धारयते मनःप्राणेन्द्रियक्रियाः ।
योगेनाव्यभिचारिण्या धृतिः सा पार्थ सात्त्विकी ।। ३३

पार्थ O Pārtha अव्यभिचारिण्या unswerving यया which धृत्या by fortitude मनःप्राणेन्द्रियक्रियाः the functions of the mind, the *Prāṇa*, and the senses योगेन through Yoga धारयते (one) regulates सा that धृतिः fortitude सात्त्विकी *Sāttvika*.

33. The fortitude by which the functions of the mind, the *Prāṇa*, and the senses, O Pārtha, are regulated, that fortitude, unswerving through Yoga, is *Sāttvika*.

यया तु धर्मकामार्थान् धृत्या धारयतेऽर्जुन ।
प्रसङ्गेन फलाकाङ्क्षी धृतिः सा पार्थ राजसी ।। ३४

पार्थ O Pārtha अर्जुन O Arjuna यया which धृत्या by fortitude तु but धर्मकामार्थान् Dharma, desire, and wealth धारयते (one) regulates प्रसङ्गेन from attachment फलाकाङ्क्षी desirous of the fruit of action सा that धृतिः fortitude राजसी *Rājasika*.

34. But the fortitude by which one regulates (one's mind) to Dharma, desire, and wealth, desirous of the fruit of each from attachment, that fortitude, O Pārtha, is *Rājasika*.

यया स्वप्नं भयं शोकं विषादं मदमेव च।
न विमुञ्चति दुर्मेधा धृतिः सा पार्थ तामसी॥ ३५

पार्थ O Pārtha दुर्मेधा a stupid man यया by which स्वप्नं sleep भयं fear शोकं grief विषादं despondency मदम् overweening conceit एव च and also न not विमुञ्चति gives up सा that धृतिः fortitude तामसी *Tāmasika*.

35. That by which a stupid man does not give up sleep, fear, grief, despondency, and also overweening conceit, that fortitude, O Pārtha, is *Tāmasika*.

Does not give up sleep, etc.: is inordinately addicted to sleep, etc., regarding these to be only proper.

सुखं त्विदानीं त्रिविधं शृणु मे भरतर्षभ।
अभ्यासाद्रमते यत्र दुःखान्तं च निगच्छति॥ ३६

भरतर्षभ O bull of the Bhāratas इदानीं now त्रिविधं threefold सुखं happiness तु and मे from Me शृणु hear यत्र in which अभ्यासाद् by habit रमते learns to enjoy दुःखान्तं the end of pain च and निगच्छति (he) attains to.

36. And now hear from Me, O bull of the Bhāratas, of the threefold happiness that one learns

to enjoy by habit, and by which one comes to the end of pain.

यत्तदग्रे विषमिव परिणामेऽमृतोपमम्।
तत्सुखं सात्त्विकं प्रोक्तमात्मबुद्धिप्रसादजम्॥ ३७

यत् which तद् that अग्रे at first विषम् poison इव like परिणामे at the end अमृतोपमम् like nectar आत्मबुद्धिप्रसादजम् born of the translucence of intellect due to Self-realisation तत् that सुखं happiness सात्त्विकं *Sāttvika* प्रोक्तम् is declared (to be).

37. That which is like poison at first, but like nectar at the end—that happiness is declared to be *Sāttvika*, born of the translucence of intellect due to Self-realisation.

विषयेन्द्रियसंयोगाद्यत्तदग्रेऽमृतोपमम्।
परिणामे विषमिव तत्सुखं राजसं स्मृतम्॥ ३८

विषयेन्द्रियसंयोगाद् From the contact of object with sense यद् which तद् that अग्रे at first अमृतोपमम् like nectar परिणामे at the end विषम् poison इव like तत् that सुखं happiness राजसं *Rājasika* स्मृतम् is declared.

38. That which arises from the contact of object with sense, at first like nectar, but at the end like poison, that happiness is declared to be *Rājasika*.

At the end like poison: because it leads to deterioration in strength, vigour, complexion, wisdom, intellect, wealth, and energy.

यदग्रे चानुबन्धे च सुखं मोहनमात्मनः।
निद्रालस्यप्रमादोत्थं तत्तामसमुदाहृतम्॥ ३९

निद्रालस्यप्रमादोत्थं Arising from निद्रा sleep आलस्यं indolence and प्रमाद: miscomprehension यत् what सुखं happiness अग्रे in the beginning अनुबन्धे in the sequel च and आत्मन: to the self मोहनम् causing delusion तत् that तामसम् *Tāmasika* उदाहृतम् is declared.

39. That happiness which begins and results in self-delusion arising from sleep, indolence, and miscomprehension, that is declared to be *Tāmasika*.

न तदस्ति पृथिव्यां वा दिवि देवेषु वा पुनः।
सत्त्वं प्रकृतिजैर्मुक्तं यदेभिः स्यात्त्रिभिर्गुणैः॥ ४०

पृथिव्यां On earth दिवि in heaven वा or देवेषु among the *Devas* तु again तत् that सत्त्वं entity न no अस्ति there is यद् which एभि: these प्रकृतिजै: born of *Prakṛti* त्रिभि: three गुणै: (by) *Guṇas* मुक्तं devoid of स्यात् is.

40. There is no entity on earth, or again in heaven among the *Devas*, that is devoid of these three *Guṇas* born of *Prakṛti*.

ब्राह्मणक्षत्रियविशां शूद्राणां च परन्तप।
कर्माणि प्रविभक्तानि स्वभावप्रभवैर्गुणैः॥ ४१

परन्तप O scorcher of foes ब्राह्मणक्षत्रियविशां of Brāhmaṇas Kṣatriyas, and Vaiśyas शूद्राणां of Śūdras च as also कर्माणि

duties स्वभावप्रभवैः born of (their) own nature गुणैः according to the *Guṇas* प्रविभक्तानि are distributed.

41. Of Brāhmaṇas and Kṣatriyas and Vaiśyas, as also of Śūdras, O scorcher of foes, the duties are distributed according to the *Guṇas* born of their own nature.

According to the *Karma* or habits and tendencies formed by desire, action, and association in the past life manifesting themselves in the present as effects. Or, nature (*Svabhāva*) may here mean the Māyā made up of the three *Guṇas*, the *Prakṛti* of the Lord.

शमो दमस्तपः शौचं क्षान्तिरार्जवमेव च।
ज्ञानं विज्ञानमास्तिक्यं ब्रह्मकर्म स्वभावजम्॥ ४२

शमः Control of mind दमः control of the senses तपः austerity शौचं purity क्षान्तिः forbearance आर्जवम् uprightness ज्ञानं knowledge विज्ञानम् realisation आस्तिक्यं belief in a hereafter एव also च and स्वभावजम् born of the nature ब्रह्मकर्म (are) the duties of Brāhmaṇas.

42. The control of the mind and the senses, austerity, purity, forbearance, and also uprightness, knowledge, realisation, and belief in a hereafter—these are the duties of the Brāhmaṇas, born of (their own) nature.

शौर्यं तेजो धृतिर्दाक्ष्यं युद्धे चाप्यपलायनम्।
दानमीश्वरभावश्च क्षात्रं कर्म स्वभावजम्॥ ४३

शौर्यं Prowess तेजः boldness धृतिः fortitude दाक्ष्यं dexterity युद्धे in the battle च and अपि also अपलायनम् not flying दानम् generosity ईश्वरभावः sovereignty च and स्वभावजम् born of the nature क्षात्रं of Kṣatriyas कर्म the duties.

43. Prowess, boldness, fortitude, dexterity, and also not flying from battle, generosity and sovereignty are the duties of the Kṣatriyas, born of (their own) nature.

कृषिगौरक्ष्यवाणिज्यं वैश्यकर्म स्वभावजम् ।
परिचर्यात्मकं कर्म शूद्रस्यापि स्वभावजम् ।। ४४

कृषिगौरक्ष्यवाणिज्यं agriculture, cattle-rearing, and trade स्वभावजम् born of the nature वैश्यकर्म the duties of Vaiśya शूद्रस्य of a Śūdra अपि also परिचर्यात्मकं consisting of service कर्म action स्वभावजम् born of the nature.

44. Agriculture, cattle-rearing, and trade are the duties of the Vaiśyas, born of (their own) nature; and action consisting of service is the duty of the Śūdras, born of (their own) nature.

स्वे स्वे कर्मण्यभिरतः संसिद्धिं लभते नरः ।
स्वकर्मनिरतः सिद्धिं यथा विन्दति तच्छृणु ।। ४५

स्वे स्वे Each his own कर्मणि to duty अभिरतः devoted नरः man संसिद्धिं the highest perfection लभते attains स्वकर्मनिरतः engaged in his own duty यथा how सिद्धिं perfection विन्दति attains तत् that शृणु hear.

45. Being devoted to his own duty, man attains the highest perfection. How engaged in his own duty, he attains perfection, that hear.

Own: according to his nature.

The Āpastaṁba Dharma-Śāstra says: "Men of several castes and orders, each devoted to his respective duties, reap the fruits of their actions after death, and then by the residual *Karma* attain to births in superior countries, castes, and families, possessed of comparatively superior Dharma, span of life, learning, conduct, wealth, happiness, and intelligence."

यतः प्रवृत्तिर्भूतानां येन सर्वमिदं ततम् ।
स्वकर्मणा तमभ्यर्च्य सिद्धिं विन्दति मानवः ।। ४६

यत: From whom भूतानां of all beings प्रवृत्ति: (is) the evolution येन by whom इदं this सर्वम् all ततम् is pervaded मानव: man स्वकर्मणा with his own duty तम् Him अभ्यर्च्य worshipping सिद्धिं perfection विन्दति attains.

46. From whom is the evolution of all beings, by whom all this is pervaded, worshipping Him with his own duty, a man attains perfection.

The highest worship to the Lord consists in the closest approach to Him. The veil of Māyā comprising *Karma* or habits, tendencies and actions prevents a man from nearing the Lord, i.e., realising his own Self. By working out one's *Karma* alone, according to the law of one's being, can this veil be rent and the end accomplished.

श्रेयान् स्वधर्मो विगुणः परधर्मात्स्वनुष्ठितात् ।
स्वभावनियतं कर्म कुर्वन्नाप्नोति किल्बिषम् ।। ४७

विगुणः (Though) imperfect स्वधर्मः one's own Dharma स्वनुष्ठितात् well-performed परधर्मात् than the Dharma of another श्रेयान् better (is) स्वभावनियतं ordained by his own nature कर्म the duty कुर्वन् doing किल्बिषम् evil न no आप्नोति (he) incurs.

47. Better is one's own Dharma, (though) imperfect than the Dharma of another well-performed. He who does the duty ordained by his own nature incurs no evil.

As a poisonous substance does not injure the worm born in that substance, so he who does his *Svadharma* incurs no evil.

सहजं कर्म कौन्तेय सदोषमपि न त्यजेत् ।
सर्वारम्भा हि दोषेण धूमेनाग्निरिवावृताः ।। ४८

कौन्तेय O son of Kuntī सदोषम् attended with evil अपि though सहजं to which one is born कर्म the duty न not त्यजेत् one should relinquish हि for सर्वारम्भाः all undertakings धूमेन by smoke अग्निः fire इव as दोषेण by evil आवृताः are enveloped.

48. One should not relinquish, O son of Kuntī, the duty to which one is born, though it is attended with evil; for all undertakings are enveloped by evil, as fire by smoke.

Duty, etc.: this need not mean caste duty.

All undertakings: one's own as well as others' duties.

The greatest evil is bondage, and this endures so long as one lives in the realm of the *Guṇas*, except in the case of a freed soul. All action is comprised in one or the other of the *Guṇas*. All action therefore involves the evil of bondage.

असक्तबुद्धिः सर्वत्र जितात्मा विगतस्पृहः ।
नैष्कर्म्यसिद्धिं परमां सन्न्यासेनाधिगच्छति ।। ४९

सर्वत्र Everywhere असक्तबुद्धिः whose intellect is unattached जितात्मा who has subdued his heart विगतस्पृहः whose desires have fled सन्न्यासेन by renunciation परमां the supreme नैष्कर्म्यसिद्धिं the perfection consisting in freedom from action अधिगच्छति (he) attains to.

49. He whose intellect is unattached everywhere, who has subdued his heart, whose desires have fled, he attains by renunciation to the supreme perfection, consisting of freedom from action.

He attains ... renunciation: This may also be interpreted to mean: he attains the supreme state in which he remains as the actionless Self, by his renunciation of all actions, for which he is prepared by his right knowledge.

सिद्धिं प्राप्तो यथा ब्रह्म तथाप्नोति निबोध मे ।
समासेनैव कौन्तेय निष्ठा ज्ञानस्य या परा ।। ५०

कौन्तेय O son of Kuntī सिद्धिं perfection प्राप्तः reaching यथा how ब्रह्म Brahman आप्नोति he attains to तथा that समासेन

in brief मे from Me निबोध learn ज्ञानस्य of knowledge या which परा supreme निष्ठा consummation.

50. Learn from Me in brief, O son of Kuntī, how reaching such perfection, he attains to Brahman, that supreme consummation of knowledge.

बुद्ध्या विशुद्धया युक्तो धृत्यात्मानं नियम्य च।
शब्दादीन्विषयांस्त्यक्त्वा रागद्वेषौ व्युदस्य च॥ ५१

विशुद्धया Pure बुद्ध्या with an intellect युक्तः endued धृत्या with fortitude आत्मानं the body and the senses नियम्य subduing च and शब्दादीन् sound and such other विषयान् sense-objects त्यक्त्वा relinquishing रागद्वेषौ attraction and hatred च and व्युदस्य abandoning;

51. Endued with a pure intellect; subduing the body and the senses with fortitude; relinquishing sound and such other sense-objects; abandoning attraction and hatred;

Pure: free from doubt and misconception, being merged in Brahman through the elimination of all alien attributes ascribed to it.

Relinquishing sound, etc.: abandoning all superfluous luxuries, all objects, except those only which are necessary for the bare maintenance of the body, and laying aside attraction and hatred even for those objects.

विविक्तसेवी लघ्वाशी यतवाक्कायमानसः।
ध्यानयोगपरो नित्यं वैराग्यं समुपाश्रितः॥ ५२

विविक्तसेवी Resorting to a sequestered spot लघ्वाशी eating but little यतवाक्कायमानस: body, speech, and mind controlled नित्यं ever ध्यानयोगपर: engaged in meditation and concentration वैराग्यं dispassion समुपाश्रित: possessed of;

52. Resorting to a sequestered spot; eating but little; body, speech, and mind controlled; ever engaged in meditation and concentration; possessed of dispassion;

Eating but little: as conducive to the serenity of thought by keeping off languor, sleepiness, and the like.

Meditation: upon the nature of the Self.

Concentration: one-pointedness of thought, on one feature of the Self.

Dispassion: for the seen and the unseen.

अहंकारं बलं दर्पं कामं क्रोधं परिग्रहम्।
विमुच्य निर्ममः शान्तो ब्रह्मभूयाय कल्पते ।। ५३

अहंकारं Egoism बलं power दर्पं pride कामं lust क्रोधं wrath परिग्रहम् property विमुच्य forsaking निर्मम: freed from the notion of "mine" शान्त: tranquil ब्रह्मभूयाय for becoming Brahman कल्पते (he) is fit.

53. Forsaking egoism, power, pride, lust, wrath, and property; freed from the notion of "mine"; and tranquil—he is fit for becoming Brahman.

Power: that power which is combined with passion and desire.

Property: Though a man who is free from all passions of the mind and the senses, may own so much of external belongings as is necessary for bodily sustenance and for the observance of his religious duties (Dharma), yet this the aspirant abandons, even if this comes of itself, because he does not regard the bodily life as his; thus he becomes a *Paramahaṁsa Parivrājaka*, a Sannyāsin of the highest order.

ब्रह्मभूतः प्रसन्नात्मा न शोचति न काङ्क्षति।
समः सर्वेषु भूतेषु मद्भक्तिं लभते पराम्॥ ५४

ब्रह्मभूतः Brahman-become प्रसन्नात्मा tranquil-minded न neither शोचति (he) grieves न nor काङ्क्षति desires सर्वेषु all भूतेषु to beings समः the same पराम् supreme मद्भक्तिं devotion unto Me लभते attains to.

54. Brahman-become, tranquil-minded, he neither grieves nor desires; the same to all beings, he attains to supreme devotion unto Me.

Brahman-become: not that he is yet freed and become the Absolute, but is firmly grounded in the knowledge that he is Brahman. His attainment of freedom is described in the next verse.

Supreme devotion: the devotion stated in VII. 17.

भक्त्या मामभिजानाति यावान्यश्चास्मि तत्त्वतः।
ततो मां तत्त्वतो ज्ञात्वा विशते तदनन्तरम्॥ ५५

यावान् What यः who च and अस्मि I am माम् Me भक्त्या by devotion तत्त्वतः in reality अभिजानाति (he) knows ततः

then मां Me तत्त्वत: in reality ज्ञात्वा having known तदनन्तरम् forthwith (मां into Me) विशते enters.

55. By devotion he knows Me in reality, what and who I am; then having known Me in reality, he forthwith enters into Me.

सर्वकर्माण्यपि सदा कुर्वाणो मद्व्यपाश्रयः ।
मत्प्रसादादवाप्नोति शाश्वतं पदमव्ययम् ।। ५६

सदा Always सर्वकर्माणि all actions कुर्वाण: doing अपि even मद्व्यपाश्रय: taking refuge in Me मत्प्रसादात् by My grace शाश्वतं the eternal अव्ययम् immutable पदम् State अवाप्नोति (he) attains to.

56. Even doing all actions always, taking refuge in Me—by My grace he attains to the eternal, immutable State.

चेतसा सर्वकर्माणि मयि सन्न्यस्य मत्परः ।
बुद्धियोगमुपाश्रित्य मच्चित्तः सततं भव ।। ५७

चेतसा Mentally सर्वकर्माणि all deeds मयि in Me सन्न्यस्य resigning मत्पर: having Me as the highest goal बुद्धियोगम् *Buddhi-Yoga* उपाश्रित्य resorting to सततं ever मच्चित्त: with the mind fixed on Me भव be.

57. Resigning mentally all deeds to Me, having Me as the highest goal, and resorting to *Buddhi-Yoga,* do thou ever fix thy mind on Me.

मच्चित्तः सर्वदुर्गाणि मत्प्रसादात्तरिष्यसि।
अथ चेत्त्वमहंकारान्न श्रोष्यसि विनंक्ष्यसि ॥ ५८

त्वम् Thou मच्चित्तः fixing the mind on Me मत्प्रसादात् by My grace सर्वदुर्गाणि all obstacles तरिष्यसि (thou) shalt overcome अथ but चेत् if अहंकारात् from self-conceit न not श्रोष्यसि (thou) wilt hear विनंक्ष्यसि (thou) shalt perish.

58. Fixing thy mind on Me, thou shalt, by My grace, overcome all obstacles; but if from self-conceit thou wilt not hear Me, thou shalt perish.

यदहंकारमाश्रित्य न योत्स्य इति मन्यसे।
मिथ्यैष व्यवसायस्ते प्रकृतिस्त्वां नियोक्ष्यति ॥ ५९

अहंकारम् Self-conceit आश्रित्य abiding in न not योत्स्ये (I) will fight यद् if इति thus मन्यसे (thou) thinkest ते thy एषः this व्यवसायः resolve मिथ्या (is) vain प्रकृतिः (thy) *Prakṛti* त्वां thee नियोक्ष्यति will constrain.

59. If, filled with self-conceit, thou thinkest, "I will not fight", vain is this thy resolve; thy *Prakṛti* will constrain thee.

Thy Prakṛti: Thy nature as a Kṣatriya.

स्वभावजेन कौन्तेय निबद्धः स्वेन कर्मणा।
कर्तुं नेच्छसि यन्मोहात्करिष्यस्यवशोऽपि तत् ॥ ६०

कौन्तेय O son of Kunti मोहात् from delusion यत् what कर्तुं to do न not इच्छसि thou desirest स्वभावजेन born of (thy) own nature स्वेन (thy) own कर्मणा by *Karma* निबद्धः fettered अवशः helpless, in spite of thyself तत् that अपि even करिष्यसि (thou) shalt (have to) do.

60. Fettered, O son of Kuntī, by thy own *Karma*, born of thy own nature, what thou, from delusion, desirest not to do, thou shalt have to do in spite of thyself.

ईश्वरः सर्वभूतानां हृद्देशेऽर्जुन तिष्ठति।
भ्रामयन्सर्वभूतानि यन्त्रारूढानि मायया ॥ ६१

अर्जुन O Arjuna ईश्वरः the Lord मायया by Māyā यन्त्रारूढानि mounted on a machine सर्वभूतानि all beings भ्रामयन् causing to revolve सर्वभूतानां of all beings हृद्देशे in the hearts तिष्ठति dwells.

61. The Lord, O Arjuna, dwells in the hearts of all beings, causing all beings, by His Māyā, to revolve, (as if) mounted on a machine.

See commentary to IX. 10.
Arjuna means "white", and here it signifies—"O pure-hearted one"

तमेव शरणं गच्छ सर्वभावेन भारत।
तत्प्रसादात्परां शान्तिं स्थानं प्राप्स्यसि शाश्वतम् ॥ ६२

भारत O Bhārata सर्वभावेन with all thy heart तम् in Him एव even शरणं गच्छ take refuge तत्प्रसादात् by His grace परां supreme शान्तिं peace शाश्वतम् eternal स्थानं the abode प्राप्स्यसि shalt (thou) attain.

62. Take refuge in Him with all thy heart, O Bhārata; by His grace shalt thou attain supreme peace (and) the eternal abode.

इति ते ज्ञानमाख्यातं गुह्याद् गुह्यतरं मया।
विमृश्यैतदशेषेण यथेच्छसि तथा कुरु ॥ ६३

इति Thus गुह्याद् than all profundities गुह्यतरं more profound ज्ञानम् wisdom ते to thee मया by Me आख्यातं has been declared अशेषेण fully एतद् it विमृश्य reflecting over यथा as इच्छसि thou likest तथा so कुरु act.

63. Thus has wisdom, more profound than all profundities, been declared to thee by Me; reflecting over it fully, act as thou likest.

It: the *Śāstra*, the teaching as declared above.

सर्वगुह्यतमं भूयः शृणु मे परमं वचः।
इष्टोऽसि मे दृढमिति ततो वक्ष्यामि ते हितम् ॥ ६४

मे My सर्वगुह्यतमं the profoundest of all परमं supreme वचः word भूयः again शृणु hear thou मे of Me दृढम् dearly इष्टः beloved असि thou art ततः therefore ते to thee हितम् what is good वक्ष्यामि will I speak.

64. Hear thou again My supreme word, the profoundest of all; because thou art dearly beloved of Me, therefore, will I speak what is good to thee.

Again: though more than once declared.

मन्मना भव मद्भक्तो मद्याजी मां नमस्कुरु।
मामेवैष्यसि सत्यं ते प्रतिजाने प्रियोऽसि मे ॥ ६५

मन्मना: With mind occupied with me मद्भक्त: devoted to Me मद्याजी sacrificing to Me भव be thou मां to Me नमस्कुरु bow down मामेव Myself एष्यसि thou shalt reach अहं I ते unto thee सत्यं truly प्रतिजाने promise मे to Me प्रिय: dear असि thou art.

65. Occupy thy mind with Me, be devoted to Me, sacrifice to Me, bow down to Me. Thou shalt reach Myself; truly do I promise unto thee, (for) thou art dear to Me.

Thou shalt reach Myself: Thus acting, i.e., looking upon the Lord alone as thy aim, means and end—thou shalt attain the Highest.

Truly do I promise unto thee: Have implicit faith in the declarations of Me, the Lord, as I pledge thee My troth.

सर्वधर्मान्परित्यज्य मामेकं शरणं व्रज।
अहं त्वा सर्वपापेभ्यो मोक्षयिष्यामि मा शुचः ॥ ६६

सर्वधर्मान् All Dharmas परित्यज्य relinquishing एकं alone माम् in Me शरणं refuge व्रज take अहं I त्वा thee सर्वपापेभ्य: from all sins मोक्षयिष्यामि will liberate मा (do) not शुच: grieve.

66. Relinquishing all Dharmas take refuge in Me alone; I will liberate thee from all sins; grieve not.

All Dharmas: including *Adharma* also: all actions, righteous or unrighteous, since absolute freedom from the bondage of all action is intended to be taught here.

Take refuge in Me alone: knowing that there is naught else except Me, the Self of all, dwelling the same in all.

Liberate thee: by manifesting Myself as thy own Self.

All sins: all bonds of Dharma and *Adharma*.

Śaṅkara in his commentary here very strongly combats the opinion of those who hold that highest spiritual realisation (*Jñāna*) and ritualistic work (*Karma*) may go together in the same person. For *Karma* is possible only in the relative world (*Saṁsāra*), which is the outcome of ignorance; and knowledge dispels this ignorance. So neither the conjunction of *Jñāna* with *Karma*, nor *Karma* alone conduces to the absolute cessation of *Saṁsāra*, but it is only the Right Knowledge of the Self which does so.

इदं ते नातपस्काय नाभक्ताय कदाचन।
न चाशुश्रूषवे वाच्यं न च मां योऽभ्यसूयति।। ६७

अतपस्काय To one who is devoid of austerities ते by thee इदं this न कदाचन never वाच्यं to be spoken न nor अभक्ताय to one without devotion न च nor अशुश्रूषवे to one who does not render service यः who मां at Me अभ्यसूयति cavils न च nor.

67. This is never to be spoken by thee to one who is devoid of austerities or devotion, nor to one who does not render service, nor to one who cavils at Me.

This: *Śāstra* which has been taught to you.

Service: to the Guru; अशुश्रूषवे also means—to one who does not wish to hear.

य इदं परमं गुह्यं मद्भक्तेष्वभिधास्यति ।
भक्तिं मयि परां कृत्वा मामेवैष्यत्यसंशयः ॥ ६८

यः Who परमं deeply गुह्यं profound philosophy इदं this मद्भक्तेषु to My devotees अभिधास्यति will teach मयि to Me परां supreme भक्तिं devotion कृत्वा doing असंशयः (being) doubtless माम् एव Me alone एष्यति shall come to.

68. He who with supreme devotion to Me will teach this deeply profound philosophy to My devotees, shall doubtless come to Me alone.

Teach: in the faith that he is thus doing service to the Lord, the Supreme Teacher.

Doubtless: or, freed from doubts.

न च तस्मान्मनुष्येषु कश्चिन्मे प्रियकृत्तमः ।
भविता न च मे तस्मादन्यः प्रियतरो भुवि ॥ ६९

मनुष्येषु Among men तस्मात् than he कश्चित् any मे to Me प्रियकृत्तमः one who does dearer service च and न not तस्माद् than he अन्यः another मे to Me प्रियतरः dearer च and भुवि on earth न not भविता shall be.

69. Nor among men is there any who does dearer service to Me, nor shall there be another on earth dearer to Me, than he.

He: who hands down the *Śāstra* to a fit person.

अध्येष्यते च य इमं धर्म्यं संवादमावयोः ।
ज्ञानयज्ञेन तेनाहमिष्टः स्यामिति मे मतिः ।। ७०

यः Who च and आवयोः of ours इमं this धर्म्यं sacred संवादम् dialogue अध्येष्यते will study तेन by him अहम् I ज्ञानयज्ञेन by the *Yajñā* of knowledge इष्टः worshipped स्याम् (I) shall have been इति such मे My मतिः conviction.

70. And he who will study this sacred dialogue of ours, by him shall I have been worshipped by the *Yajña* of knowledge; such is My conviction.

Yajña of knowledge: *A Yajña* can be performed in four ways, such as (1) *Vidhi* or ritual, (2)*Japa*, (3) *Upāṁśu*, or a prayer uttered in a low voice, or (4) *Mānasa* or prayer offered with the mind. *Jnāna-yajña* or the *Yajña* of knowledge comes under the head of *Mānasa*, and is therefore the highest.

The study of the Gītā will produce an effect equal to that of the *Yajña* of knowledge.

श्रद्धावाननसूयश्च शृणुयादपि यो नरः ।
सोऽपि मुक्तः शुभाँल्लोकान्प्राप्नुयात्पुण्यकर्मणाम् ।। ७१

श्रद्धावान् Full of *Śraddhā* अनसूयः free from malice च and यः who नरः man शृणुयात् will hear अपि even सः he अपि too मुक्तः liberated पुण्यकर्मणाम् of those of righteous deeds शुभान् happy लोकान् the worlds प्राप्नुयात् shall attain to.

71. And even that man who hears this, full of *Śraddhā* and free from malice, he too, liberated, shall attain to the happy worlds of those of righteous deeds.

Even that man: much more so he who understands the doctrine.

कच्चिदेतच्छ्रुतं पार्थ त्वयैकाग्रेण चेतसा।
कच्चिदज्ञानसंमोहः प्रनष्टस्ते धनञ्जय॥ ७२

पार्थ O Pārtha त्वया by thee एकाग्रेण attentive चेतसा with mind एतत् this कच्चित् whether श्रुतं has been heard धनञ्जय O Dhanañjaya ते thy अज्ञानसंमोहः the delusion of ignorance कच्चित् whether प्रनष्टः has been destroyed?

72. Has this been heard by thee, O Pārtha, with an attentive mind ? Has the delusion of thy ignorance been destroyed, O Dhanañjaya ?

अर्जुन उवाच

नष्टो मोहः स्मृतिर्लब्धा त्वत्प्रसादान्मयाच्युत।
स्थितोऽस्मि गतसन्देहः करिष्ये वचनं तव॥ ७३

अर्जुनः Arjuna उवाच said:

अच्युत O Acyuta मोहः the delusion नष्टः is destroyed मया by me त्वत्प्रसादात् through Thy grace स्मृतिः memory लब्धा has been gained स्थितः firm अस्मि I am गतसन्देहः freed from doubts तव Thy वचनं word करिष्ये I will do.

Arjuna said:

73. Destroyed is my delusion, and I have gained my memory through Thy grace, O Acyuta. I am firm; my doubts are gone. I will do Thy word.

***Memory*: of the true nature of the Self.**

Firm: in Thy command.

The purpose of the knowledge of the *Śāstras* is the destruction of doubts and delusions, and the recognition of the true nature of the Self. Here the answer of Arjuna conclusively shows that purpose has been fulfilled in him.

The teaching of the *Śāstra* is over here. The rest is only to connect it with the main narrative.

सञ्जय उवाच

इत्यहं वासुदेवस्य पार्थस्य च महात्मनः ।
संवादमिममश्रौषमद्भुतं रोमहर्षणम् ।। ७४

सञ्जयः Sañjaya उवाच said:

अहं I इति thus वासुदेवस्य of Vāsudeva महात्मनः high-souled पार्थस्य of Pārtha च and इमम् this रोमहर्षणम् which cause the hair to stand on end अद्भुतं wonderful संवादम् dialogue अश्रौषम् (I) have heard.

Sañjaya said:

74. Thus have I heard this wonderful dialogue between Vāsudeva and the high-souled Pārtha, causing my hair to stand on end.

व्यासप्रसादाच्छ्रुतवानिमं गुह्यमहं परम् ।
योगं योगेश्वरात्कृष्णात्साक्षात्कथयतः स्वयम् ।। ७५

अहं I व्यासप्रसादात् through the grace of Vyāsa इमं this परम् supreme गुह्यम् most profound योगं Yoga कथयतः speaking स्वयम् Himself साक्षात् direct योगेश्वरात् from the Lord of Yoga कृष्णात् from Kṛṣṇa श्रुतवान् I have heard.

75. Through the grace of Vyāsa have I heard this supreme and most profound Yoga, direct from Kṛṣṇa, the Lord of Yoga, Himself declaring it.

Through . . . Vyāsa: by obtaining from him the *Divya-cakṣu* or divine vision.

राजन्संस्मृत्य संस्मृत्य संवादमिममद्भुतम् ।
केशवार्जुनयोः पुण्यं हृष्यामि च मुहुर्मुहुः ॥ ७६

राजन् O King केशवार्जुनयो: between Keśava and Arjuna इमम् this पुण्यं holy अद्भुतम् wonderful संवादम् dialogue संस्मृत्य संस्मृत्य as I remember and remember मुहु: मुहु: again and again हृष्यामि I rejoice.

76. O King, as I remember and remember this wonderful and holy dialogue between Keśava and Arjuna, I rejoice again and again.

King: Dhṛtaraṣṭra.

तच्च संस्मृत्य संस्मृत्य रूपमत्यद्भुतं हरेः ।
विस्मयो मे महान् राजन् हृष्यामि च पुनः पुनः ॥ ७७

राजन् O King हरे: of Hari तत् that अत्यद्भुतं most wonderful रूपम् Form संस्मृत्य संस्मृत्य as I remember and remember च and मे my महान् great विस्मय: wonder च and अहं I पुन: पुन: again and again हृष्यामि rejoice.

77. And as I remember and remember that most wonderful Form of Hari, great is my wonder, O King; and I rejoice again and again.

Form: *Viśvarūpa*, the Universal Form.

यत्र योगेश्वरः कृष्णो यत्र पार्थो धनुर्धरः ।
तत्र श्रीर्विजयो भूतिर्ध्रुवा नीतिर्मतिर्मम ।। ७८

यत्र Wherever योगेश्वरः the Lord of Yoga कृष्णः Kṛṣṇa यत्र wherever धनुर्धरः the wielder of the bow पार्थः Pārtha तत्र there श्रीः prosperity विजयः victory भूतिः expansion ध्रुवा sound नीतिः policy इति such मे my मतिः conviction.

78. Wherever is Kṛṣṇa, the Lord of Yoga, wherever is Pārtha, the wielder of the bow, there are prosperity, victory, expansion, and sound policy: such is my conviction.

The bow: called the *Gāṇḍīva*.

इति श्रीमद्भगवद्गीतासूपनिषत्सु ब्रह्मविद्यायां
योगशास्त्रे श्रीकृष्णार्जुनसंवादे मोक्ष-सन्न्यासयोगो
नामाष्टादशोऽध्यायः ।।

Thus in the Śrīmad-Bhagavad-Gītā, the
Essence of the Upaniṣads, the Science
of the Brahman, the Scripture of
Yoga, the Dialogue between Śrī Kṛṣṇa and
Arjuna, ends the eighteenth chapter, designated,

The Way of Liberation in Renunciation.
Here the Bhagavad-Gītā ends.

ॐ शान्तिः शान्तिः शान्तिः ।।

Om! Peace! Peace! Peace be to all!

॥ अथ श्रीगीतामाहात्म्यम् ॥

THE GREATNESS OF THE GĪTĀ

श्रीगणेशाय नमः ॥ श्रीराधारमणाय नमः ॥

Salutation to Śrī Gaṇeśa!
Salutation to Śri Rādhāramaṇa!

Gaṇeśa is the god of wisdom and remover of obstacles; hence he is invoked and worshipped at the commencement of every important undertaking. Rādhāramaṇa, the Lover of Rādhā, is Sri Kṛṣṇa.

धरोवाच

भगवन्परमेशान भक्तिरव्यभिचारिणी ।
प्रारब्धं भुज्यमानस्य कथं भवति हे प्रभो ॥ १

Dharā (the Earth) said:

1. O Blessed Lord, O Supreme Ruler, how may one, who is held back by his *Prārabdha Karma*, obtain unswerving devotion?

Prārabdha Karma: There are three kinds of *Karma*: (1) *Sañcita* or accumulated and stored up in past lives; (2) *Āgāmī* or that which is yet to be done; (3) *Prārabdha* or that which is already bearing fruit. This last is that part of the accumulated actions (*Sañcita*) which has brought about the present life and will influence it until its close.

The knowledge of Brahman destroys all accumulated *Karma* and makes the current work abortive. But the *Prārabdha Karma* must run out its course, though the balanced mind of a liberated man is not affected by it.

श्रीविष्णुरुवाच

प्रारब्धं भुज्यमानो हि गीताभ्यासरतः सदा।
स मुक्तः स सुखी लोके कर्मणा नोपलिप्यते॥ २

The Lord Viṣṇu said:

2. If one be devoted to the constant practice of the Gītā, even though he be restrained by *Prārabdha Karma*, yet is he *Mukta*, happy, in this very world. He is not tainted by (new) *Karma*.

महापापातिपापानि गीताध्यानं करोति चेत्।
क्वचित्स्पर्शं न कुर्वन्ति नलिनीदलमम्बुवत्॥ ३

3. No evil, however great, can affect him who meditates on the Gītā. He is like the lotus leaf untouched by the water.

गीतायाः पुस्तकं यत्र यत्र पाठः प्रवर्तते।
तत्र सर्वाणि तीर्थानि प्रयागादीनि तत्र वै॥ ४
सर्वे देवाश्च ऋषयो योगिनः पन्नगाश्च ये।
गोपाला गोपिका वापि नारदोद्धवपार्षदैः॥ ५

4–5. Where there is the book of the Gītā, where its study is proceeded with, there are present all the holy places, there verily, are Prayāga and the rest.

There also are all the *Devas*, *Ṛṣis*, *Yogis* and *Pannagas*, so also the *Gopālas* and *Gopikās*, with Nārada, Uddhava, and their whole train of comrades.

सहायो जायते शीघ्रं यत्र गीता प्रवर्तते ।
यत्र गीताविचारश्च पठनं पाठनं श्रुतम् ।
तत्राहं निश्चितं पृथ्वि निवसामि सदैव हि ।। ६

6. Where the Gītā is read, forthwith comes help. Where the Gītā is discussed, recited, taught, or heard, there, O Earth, beyond a doubt, do I Myself unfailingly reside.

गीताश्रयेऽहं तिष्ठामि गीता मे चोत्तमं गृहम् ।
गीताज्ञानमुपाश्रित्य त्रीन्लोकान्पालयाम्यहम् ।। ७

7. In the refuge of the Gītā, I abide; the Gītā is My chief abode. Standing on the wisdom of the Gītā, I maintain the three worlds.

गीता मे परमा विद्या ब्रह्मरूपा न संशयः ।
अर्धमात्राक्षरा नित्या स्वानिर्वाच्यपदात्मिका ।। ८
चिदानन्देन कृष्णेन प्रोक्ता स्वमुखतोऽर्जुनम् ।
वेदत्रयी परानन्दा तत्त्वार्थज्ञानसंयुता ।। ९

8-9. The Gītā is My Supreme Knowledge; it is undoubtedly inseparable from Brahman—this Knowledge is absolute, imperishable, eternal, of the essence of My inexpressible State—the Knowledge comprising the whole of the three Vedas, supremely blissful, and consisting of the realisation of the true nature of the Self—declared by the All-knowing and Blessed Kṛṣṇa, through His own lips, to Arjuna.

Ardhamātrā: lit., the half-syllable, and refers to the dot on the ॐ; symbolically, it stands for the *Turīya* state, hence the Absolute.

योऽष्टादश जपेन्नित्यं नरो निश्चलमानसः ।
ज्ञानसिद्धिं स लभते ततो याति परं पदम् ।। १०

10. That man who with steady mind recites the eighteen chapters daily, attains the perfection of knowledge, and thus reaches the highest plane.

पाठे समग्रेऽसम्पूर्णे ततोऽर्धं पाठमाचरेत् ।
तदा गोदानजं पुण्यं लभते नात्र संशयः ।। ११

11. If the whole cannot be recited, then half of it may be read; and he who does this acquires merit, equal to that of the gift of a cow. There is no doubt about this.

त्रिभागं पठमानस्तु गङ्गास्नानफलं लभेत् ।
षडंशं जपमानस्तु सोमयागफलं लभेत् ।। १२

12. By the recitation of a third part, he gains the same merit as by bathing in the Gaṅgā. By the repetition of a sixth part, he obtains the fruit of the *Soma*-sacrifice.

एकाध्यायं तु यो नित्यं पठते भक्तिसंयुतः ।
रुद्रलोकमवाप्नोति गणो भूत्वा वसेच्चिरम् ।। १३

13. He who reads, full of devotion, even one chapter daily, attains to the *Rudraloka*, and lives there for a long time, having become one of those who wait on Śiva.

Become, etc.: lit., attained to Gaṇahood.

अध्यायं श्लोकपादं वा नित्यं यः पठते नरः ।
स याति नरतां यावन्मन्वन्तरं वसुन्धरे ।। १४

14. The man who daily reads a quarter of a chapter, or of a *Śloka*, O Earth, attains to human birth throughout the duration of a Manu.

Attains to human birth: is born every time in a man-body.

गीतायाः श्लोकदशकं सप्त पञ्च चतुष्टयम् ।
द्वौ त्रीनेकं तदर्धं वा श्लोकानां यः पठेन्नरः ।। १५
चन्द्रलोकमवाप्नोति वर्षाणामयुतं ध्रुवम् ।
गीतापाठसमायुक्तो मृतो मानुषतां व्रजेत् ।। १६

15–16. The man who recites ten, seven, five, four, three, or two *Ślokas*, or even one or half a *Śloka* of the Gītā, certainly lives in *Candraloka* for ten thousand years. He who leaves the body while reading the Gītā, obtains the world of Man.

गीताभ्यासं पुनः कृत्वा लभते मुक्तिमुत्तमाम्।
गीतेत्युच्चारसंयुक्तो म्रियमाणो गतिं लभेत्॥ १७

17. Again, practising the Gītā, he attains Supreme *Mukti*. The dying man uttering the word "Gītā" will attain the goal.

गीतार्थश्रवणासक्तो महापापयुतोऽपि वा।
वैकुण्ठं समवाप्नोति विष्णुना सह मोदते॥ १८

18. One who loves to hear the meaning of the Gītā, even though he has committed heinous sins, attains to heaven, and lives in beatitude with Viṣṇu.

गीतार्थं ध्यायते नित्यं कृत्वा कर्माणि भूरिशः।
जीवन्मुक्तः स विज्ञेयो देहान्ते परमं पदम्॥ १९

19. He who constantly meditates on the meaning of the Gītā, even though he performs *Karma* incessantly, he is to be regarded as a *Jīvanmukta*; and after the destruction of his body he attains to the highest plane of knowledge.

गीतामाश्रित्य बहवो भूभुजो जनकादयः।
निर्धूतकल्मषा लोके गीता याताः परं पदम्॥ २०

20. With the help of the Gītā, many kings like Janaka in (this) world became free from (their) impurities and attained to the highest goal. It is so sung.

गीतायाः पठनं कृत्वा माहात्म्यं नैव यः पठेत् ।
वृथा पाठो भवेत्तस्य श्रम एव ह्युदाहृतः ।। २१

21. He, who having finished the reading of the Gītā, does not read its *Māhātmya* as declared here, his reading is in vain; it is all labour wasted.

एतन्माहात्म्यसंयुक्तं गीताभ्यासं करोति यः ।
स तत्फलमवाप्नोति दुर्लभां गतिमाप्नुयात् ।। २२

22. He who studies the Gītā, accompanied with this discourse on its *Māhātmya*, obtains the fruit stated herein, and reaches that goal which is difficult to attain.

सूत उवाच

माहात्म्यमेतद् गीताया मया प्रोक्तं सनातनम् ।
गीतान्ते च पठेद्यस्तु यदुक्तं तत्फलं लभेत् ।। २३

Sūta said:

23. He who will read this eternal Greatness of the Gītā, declared by me, after having finished the reading of the Gītā itself, will obtain the fruit described herein.

These declarations will, no doubt, seem to be mere flights of extravagant fancy, if they are taken in their literal sense. They may be explained either (1) as mere *Arthavāda* or a statement of glorification meant to stimulate a strong desire for the study of the Gītā, which being performed from day to day, may, by the force of the truth and grandeur of one or other of its teachings, strike an inner chord of the heart some time, so much so as to change the whole nature of the man for good; (2) or, the "reading" and "reciting" and so forth, of the whole or a part, may not perhaps be taken in their ordinary sense, as meaning lip-utterance and the like; but in view of the great results indicated, they may be reasonably construed to mean the assimilation of the essence of the Gītā teaching into the practical daily life of the individual. What wonder, then, that such a one who is the embodiment of the Gītā would be a true *Jñāni*, or a *Jivanmukta*, or that he would, in proportion to his success of being so, attain the intermediate spheres of evolution and finally obtain *Mukti?*

इति श्रीवाराहपुराणे श्रीगीतामाहात्म्यं संपूर्णम् ॥

Thus ends in the Vārāha Purāṇa the discourse designated, *The Greatness of the Gītā*.

INDEX TO FIRST LINES